THE ANATOMY OF A SPY

A HISTORY OF ESPIONAGE AND BETRAYAL

MICHAEL SMITH

The History Press

First published 2019

The History Press
97 St George's Place, Cheltenham,
Gloucestershire, GL50 3QB
www.thehistorypress.co.uk

British Library Cataloguing in Publication Data.
A catalogue record for this book is available from the British Library.

ISBN 978 0 7509 9257 2

Typesetting and origination by Geethik Technologies
Printed and bound in Great Britain by TJ International Ltd.

MIX
Paper from
responsible sources
FSC® C013056

For my mother,
Joyce Marguerite Smith

CONTENTS

PROLOGUE

Rinat Rafkatovitch Akhmetshin was a bit of a showman, an idiosyncratic lobbyist for Russian oligarchs known for riding around Washington DC on a gaudy orange bicycle and his supposed ties to Russian spies, including a spell with military intelligence and a claim that half his family had worked for the FSB, the Russian Federal Security Service, all of which he was happy to admit before the 2016 presidential elections.

Akhmetshin arrived in New York on the morning of 9 June 2016 supposedly intent only on watching the beautiful Russian actress Chulpan Khamatova appear that night in a play at the New York City Center.

So casual was his visit that he was wearing pink jeans, fashionably ripped at the knees with a matching pink T-shirt. It was, of course, pure coincidence that Natalia Veselnitskaya, a Russian lawyer with close ties to the Russian Prosecutor-General, heard he was in town and invited him to lunch at Nello, a fashionable Italian restaurant on the Upper East Side, popular with movie stars and other celebrities.

Veselnitskaya needed his advice. She had a meeting that afternoon with Donald Trump Jr, the son of the would-be president, ostensibly to talk about the Magnitsky Act, which froze the assets of Russian oligarchs seen as being in breach of human rights and prevented them entering the US. The Putin government was determined to try to get the act overturned and, as a lobbyist for some of Russia's richest oligarchs, Akhmetshin was as much of an expert on the subject as she was.

She had her own briefing paper on what she wanted to say at the meeting but that was not all she was expected to discuss.

She also had an additional four pages in Russian focusing on money-laundering and tax evasion by key supporters of both the Magnitsky Act and the Democratic Party. How did Rinat Rafkatovitch think she should handle the meeting?

Akhmetshin was relaxed and reassuring. She shouldn't rush into the Magnitsky Act. Start with stuff they'd be interested in – the Democratic donors involved in tax evasion. They'd love any dirt they could throw at Hillary. That would grab their attention. Then she could start talking about how, with Trump Senior so keen to improve relations with Russia, getting rid of the Magnitsky Act would be a good way forward. Akhmetshin agreed to come with her to give her support.

After arriving at the glitzy, glass-fronted Trump Tower in Midtown Manhattan, they were shown up to Donald Jr's offices on the twenty-fifth floor and ushered into a conference room with stunning views out over Manhattan. The room seemed to be the size of a basketball court, dominated by a large wooden table, the walls lined with stylish framed photographs of Trump trophy properties. Paul Manafort, Trump's newly appointed campaign manager, was sat at one end of the table concentrating on something he was tapping into his phone. Akhmetshin seemed to recognise him and walked over to him.

'Right before the meeting started, Mr Akhmetshin approached Mr Manafort and suggested that they'd met previously at some kind of meeting in Washington DC,' one of those present recalled. 'There was no response from Mr Manafort. I don't think he even lifted his eyes off his phone.'

Akhmetshin just smiled and sat down. He had been right at lunch. Donald Jr and his brother-in-law, Jared Kushner, were looking for dirt on Hillary. It was the only reason they were there. A contact linked to the Russians who helped Trump stage a Miss Universe contest in Moscow three years earlier had emailed Donald Jr to suggest the meeting with Veselnitskaya, claiming that she had 'official documents and information that would incriminate Hillary'. The email from the contact said the information on offer was 'part of Russia and its government's support for Mr Trump'.

Kushner arrived a few minutes late and after some brief introductions, Donald Jr sat down opposite Veselnitskaya. 'I believe you have some information for us,' he said. 'Yes, indeed I do,' she replied, launching into a spiel about how key supporters of the Magnitsky Act had evaded tax on hundreds of millions of dollars of 'bad money' that had made its way into the US, with a large chunk of it donated to the Democratic Party and no doubt used to fund the Clinton campaign.

'So, can you show us how this money goes to Hillary?' Donald Jr asked. 'Do you have paperwork?'

Veselnitskaya replied that she had traced it as far as America, and it was clear the people involved had donated large sums to the Democratic National Committee. Donald Jr and his colleagues were in a far better position to track how much of it went to Hillary. 'I don't have that capacity to track it down,' she said. 'But I can tell you that bad money from criminal money came back to New York.'

The disappointment on the other side of the table was tangible. Donald Jr was clearly frustrated with the lack of any evidence that would make such charges stick. Veselnitskaya launched into her brief on the Magnitsky Act, but she had lost the room before she even began. Donald Jr nodded politely but was clearly no longer interested. Kushner couldn't hide his irritation, tapping into his phone to have an aide call him to give him an excuse to leave. Akhmetshin intervened to point out how repealing the Act would help Mr Trump show his commitment to better ties with Russia, but no one was listening.

Kushner had already left, not even making his excuses. Manafort was still head down tapping away on his phone. When Veselnitskaya tailed off, Donald Jr politely explained that at this point his father was just a private citizen with no influence over the situation. Once he was elected president, they could revisit the issue. A sense of embarrassment hung in the air. Everyone made their excuses and left.

Donald Jr later dismissed the idea of 'official documents and information that would incriminate Hillary' as just a pretext to get Veselnitskaya and Akhmetshin through the door, and in a way he was right, but he was wrong to imagine that the real purpose of the meeting was to discuss the Magnitsky Act. The real purpose of the meeting, so far as the Russian intelligence operatives who had engineered it were concerned, was to find out how amenable the Trump Campaign was to taking dirt on Clinton from Moscow, which would have been illegal under US election law.

Donald Jr's response to the initial offer had already made his position clear. 'I love it,' he said. His father claimed to have no idea about the offer but, in what must therefore have been a complete coincidence, announced a couple of days before the meeting that he would soon be giving 'a major speech' about 'all of the things that have taken place with the Clintons', a speech that oddly never took place.

Jared Kushner's impatient response to the lack of any dirt and his early exit confirmed his position and, despite the illegality of obtaining assistance from the Russians, there was not a single campaign lawyer at the meeting, someone who might have urged caution should any real dirt have emerged. The Russian intelligence officers running the 'Active Measures' operation against Clinton had their answer.

Six days later, they released the first batch of highly embarrassing emails and documents hacked from the Democratic National Committee computers, causing incalculable damage to the Clinton campaign.

Chapter 1

WHY SPIES SPY

Why did she betray him?

That most masculine of questions has been a dominant theme for storytellers ever since the ancient biblical tale of Samson and Delilah – someone whose name has become so associated with betrayal that it is even now frequently used to describe a woman who has been unfaithful to her husband or lover. The adulteress terrified male-dominated society. The cuckold was a laughing stock. Stories set around the activities of an unfaithful wife evoked an irresistible mix of sex and horror for the male reader, while creating a disquieting sense of female empowerment. This fascination with female sexual betrayal has been a dominant theme of such literary classics as *Madame Bovary*, *Anna Karenina*, *Ulysses* and *Lady Chatterley's Lover*.

But while Delilah has come to epitomise female sexual infidelity, her betrayal of Samson had nothing whatsoever to do with adultery. Her actions were those of a spy, an enemy agent inside the unsuspecting hero's camp. She exploited her sexual power over Samson to destroy him at the behest of Israel's enemy, the Philistines, repeatedly using the post-coital slumber induced by their love-making to test ways of rendering him helpless.

Samson was so hopelessly in love with her, or more likely so possessed by lust, that he failed to realise what was happening and eventually admitted that if his hair were shaved off, he would lose his strength and become 'just like any other man'. Delilah duly made love to him one more time, and when he fell asleep, she had his hair cut off before handing him over to the Philistines in what is still seen as one of the greatest betrayals in history.

So why did she betray him?

The Book of Judges says that every one of the Philistine leaders promised to pay her 1,100 pieces of silver. This would have been a substantial sum and a considerable financial inducement to betrayal. Money is often a factor in agent motivation, but it is rarely the only one. Here was a man, and a powerful one – not just a legendary strongman in the tradition of Heracles or Goliath, but the Jewish leader, who according to the Bible 'judged' Israel for twenty years. He had fallen in love with Delilah. He could have transformed her life.

Yet her loyalty to him was not so deep as to prevent her betraying him. The Bible tells us very little about their relationship or Delilah herself, but it says enough to provide some clues as to other possible motives for the betrayal.

It might simply be that her loyalty was to the Philistines and not to Israel. She lived in the Valley of Sorek, west of Jerusalem, which formed the boundary between the coastal strip controlled by the Philistines and the lands of Israel. Samson is known to have had a penchant for Philistine women but, while the Bible does not state Delilah's ethnic origins, if she were a Philistine, the writer of the very moralistic tale of Samson's downfall would surely have said so. Nevertheless, people living in areas separating warring communities frequently suffer at the hands of one side or the other. Revenge is one of the most powerful motives for any agent. Had Delilah or her family suffered ill by the Israelites? Any examination of her motives would need to investigate the possibility that she was already a supporter of the Philistines, perhaps under their control from the start of the relationship and had been instructed by them to seduce Samson.

Even if their relationship was a genuine love affair, there is a strong suggestion that she was either trying to gain control over him or testing him. Did this powerful man really love her or was he just using her? She asked him three times how he could lose his strength and each time he fed her a different line. She bound him with green tree stems, new ropes and even plaited locks of his hair. All of these failed. Could he really be in love with her if he would not tell her the truth?

'How canst thou say, I love thee, when thine heart is not with me?' she complained. 'And it came to pass, when she pressed him daily with her words, and urged him, that his soul was vexed unto death, that he told her all his heart.'

Money, tribal loyalty, revenge, control or doubt over his sincerity. There are any number of possible reasons for Delilah's betrayal of Samson, of which those silver pieces are only the most obvious. The Philistines' money gave her a powerful motive but it is unlikely to have been her sole reason. The one thing that is clear is that the reason she succeeded was her sexual power over Samson.

If Delilah was one of the first spies, how does her modern fictional counterpart, James Bond, compare? The intelligence services repeatedly claim that the work of the real spies is nothing like that portrayed in the films. James Bond's escapades for the British Secret Intelligence Service (SIS), better known as MI6, have blurred the lines between fact and fiction. SIS chiefs insist that most intelligence officers sit behind desks, never using a gun and certainly not living a life of glamour, seducing foreign spies and drinking cocktails (whether shaken or stirred). While this is to a large extent true, at one level it is misleading. SIS intelligence officers who need weapons training are taught how to use small-arms by a former special forces warrant officer based at their Fort Monckton training base in Hampshire and, given that they have to run agents in very difficult situations, in dangerous areas such as Libya, Syria, Iraq or Afghanistan, this is scarcely surprising.

One former senior SIS officer said:

MI6 officers certainly do not routinely carry weapons, but there is a difference between for instance an officer working under diplomatic cover, who would not be armed, and one employed on a particular operation which may or may not involve an element of risk. Just because you were taking part in an operation you wouldn't necessarily say: 'Oh, I must go to the safe and get out a gatt [gun].' But where there is some likelihood of weapons being needed, given the proper authorisation, they are available.

Whatever his bosses might say, James Bond still has recourse to a gun and, when operating on the front line, he (or she) retains a licence to kill. All of the world's leading foreign intelligence services employ special operations teams who carry out difficult operations such as protecting intelligence officers, making contact with people whose reliability has not been tested, exfiltrating agents, or removing captured material and equipment from enemy territory.

Nevertheless, even in a war zone, the intelligence officer is only rarely carrying out the spying. That is the job of the agent. There is a key difference between officers and agents. Unlike officers, agents are not on the staff of the intelligence service; they are recruited by an individual officer for a specific role. It might be because they have direct access to the intelligence that is being sought, such as a traitor inside the target country or organisation, or because for some reason they have access to a region where the intelligence officer cannot operate, such as a businessman selling his wares in a country such as North Korea, which it is difficult for Westerners to visit. They might have a specific skill that is needed to acquire the intelligence, such as the local knowledge and linguistic ability to impersonate an insider. It is these agents, and only rarely the intelligence officers themselves, who are the real spies.

So why are they prepared to put their lives and their loved ones at risk in order to collect intelligence, often for a country to which they have no natural allegiance? How do the intelligence services induce ordinary men and women to spy for them? How do they ensure that the agents they recruit do what they want and produce the intelligence required? How can they be confident the agent will not betray them? What makes the perfect spy? Why do spies spy?

There is no simple answer to these questions. There are common denominators that occur frequently, but every case is different, just as every human being is different. Many people are prepared to spy for money. It is the simplest of motives, but even with money there has to be another reason in the background that led the agent to decide it was worthwhile taking that money.

It is imperative for the intelligence officer running an operation or handling a specific agent to understand why he or she is betraying their country or their colleagues, to know the triggers that they can use to control the agent, but also to understand those that might lead to a loss of control, blowing the operation. How far can the agent be pushed? Someone who has already betrayed one side is likely to react badly if he or she is asked to do something that conflicts with their original motivation for betrayal. Those motivations can also change over time, creating addition problems. Getting it wrong risks seeing an operation fall apart, often with catastrophic results.

'The motivation of a continuing agent is, or should be, the subject of constant study on the part of his case officer,' one former CIA officer said. 'Unless a case officer knows what it is that drives his agent, he cannot know to what lengths the man will go, freely or under pressure, what risks he is willing to take, at what point he will break, tell another intelligence service what he is doing, or simply stop producing.'

Knowing what motivates the agent offers far greater control, and so long as the officer handling the agent has grown close enough to build up the necessary relationship of trust that has to exist between two people who can often hold the other's fate, even their life, in their hands, the motivation can even be adjusted in order to improve the degree of control.

'An agent's motivation can be changed, either by circumstances or through the efforts of an interested and patient case officer,' the former CIA officer said. 'Some of the less desirable motives – money, hatred, love of adventure, fear – can be redirected and tempered by a careful programme of indoctrination designed to bring out whatever finer purposes the agent has.'

Most intelligence agencies have teams of intelligence officers and psychologists looking at this issue. The CIA has a Behavioural Activities Branch specifically tasked to look at agent motivation and provide psychological assessments on request, although even obtaining the data needed for such studies from the agents risks pushing them too far. The FBI uses an acronym for agent motives. MICE stands for money, ideology, compromise or ego, but this is far too simplistic. Agents do things for the same reasons any human being does things, anything.

It used to be said, not least by the KGB, that British traitors, such as the Cambridge Five, Kim Philby, Donald Maclean, Guy Burgess, Anthony Blunt and John Cairncross, spied for ideological reasons, while American traitors spied for money. This has a certain truth to it but is overstated. Philby, for example, began by spying for ideological reasons, but it very quickly developed into an egotistical adventure. Burgess began as an ideological traitor but was soon much more concerned with being needed by the Russians and was even hurt when they decided to put all five of the Cambridge Spy Ring on hold, believing they were too good to be true. Ultimately, Burgess needed someone, the KGB in this case, to need him, and to make him believe that he was someone who mattered.

'Motives are often mixed or become mixed even if they aren't to start with,' one former SIS officer said. 'Motives for spying are as varied as motives for not spying and sometimes genuinely change over time. That's partly what makes it so fascinating. Agents will often give different accounts of their motives depending on when they're asked, just as we all do in other areas of life, for example: why did you marry X, not marry Y, become a journalist, move to Scotland?'

So, why do spies spy?

Chapter 2

SEXUAL RELATIONSHIPS

Agent motivation – why spies spy – is a complex subject. As in the case of Delilah, what seems at first sight to be the reason for betrayal is often not the sole one, or even the defining one. A short list of what appear to be the most common motivations: money, sex, revenge, love, hatred, patriotism, ideology, ego and fear, only scrapes the surface. The answer to the question why do spies spy is only rarely simple and straightforward. However, as with Samson and Delilah, sex can be an extremely powerful inducement, particularly when employed by a woman.

During the American Civil War, between 1861 and 1865, a number of female spies from the South seduced senior Union officers and politicians into indiscretions that helped the Confederate cause. Most of these men were unwitting traitors to the North's cause – what would now be known as 'unconscious' or 'unwitting' agents – although some undoubtedly realised what was going on and just did not care. Their lust for the women overwhelmed any sense of loyalty.

Rose O'Neal Greenhow, a society hostess in Washington DC, entertained prominent admirers at her fashionable home close to the White House and from these guests she extracted vital intelligence that she passed on to the Confederacy. Jefferson Davis, the Confederate President, credited her early intelligence reports as being the key factor in the Confederate Army's victory in the First Battle of Bull Run in July 1861, the first major clash in the war.

'Wild Rose' ran a network of conscious and unconscious agents in the US capital, and although some of those were motivated by a belief in the southern cause, a substantial number were simply

20   *The Anatomy of a Spy*

beguiled by her seductive personality. The Confederate Naval Secretary Stephen Mallory said, with no little amount of admiration, that Greenhow 'hunted man with resistless zeal and unfailing instinct', enjoying, and using, romantic trysts with Union officers and politicians alike. Henry D. Wilson, a Republican senator, who as chairman of Abraham Lincoln's Committee on Military Affairs was fully aware of the Union forces' plans, wrote passionate, even obsessive, love letters to Greenhow. 'You know that I do love you,' Wilson said in one signed simply 'H'. 'I am sick physically and mentally and know nothing that would soothe me so much as an hour with you. And tonight, at whatever cost, I will see you.' The Union Army officer Colonel Erasmus D. Keyes, another who spent many hours alone with 'Wild Rose', described her as 'one of the most persuasive women that was ever known in Washington'.

Another female spy, Ginnie Moon, whose equally attractive sister, Lottie, also spied for the Confederates, was at one point engaged to sixteen different Union soldiers, all of whom sent her regular love letters in which they inadvertently included details of what they and their units were doing, producing useful intelligence that she passed on to her Confederate contact, Lieutenant-General Nathan Bedford Forrest.

Undoubtedly, the most brazen of the leading Civil War female spies was Belle Boyd, who was described by one jealous love rival as 'the fastest girl in Virginia, or anywhere else for that matter'. When the Boyds' home town of Martinsburg, at the lower end of the Shenandoah Valley, was taken by Union forces in mid May 1862, her mother sent Belle, then just 17, up the valley to the town of Fort Royal, where her aunt owned the Fishback Hotel. Belle and her maid arrived there around the same time as the advancing Federal forces to find that the Union general James Shields had taken over her aunt's hotel as his headquarters. Undeterred, Belle seduced Shields, spending four hours 'closeted' alone with him, and then moved on to his aide-de-camp Captain Daniel Kelly who was so entranced by her beauty that he bombarded her with flowers and love poems. She recorded in her memoirs that she was indebted to him for 'some very remarkable effusions, some withered flowers, and last, but not least, for a great deal of very important information'. The most significant thing Kelly told her was the date and time of the next meeting of the general's war council which was to be held in the hotel. Boyd drilled a small hole through the floor of the room above and watched the meeting taking place, making a transcript of all that was discussed before sneaking out and crossing the lines to pass it on to the Confederate forces.

While the male sex drive might seem to make men more susceptible to the use of seduction, women have proven just as vulnerable. The very human need for physical and emotional sexual intimacy with another person has been almost as much of a boon for espionage as it has for prostitution. It is no accident that the two are deemed to be the world's two oldest professions.

Britain's modern espionage apparatus dates from 1909 when a Secret Service Bureau was set up in response to the increasing threat of war with Germany. The Bureau was instructed 'to deal both with espionage in this country and with our own foreign agents abroad'.

The first head of its foreign section, the organisation that would become the Secret Intelligence Service, was a 50-year-old Royal Navy commander who had been forced off the active list because he was prone to chronic seasickness. Although an apparently unpromising candidate for the job, Mansfield Cumming established many of the traditions still followed by the service he created. Cumming was known only as 'C', from the first letter of his name. To this day the head of SIS is still known as 'C', albeit now referring to the initial for 'Chief', the formal title, and 'C' still uses green ink to sign his correspondence, a naval tradition adopted by Cumming from the start.

The first 'C' inherited a ragbag of agents from his military intelligence predecessors, most of whose motives were highly dubious, but he noted in his diary that Danish naval officer Captain Walter Christmas 'seemed straightforward'. The 48-year-old Christmas was in charge of the Danish Navy's intelligence reports on German ships passing between northern Denmark and Sweden, so he was a very useful source of intelligence on enemy ships leaving the Baltic and entering the North Sea.

Cumming's assessment of Christmas's reliability rested on the Danish officer's favoured method of passing on his reports and collecting his payment. Christmas received a salary of £200 a year. This was a relatively useful sum, equivalent to around £20,000 at today's prices, coming as it did on top of his salary as a Danish naval captain, but it was by no means his only reward.

The twice-married Christmas insisted that the courier who collected his reports should be a 'pretty girl' who would meet him at a hotel in Skagen, the fishing port at the northernmost tip of Denmark. A succession of attractive prostitutes was selected to keep him happy and when, in 1915, one of them inadvertently gave him away and he had to be exfiltrated from Denmark, the British secret service obtained a flat for him in Shepherd Market, the traditional red-light district of London's Mayfair.

The link between the world's two oldest professions was cemented early on in the history of SIS. According to Cumming's biographer, Alan Judd, who served in SIS himself, the service subsequently 'developed something of a tradition in pretty girls'. Sometimes, of course, as the Russians recognised more than most, pretty boys were just as useful.

The Russians had realised very early on that sex was a valuable tool in the recruitment of spies, not least for the British secret service, whose remarkably extensive agent networks in the Soviet Union were rounded up during the 1930s by the predecessors of the KGB. The United Kingdom was then regarded by Moscow as 'the Main Enemy' and Andrei Vyshinsky, the Soviet State Prosecutor, gave a series of lectures in 1937 warning Russians that 'however innocent and naive foreigners appeared, they were probably secret agents sent to the USSR to exploit the human weaknesses and vices of unsuspecting Soviet citizens of both sexes, to get these citizens into their diabolical power and to force them to work as wreckers, terrorists, and spies'.

The Russians were in fact just as happy as the British 'to exploit human weaknesses and vices' to recruit their own agents. The first CIA officer to be sent to Moscow in the early 1950s was Edward Ellis Smith, who was ordered to arrange drops for Pyotr Semyonovich Popov, an officer in the GRU, Soviet military intelligence, who served in Austria during the post-war Allied occupation. Popov was a 'walk-in', an agent who volunteered his services to the Americans during this period (rather than being actively recruited) and he was run by their Vienna station until 1955, when the Russians withdrew from Austria. He was then posted back to Moscow, where Smith was assigned to run him. It was not a successful relationship. The new CIA handler's choice of dead drops was so inept that Popov asked him if he was trying to get him killed.

Smith was reckless in more ways than one. Yuri Nosenko, who defected to the Americans in the early 1960s, said the KGB used a honeytrap, or a sexual compromise, to recruit Smith in September 1956. 'We gave him the code name *Rhyzhiy* (redhead),' Nosenko said, revealing that the KGB had just as little respect for the American as Popov. 'We used to call him *Rhyzhiy Khui*, red-headed prick. He went to bed with his Russian maid, our agent, and we staged a scene that made it look like a criminal offence.'

Smith initially considered not reporting the incident and continuing with his relationship with the maid, an 'alluring' young woman called Valya. But eventually, after a further meeting with Vladislav Kovshuk, the KGB officer who ran the sting, he decided to tell his bosses in Washington. He was immediately recalled and the resulting investigation led to his dismissal.

In an attempt to keep him on side, Smith was set up with a research post at the Hoover Institution but was nevertheless furious at being sacked. Whether he then contacted the Russians, or they found out about his predicament in another way, is unclear, but in the summer of 1958, Kovshuk travelled to the US and spent a lot of time commiserating with Smith over his dismissal, treating him like an old friend. Eventually, Smith gave the KGB officer enough information to allow the KGB to track down Popov. The Soviet intelligence service then ran him back against the Americans as a double agent for a brief while before shooting him.

Smith denied any role in Popov's betrayal and died in 1982, but in 2001, as part of a spate of books trumpeting its successes, the KGB confirmed that he had been successfully recruited as an agent. Although it was sexual compromise that initiated his relationship with an enemy intelligence service, the situation was – as with so many spies – more complex than that and Smith's ultimate motive was anger over his dismissal and a desire for revenge.

Oleg Kalugin, a senior officer in the KGB from 1951 to 1990, recalled that during the Cold War its Second Chief Directorate, which was responsible for internal security, had a number of different departments targeting tourists, businessmen or diplomats to entice them into compromising situations which could be used to force them to become KGB agents. An agent would be sent, normally an actress, dancer or professional woman rather than a prostitute – 'because they generally were more intelligent and therefore more credible to foreigners' – to pick up the target, usually in the bar of his hotel. The women, known as 'Swallows' – their male counterparts were 'Ravens' – were persuaded to have sex with potential agents by offers of money, a better apartment, a promotion, or even a job overseas, although it seems unlikely that many would have seen it as wise to turn down a request for assistance from the KGB.

'I was forever amazed at how much trouble people got into over sex,' Kalugin said. 'Catching people with their pants down was a prime way of compromising and recruiting them. As long as men would be men and women would be women, lust would play a role in the spy wars.'

★★★

Having been burned by the Ellis Smith case, the CIA was initially keen to follow suit. In the early 1950s, under a programme appropriately code-named Midnight Climax, it set up 'brothels' in safe houses in the Bay Area of San Francisco and New York's Greenwich Village to test the combined effects of alcohol, drugs and sex on unwitting men. Prostitutes employed by the CIA took their clients back to the safe houses and plied them with drinks laced with a wide range of different drugs, including LSD, to determine the effect this might have on them. The victims' reactions were observed through two-way mirrors, with the possibility that men might be induced to talk more freely during sex a particular focus of the tests.

CIA experimented with the idea of the prostitute offering the men an extra sexual service to see if this would make them more likely to open up and talk, but this proved unnecessary; one of the CIA officers working on Midnight Climax recalled: 'We found the guy was focused solely on hormonal needs. He was not thinking of his career or anything else at that point.' The main conclusion – that the men were at their most emotionally vulnerable, and therefore most likely to reveal secrets, during the post-coital period – was scarcely a revelation to anyone familiar with Delilah's effect on Samson.

Kalugin was dismissive of the CIA's efforts in using sex as a means of obtaining intelligence, claiming with some justification that the KGB and the other Eastern Bloc intelligence services had turned the use of honeytraps into something of an industry. 'On the sexual espionage front, we usually got the better of the CIA and hostile intelligence agencies for the simple reason that we were far more willing to use sex as a weapon, and generally had fewer scruples.'

The last point was in fact a key obstacle for the Western agencies. At least in the modern era, it has been forbidden for CIA officers to use sex to recruit agents. 'New candidates are informed early on in the interviewing process that such techniques are prohibited,' one long-serving CIA officer said. 'Such practices are operationally risky.' The use of sexual relationships to control an agent runs the risk that the agent could come to dominate the relationship. 'It gives them leverage over the officer running them, a very undesirable circumstance. Operational control is vital. If the officer is married, additional risks are incurred.'

SIS, the main British intelligence service, has tended to take a more nuanced view, but in general follows the same principles as the CIA. One former officer said:

> We hardly ever used sex to recruit agents. I know of no case where it was a dominant factor. Even to propose an operation that depended on sex (with or without blackmail) was frowned upon. I recall one case where the target, a Russian, was

a rampant homosexual who fraternised homosexual haunts in
the country where he was posted. At a target meeting, one
officer proposed an operation to seduce and then blackmail
him. The officer was warned that this was wholly unacceptable
– and thereafter was regarded with caution.

But a second former officer stated that, unlike the CIA, SIS did
not have an absolute ban on using sex and that he knew of two
cases where it had been used, although in one of these it had
occurred as an unplanned part of the recruitment case rather
than the central plank. 'It's very much a case-by-case decision,' he
said. 'But it's certainly not commonly done. As a rule, you seek to
recruit an agent on more solid grounds than personal affection
and make them transferable, i.e. you can hand them over to a new
case officer without threat to the case.'

At any event, the ability to use sexual compromise has dimin-
ished over time as a result of changes in society's attitudes towards
sex. In 1991, the Iraqi secret service the *Mukhabarat* used a female
agent on the domestic staff of Baghdad's Hyatt Hotel to seduce
a German member of the UNSCOM weapons inspection team.
The German dismissed the subsequent threat of blackmail, asking
the *Mukhabarat* officers for a copy of the video so that he could
show it to his wife, who was 'very liberal in such matters' and
would, he said, enjoy watching it with him. Even in the 1970s, the
KGB had begun to find that many of those caught in honeytraps
would initially agree to spy in order to get out of an awkward
situation but once they returned home refused to help.

Coercion based on illicit homosexual activity was generally more successful. Even after it was legalised, the potential
for embarrassment to those who had not 'come out' meant that
someone working in jobs handling secrets would be removed
from their post. It was, therefore, generally a fruitful area for
blackmail by intelligence operatives. The KGB employed homosexual officers specifically to target foreign embassy staff.

One of the most successful of these cases was that of John
Vassall, a British civil servant who worked for the Admiralty.
He was posted to the British embassy in Moscow in 1954 as an

assistant to the naval attaché, a post for which he volunteered, apparently seeing it as an entrée into an elite social world of embassy parties at which he would mix as an equal with diplomats from around the world. As a junior member of the embassy's administrative staff, not even a Foreign Office employee, the 29-year-old Vassall was soon disabused of this notion. Clearly trying to find his way in life, with no apparent sexual interest in women and with ready access to British naval secrets, it was not long before Vassall was talent-spotted by the KGB. He was befriended by a locally employed embassy interpreter, Sigmund Mikhailski, a Pole who, if not homosexual, was certainly bisexual and had been planted on the embassy by the KGB. Mikhailski became close to Vassall, easily luring him into Moscow's illegal homosexual underworld. Over the next few months, the Pole introduced Vassall to a number of new Russian friends, who seemed to accept him for what he was and, unlike the senior embassy staff, did not see him as an inconsequential young man with ideas above his station.

The trap was now set. Mikhailski introduced Vassall to three new 'friends', KGB officers who, in a private dining room of a Russian restaurant near the Bolshoi, gave him alcohol laced with drugs and induced him into taking part in a staged homosexual orgy.

'We had drinks, a large dinner and I was plied with very strong brandy, and after half an hour I remember everybody taking off their jackets and somebody assisted me to take off mine,' Vassall said. 'I remember the lighting was very strong, and gradually most of my clothes were removed. There was a divan in the corner. I remember two or three people getting on the bed with me, all in a state of undress. Then certain compromising sexual actions took place. I remember someone in the party taking photographs. It all seemed beyond my control. I did not know where I was, or what was going on, or why it was happening.'

Predictably, the photos were then shown to Vassall and used to blackmail him into working for the Russians. 'After about three photographs, they made me feel ill,' Vassall said. 'There I was caught by the camera enjoying every possible sexual activity. If you were a man and saw photographs of yourself having oral, anal, or a complicated array of sexual activity with a number of different men, what would your feelings be?'

The KGB officers were so well aware of Vassall's social weaknesses that one of the first people they threatened to show the photos to was Lady Hayter, the wife of the ambassador. Faced with the prospect of being exposed as a homosexual, which was then illegal in both the Soviet Union and the United Kingdom, Vassall agreed to provide seemingly innocuous details of the staff of the British embassy. At first, this was simply who he liked and didn't like. His handlers were careful to make clear that nothing they requested was secret. He wasn't being asked to put his country at risk. They pointedly claimed that giving them minor details about who did what in the embassy would not be illegal – unlike his homosexual activities. As time went on, the KGB's demands grew, and Vassall began passing them secret information. At that point, they paid him 2,000 roubles (then about £50, or the equivalent of several weeks' pay) and had him sign a receipt for the money. There was now no turning back, one British counterintelligence officer said. 'This was a classic of KGB tradecraft. Once you sign for the money you are on the hook, however innocuous the information you are being asked to provide. It seems negligible at the time, but there is no going back.' It was the receipt – the clear evidence of betrayal – rather than the photographs, which would give Vassall's handlers the insurance they needed to ensure he continued to provide the KGB with secret documents. But by now they would have been fairly certain the threat of blackmail would never be needed. A far more powerful motivation had been brought into play from the moment that Mikhailski first befriended him. Someone cared for him. It ensured that for seven years Vassall handed over thousands of secret documents.

Shortly before he was posted back to London, in the summer of 1956, Vassall was introduced to a man he knew only as Grigori who would run him in the UK. Grigori was in fact Nikolai Korovin, the KGB *Rezident* (head of station) in London. Vassall's new job was in the Naval Intelligence Division, a post that would give him access to reports from SIS and GCHQ (the secret government communications centre), telling the Russians what the West did and did not know about Soviet activities and providing them with the opportunity to work out who the sources of the leaks might be and which of their codes had been broken. Initially, Vassall would take documents home on the night he was due to meet 'Grigori', slipping them between the pages of a magazine or newspaper and then placing them in his briefcase. There were a variety of meeting places in north London, at Frognal station on the Finchley Road, a Greek restaurant on the Cockfosters Road and on a suburban avenue close to Wembley football stadium. But this was a very haphazard way of working and soon the KGB provided Vassall with his own camera so he could take documents home at any time, photograph them and return them without anyone knowing they were missing. 'Grigori arranged with me that if I wanted to contact him urgently, I would leave a circle in pink chalk on a wooden fence directly above the trunk of a tree outside, I think, Plane Tree House, Duchess of Bedford Walk, junction of Holland Walk,' Vassall said. 'I only made use of this on one or two occasions.' There was also a Kensington telephone number for use in emergency. Vassall was to ask for 'Miss Mary'. He rang it only once.

He was paid various amounts ranging from £50 to £200 depending on the value of his last set of photographs; taking the tax on his Civil Service salary into account, this doubled Vassall's income and enabled him to pay for an expensive apartment in Pimlico's fashionable Dolphin Square. His value to the Russians continued throughout the 1950s and into the 1960s, by which time he was assistant private secretary to a Navy minister and was being run by a new KGB *Rezident*, Nikolai Karpekov.

The existence of a spy inside the Admiralty was revealed first by Anatoli Golitsyn, a KGB officer who defected to the Americans in December 1961. It was confirmed six months later by another KGB officer, Yuri Nosenko. MI5 narrowed the suspects down to Vassall and a search of his flat uncovered photographs of secret documents concealed in a hidden compartment in his wardrobe. Vassall was arrested, swiftly confessed and was jailed for eighteen years. His claims that he spied, not because of the blackmail over his homosexuality, but because the Russians seemed to regard him as someone important – whereas the senior diplomats in the embassy ignored him – were ridiculed at the time. It is clear that it was not so much the sex as the acceptance and friendship given to a lonely man by Mikhailski and his homosexual friends that drew the desperately lonely Vassall down the path that would eventually lead to treason. Even after his arrest, Vassall insisted that Mikhailski could not possibly have had any part in his recruitment by the KGB. The Pole was a 'warm-hearted' friend who was quite unlike the remote senior diplomats at the embassy.

'I felt that the general atmosphere in the embassy was an unhappy one,' Vassall told the Special Branch detectives who interviewed him. 'The senior officials mostly seemed pre-occupied with their own private and official duties and in some ways junior staff were left to fend for themselves. If we were cared for as one family, I do not think that some of us would have got into these troubles.'

Lonely people, flattered by the attention of seemingly glamorous members of the opposite sex they would never normally expect to show any kind of interest in them, are frequently easy targets for agents specialising in seduction techniques, and it was not just the British and Americans who proved vulnerable to the KGB honeytraps. In the mid-1960s, Roy Guindon, a security guard at the Canadian embassy in Moscow, was recruited by a beautiful KGB agent, Larissa Dubanova, whom he met at the Bolshoi. She seduced him and then claimed to be pregnant by him, so he agreed to marry her in what was, unbeknown to him, a fake ceremony. When he was posted to the Warsaw embassy, she followed him, persuading him to provide her with embassy ciphers and plant listening devices in the embassy conference room. Guindon was subsequently posted to Tel Aviv, where the Israeli security service *Shin Bet* spotted him meeting with a known KGB officer. The Israelis tipped off the Canadian authorities and Guindon was recalled. In return for not being prosecuted, he co-operated with a Royal Canadian Mounted Police Security Service investigation into the KGB penetration of Canadian embassy security, which was found to have involved a number of junior security staff with access to secret codes in several different embassies around the world.

The Israeli foreign intelligence service Mossad has made a speciality of operations that would have stretched the imagination of even the very best of thriller writers, including Ian Fleming, the creator of James Bond. It was responsible for what must rate as one of the most spectacular and also the most brutal of honeytraps. Operation Diamond was the culmination of a series of Mossad attempts to obtain the latest Soviet aircraft used by the Syrians and Egyptians in order to work out ways of countering them in aerial combat. The Israelis initially targeted Egyptian pilots, who were seen as most likely to be willing to defect, and, though they had some limited success, the results were largely disappointing. Then another potentially more productive source emerged.

During the 1950s, Iraq's Hashemite monarchy had enjoyed close links with the British, but a 1958 coup brought Brigadier Abd al-Karim Qasim, a Soviet-backed army officer, to power. The new regime was welcomed in Moscow, which sold it the latest Soviet fighter aircraft, the MiG-21. But in 1963, Qasim was deposed in a coup, and eventually a more pragmatic president, Abdul Salam Arif, came to power and began re-establishing friendly relations with the British and – more importantly – the Americans.

The close links with Russia were scaled back, Soviet advisers were sent home, and many of the MiG-21 pilots, having been trained in the Soviet Union, now came under suspicion as potential communist spies. Only a handful of pilots were trusted to continue to fly the aircraft. The MiG-21 was superior to the French Mirage jets the Israeli Air Force flew, and Mossad saw this as an opportunity to obtain all the data on the aircraft, information that would give the Israeli pilots the upper hand in dog fights with their Arab counterparts. Mossad contacted its agents inside Iraq and made clear its interest in contacting Iraqi pilots who might be persuaded to defect to Israel with their aircraft.

Ezra Zelkha was an Iraqi Jew who had been adopted by a prominent criminal family in Baghdad, becoming the consigliere, much in the manner of the Tom Hagen character played by Robert Duvall in the movie *The Godfather*. He was also a Mossad agent code-named 'Yusuf'. Zelkha used his extensive contacts to discover that, as a direct result of the new regime's decision to foster close relations with the United States at Moscow's expense, fifteen Iraqi Air Force officers were being sent on a United States Air Force staff course in San Antonio, Texas. Four of those officers were MiG-21 pilots. All four were targeted by female Mossad agents, who picked them up in San Antonio bars.

The first to be approached was Lieutenant Hamid Dhahe. He slept with the female agent, who was clearly of Middle East origin and called herself Zainab. But when she revealed that she was in fact an Israeli agent and wanted to help him defect, he point-blank refused. If they wanted the operation to continue with the other three pilots, the Israelis now had no choice. Dhahe had to be eliminated. Three days later, he was in a bar when the lights went out. In the darkness, a single gunshot rang out, creating panic. When power was restored and the lights went back on, Dhahe was lying on the floor with a bullet in his head.

Following Dhahe's death, the rest of the Iraqi officers were withdrawn from the course and flown back to Iraq, but the female Mossad agents who had picked up the three other MiG-21 pilots kept in touch with their lovers. The Israelis were determined that one of the three would be induced to defect. The next to be targeted with an offer to defect, which by now it was clear he could not refuse, was Captain Shakir Mahmoud Yusuf, the commander of the only Iraqi Air Force squadron flying MiG-21s. The female agent who had seduced him flew to Baghdad and met him in an apartment there. After spending time in the bedroom renewing their relationship, she proposed to him that he should defect. He would be set up for life. The Israelis would look after him. He would want for nothing. Although they appeared to be on their own, Ezra Zelkha was in another room, monitoring the situation. When Yusuf refused and said he would report the matter to the authorities who would arrest her as a spy, Zelkha entered the bedroom and shot him dead.

Mossad had more success with one of the other pilots, Captain Mohammad Raglob, who initially agreed to defect and even travelled to Europe for a meeting as a prelude to going to Israel and sealing the deal. But he became difficult and attempted to blackmail Mossad, suggesting to his contacts that he could simply inform his bosses and that would be the end of any chance the Israelis had of obtaining a MiG-21. The response was brutal. He was thrown out of a speeding train in Germany, leaving just one remaining MiG-21 pilot of the four seduced by female Israeli agents on the trip to America.

The woman who had seduced that fourth pilot during the US staff course arrived in Iraq unannounced, apparently searching for her lost love, Captain Munir Redfa. Lisa Brat, as she called herself, got in touch with Redfa, slept with him again, and then invited him to meet up with her on holiday in Greece, where she intimated they could spend much more time together.

Not long after arriving, Brat and Redfa – a Maronite Christian rather than a Muslim – were drinking in a bar when they fell into conversation with a Polish pilot who claimed to be working for an anti-Communist organisation. The two men bonded and spent several nights drinking and discussing flying. Eventually, the Pole admitted that he was a Holocaust survivor, which drew the conversation easily towards the fact that he was an Israeli. His true identity was Colonel Ze'ev Liron, head of Israeli Air Force intelligence, and he was there to make Redfa an offer, man to man, one pilot to another. The Israelis wanted him to fly a MiG-21 to Israel. They would resettle him and his family in Israel and ensure that he was financially secure and protected for life. They would also give him a million dollars. He would want for nothing. It was made clear to him precisely why he was the only one of the four MiG-21 pilots who had gone on the course in San Antonio who was still alive. There was no explicit threat, but the implication was obvious. Redfa was told to think about it overnight, a night he spent with Brat, who also now admitted that she worked for Mossad and suggested their relationship could continue in Israel. She produced a brand-new Israeli passport in his name and tickets to Tel Aviv. Next morning, Redfa told Liron that he was happy to go. The only thing he insisted on was that his extended family should be resettled in the West.

Once in Israel, his importance was reinforced by interviews with Mossad boss Meir Amit, who had taken personal control of

Operation Diamond, and the commander of the Israeli Air Force, Brigadier Mordecai Hod, who sat with Redfa and senior planners working out the route that the MiG-21 would take out of Iraq, through Jordanian airspace and into Israel. The conversations with Amit and Hod were not just about the significance of the operation. The clear message was that he was an important man, so important that he could talk in person with the head of Mossad and the chief of the Israeli Air Force. Once the Israelis were certain Redfa was confident in what he was about to do, he was sent back to Greece with Lisa Brat and from there flew back to Iraq.

Almost immediately, Ezra Zelkha began getting members of Redfa's family out. The pilot's wife, Betty, and their two daughters were flown first to Amsterdam, supposedly so Betty could be treated for a medical condition, and then on to Paris, where they thought they would be having a family holiday. When Betty was told the truth, she allegedly threw a fit and threatened to go to the Iraqi embassy but was eventually calmed down and told she and her daughters would be flown to Israel to meet her husband. Three days before the flight was planned, the rest of the Redfa's extended family, also unaware what was happening, were invited on a picnic close to the Iranian border and then smuggled out of Iraq to a waiting helicopter, which flew them to an airport. They were told that Betty was ill and they were being flown to Europe to see her. In fact, their destination was Israel.

On 16 August 1966, Munir Redfa took off from Tammuz air base west of Baghdad on a high-altitude training mission. He headed for the Jordanian border, flying in a zig-zag approach agreed with the Israeli Air Force planners in an attempt to delay the moment when the Iraqi Air Force controllers would realise what he was doing. When they did and ordered him to turn back on pain of being shot down, he simply ignored them and turned off the radio.

After an 800-kilometre (500-mile) flight, he entered Israeli airspace and was escorted into Hatzor air base east of the coastal town of Ashdod. Redfa was put up in front of a press conference alongside Brigadier Hod to explain why he had defected. He was not identified by name and what he said was clearly rehearsed. He had served more than ten years in the Iraqi Air Force, he explained, and as a Maronite Christian his position was 'awkward'. Christians were not trusted with responsible posts and he had also been angry over a campaign of bombing Kurdish rebels in which he had been forced to take part. This had led him to write a letter via a friend in Israel offering to fly the MiG-21 to Hatzor. Hod said the letter had arrived ten days earlier and at the time he had 'thought it too good to be true'. But the Israeli air defences had been warned to look out for the aircraft and when the pilot dipped his wings and lowered the undercarriage, two Mirage fighters had escorted the MiG-21 into Hatzor.

This was only the first stage of what would become an elaborate cover story for the operation. To ensure there were no rows with the US over Mossad agents operating on US soil, this carefully glossed over the multiple honeytrap during the staff course in Texas that – had it become known – would have certainly led to the US realising who had killed the Hamid Dhahe, the first Iraqi officer, and would have jeopardised Redfa's continuing loyalty. Mossad also played on his position as a Maronite Christian, reinforcing the idea that he would be treated with a higher level of respect in Israel than he could hope for at home (a promise that turned out to be mendacious).

While his complaint over the bombing of the Kurds might well have been true, Redfa's promotion prospects within the Iraqi Air Force were not affected in any way by his religion. At the time he went to the US on the staff course, he had achieved a high level of seniority, being the deputy commander of the only Iraqi Air Force squadron flying the MiG-21, one of the most effective fighter aircraft in the world (and certainly the best the Iraqis had). On his return from Texas, Redfa was then given command of the squadron, which hardly supports his claims of suffering discrimination.

Whatever the deception practised in the official account of the operation, there was one simple truth that was never in doubt. Obtaining the aircraft was a tremendous coup for the Israelis, helping ensure that they managed to outmanoeuvre the Egyptian and Syrian MiG-21s a year later during the Six-Day War. Redfa's aircraft was also subsequently passed to the Americans so they could test it and work out ways of countering its abilities.

Munir Redfa and his family found it impossible to settle in Israel, and after a few years they were given false identities and moved to Western Europe, where in 1988 Munir himself died of a heart attack. So revered was his role within Mossad that it allegedly held a slightly surreal memorial ceremony for him at which veteran officers were apparently unable to hold back their tears. But if Redfa's motivation had in reality nothing to do with religious discrimination, it was almost certainly far more complex than simply the novelty of the sexual relationship with the Mossad agent Lisa Brat. The attention paid to him by a succession of prominent Israeli officials also played to the Iraqi's own feelings of self-worth and almost certainly to his ego. The willingness of the Israeli Air Force intelligence chief Ze'ev Liron to fly to Greece to meet Redfa and spend many hours drinking with him to woo him over, the meeting in Israel with the head of Mossad Meir Amit – who deemed him so important he was taking charge of the operation himself – and the discussion of his route with Mordecai Hod, the commander of the Israeli Air Force, were all designed to make Redfa feel wanted, the indispensable player at the heart of the team stealing the Soviet aircraft. The million dollars Redfa was paid to fly to Israel represented a considerable inducement, but Liron was told that if he refused he had authorisation to double it immediately.

The money, the appeal to his ego – and inevitably the knowledge of what had happened to his colleagues – were clearly important parts of Redfa's recruitment process, but in the end, it was the sexual relationship that was the key factor in enabling it.

***

The use of sex or, more often in the case of women, a romantic liaison, to recruit agents is not restricted to the major intelligence agencies. Spies the world over have been willing to use it as a means of inducing betrayal. Sharon Scranage had only recently come out of a brief but violent marriage when the CIA posted her to the Ghanaian capital Accra in May 1983. Her subsequent betrayal had no mixed motives. The romantic relationship with a popular, good-looking man who treated her like a princess was the only motive she needed.

The pretty 27-year-old operations support assistant came from a close-knit religious Afro–American family in the town of King George in rural Virginia and was described by those who knew her as 'a shy, country girl'. Her parents, Perry and Mary-Belle, were noted on her CIA file as 'solid, self-respecting citizens' who were active in the local church. Her father worked at the Quantico US Marine Corps base, and Scranage had been part of the 'honor society' and the cheerleading team at high school. She was widely seen as 'a good kid' and had no problem passing the CIA vetting process. Scranage had never been abroad before and was reluctant to go but agreed with her bosses that she should go to Ghana and 'make the most of it'.

Missing home and still recovering from the unhappy marriage, Scranage was vulnerable to the advances of a Romeo agent working for the Ghanaian intelligence services. Michael Soussoudis, a relative of Ghana's Marxist leader Jerry Rawlings, was known as something of a playboy. Although his mother was Ghanaian, and he had been born in Accra, he had grown up in West Germany before moving to New York, where he married and then divorced an American woman. His family and friends in Accra regarded him as 'more American than Ghanaian', but he was employed by the Ghanaian domestic intelligence and security service run by Kojo Tsikata, which worked closely with the East German foreign intelligence service, the *Hauptverwaltung Aufklärung* (HVA). Soussoudis held glamorous parties to which he invited Scranage, who was vulnerable to male attention and, given her background, flattered by the interest of a sophisticated man. 'Evidently this Ghanaian, who became her lover, had captivated her,' said Robert E. Fritts, who was ambassador to Ghana at the time. 'He had money and gave lavish Ghanaian parties with an in-crowd. She was seduced physically and morally by the glamour of being selected to go where no other Western foreigner went.'

Much happier as a result of the attention she was receiving from Soussoudis, she was encouraged by him to gather low-level intelligence, which she obtained by socialising extensively with her colleagues in the CIA station and the embassy itself. 'She was quite popular and good for morale,' Fritts said.

Things began to go wrong for Scranage when, during a dinner party at her home, one of her colleagues spotted a photograph of Soussoudis tucked into her dressing table mirror. He had clearly been in Scranage's bed when the photograph was taken. All CIA employees working abroad are obliged to seek permission before forming relationships with local people and she had not done so. Nevertheless, although the colleague reported the issue, it was not until the end of her tour in Ghana, when Scranage was put through a routine polygraph lie detector test, that her betrayal was detected.

Fritts was told that 'the needle went off the chart'. Challenged over her answers, Scranage confessed to having passed the names of a number of Ghanaians who were spying for the CIA to her lover. She also admitted that Soussoudis and his friends, at least one of whom was white and German, had wanted her to look through the files at Langley for more information. She agreed to help the FBI lure Soussoudis to the United States, telephoning him and asking him to fly over because she had something to give him. She was then sent on leave for a week to get her out of the way when the Ghanaian arrived. The CIA also needed to move most of its officers and their families, and any agents who had not been arrested, to the United States.

'The first priority was to get our CIA people and compromised Ghanaians out of Ghana,' Fritts explained. 'We had the CIA folk and their families gone quickly – maybe 72 hours. We also arranged to inform many of the compromised Ghanaians, who also left the country precipitately, some real human tragedies, of course.' The CIA departures were staggered to avoid raising the suspicions of the Ghanaian government. 'If they knew what we were up to, they would round up Ghanaians they suspected, have phoney trials and execute them.'

It was not until as many as possible of those at risk had been got out of Ghana that Scranage was told to arrange a meeting with Soussoudis at a motel in Arlington, across the Potomac from Washington DC. The Ghanaian was arrested as he arrived and charged with espionage. Scranage was arrested the following day, also charged with espionage and the disclosure of the identities of intelligence agents and released back into the custody of her parents. Fritts spent the next six months arranging a complex spy swap in which most of the CIA agents who had been arrested by the Ghanaians, and members of their immediate families, were to be allowed out. Once the deal was agreed, Scranage and Soussoudis were put on trial. He received a twenty-year prison sentence but, as part of the exchange deal negotiated by Fritts, was freed on condition that he left the US within twenty-four hours. He flew home to a hero's welcome.

In return, the Ghanaian agents and their families were allowed to cross the border into Togo, from where they flew to the United States to be resettled. Sharon Scranage admitted espionage and was jailed for five years, although her initial sentence was cut to two years by an appeal judge who cited the disparity between her treatment and that of Soussoudis. She was eventually released on parole after just eighteen months in prison.

Her recruitment had been solely a result of the sexual relationship into which she had been enticed by Soussoudis. A lonely woman, away from her family for an extended period for the first time, she was flattered by the attention a popular man bestowed on her, and after he seduced her she fell in love with him. It was a very straightforward case of sex and romance as an inducement to spy.

***

Among those intelligence agencies that used honeytraps to ensnare the unwary, the Eastern Bloc services made something of a speciality of using so-called Romeo spies to seduce women who worked for Western governments, senior Western politicians or organisations such as NATO. The *Hauptverwaltung Aufklärung* (HVA), the foreign intelligence division of the Stasi,

East Germany's secret service, was adept at spotting lonely West
German women who had access to secret information and whose
loneliness could easily be exploited with the offer of romance.
The Second World War had left both the eastern and western sectors of Germany with a shortage of men, so lonely middle-aged
spinsters were relatively common, and the HVA Romeo spies
could easily blend into the local population.

Although they were trained in the art of seduction, the Romeos
were not necessarily good looking and usually targeted single,
middle-aged women working as secretaries to high-ranking politicians or NATO officials. They had to be prepared to spend a
long time building up the relationship with the agent, inspiring
her motivation. At a time when women were rarely treated as
equals, the HVA training manual instructed the Romeo spies to
give the woman 'the feeling that she is regarded as an equal partner who is appreciated and loved'. During the period when the
relationship was being established, there was never any attempt
to obtain intelligence. Only once the 'Juliet' was completely in
love with her Romeo, and therefore unlikely to blow the whistle,
did her seducer confess that he was a spy, although even then he
would of course maintain the fiction that it was a genuine, completely coincidental, romance.

One of the most successful of the Romeo spies was Karl-
Heinz Schneider. He was an unprepossessing, slightly overweight
HVA officer, who would not have been most people's idea of a
Lothario picked out and trained to seduce women into betraying
their country. Schneider and his immediate superior, Gotthold
Schramm, were based in Karl-Marx-Stadt (now Chemnitz) and
were responsible for the seduction of two West German sisters
working for the Bonn government. Marianne Lenzkow, the elder
of the two sisters, was a 31-year-old divorcee who worked as a
teleprinter operator in the Interior Ministry, typing signals for the
Bundesamt für Verfassungsschutz, the West German internal security
service. Schramm posed as a Danish army officer to seduce her
and, once their relationship was established, suggested her sister
Margarethe might like to meet one of his friends. Margarethe
Lubig was unmarried. She worked for NATO and in intelligence

terms was an even better catch than her sister, but she wasn't keen on Schneider or on another HVA Romeo spy introduced to her by Schramm. So Schneider came up with an imaginative ploy. He recruited a handsome East German actor, Roland Gandt, to seduce her. Gandt also posed as a Dane, Kai Petersen, but his cover story was that he was a journalist. Once both women had fallen in love, the two Romeos revealed themselves as Danish intelligence officers. They explained that since Denmark was one of NATO's smallest countries, the West Germans frequently kept important intelligence back from them. They were looking for help to even things up. This was a classic false-flag operation, where the intelligence officers concerned pretend to represent a completely different country to their own. Naively, the two women believed that they were indeed Danish (and therefore Allied) intelligence officers and they agreed to supply them with top-secret reports. Marianne and Margarethe were run as highly productive agents by their respective lovers – sincerely believing that they were only assisting a NATO ally – until just before the Berlin Wall came down and Germany was unified.

The sisters were just two of many West German women seduced by the HVA's Romeo spies, the best of whom was almost certainly Gabriele Gast. She was in her mid-twenties and studying for a PhD in politics at Aachen's Rheinisch-Westfalische Technical University when she was spotted as a potential target. Gast came from a well-to-do family in Remscheid in north-west Germany. Her family background was on the centre-right of German politics, and she herself was a member of the conservative Christian Democratic Youth Movement. In the summer of 1968, Gast applied via relatives living in the East to go there to research her dissertation on 'The political role of women in the German Democratic Republic'. Anyone from the West applying for permission to visit East Germany was subject to stringent checks, which were bound to be even more rigorous in the case of someone wanting to interview party officials. The initial assumption by the Stasi would have been that Gast was working for Western intelligence. The checks triggered immediate interest, because her supervisor was Professor Klaus Mehnert, one of the world's leading experts on the Soviet Union and its communist satellites. Mehnert was known to be a talent-spotter for the West German intelligence service, the *Bundesnachrichtendienst* (BND), and Gast was his star student. Either she was a spy – and there was no obvious evidence that she was – or Gast's application presented a golden opportunity to recruit a potential high-flyer in the political or bureaucratic structures of West Germany, someone who could be carefully steered by her handlers into the right job. With a bit of luck, and a little unconscious assistance from Mehnert, they would be investing in a future agent-in-place inside the BND.

Gast arrived in Karl-Marx-Stadt in August 1968 and was pleasantly surprised at how willing the East German authorities were to assist her studies into the role of women there, an approach she put down to a more emancipated attitude in the East. They even laid on a chauffeur-driven car. The driver was a friendly man in his early thirties who told her his name was Karl-Heinz Schmidt. He was a trained mechanic who had been assigned to drive her wherever she needed to go. Schmidt was more mature than men of Gabriele's own age. He had a well-worn face topped by a blond crew cut and he was well-built, albeit with a slight paunch. They were soon getting on well, drinking beer together in a local bar. Gast was recovering from the break-up of her engagement to a childhood sweetheart, who had wanted to get married and have children and could not see why she might want a career of her own. Schmidt was just a nice man. He seemed to be really interested in her research into the role of women and, unlike many of the men she knew in the West, he made her feel like an equal. It was what he was trained to do. Schmidt was not his real name. He was in fact the HVA officer who had supervised Margarethe Lubig's seduction and recruitment – Karl-Heinz Schneider.

Gast took long walks with him in the countryside and they spent their evenings drinking, dancing and flirting. Blissfully unaware of his real motives, Gast was soon calling him by a pet name, Karlizcek. He in turn called her Gabi. The backing of the East German authorities made it a very productive trip in terms of her research but being with Karl-Heinz meant it was doubly enjoyable for Gast. When the East German authorities invited her back to see more evidence of how women were treated better in the East, she grasped the opportunity eagerly, although in truth her prime motivation for going back to East Germany was the fact that Karl-Heinz was equally keen to meet up again. She had a new man in her life. They both wanted to spend more time together.

Professor Mehnert was pleased when Gast explained how helpful the East Germans had been and how officials had promised to let her interview a wide number of politically active women if she went back in the summer. He said it was an opportunity not to be missed and she must go back. Gast needed no encouragement. She told the professor that she had already agreed to return, although she did not mention that she had met someone over in the East. It was 'a private matter' and none of Mehnert's business, she told herself. In her letters to her lover Karl-Heinz, she asked him to arrange the entry permit for the end of August. But tensions were rising across Eastern Europe over the Prague Spring, the introduction by Alexander Dubček, First Secretary of the communist party of Czechoslovakia, of reforms that Moscow saw as a threat to communist control there. Gast wrote to Karl-Heinz, suggesting that it might be sensible 'given the political situation' to postpone her trip. When Soviet tanks rolled into Prague on 21 August 1968, she assumed she had no chance of going back to East Germany any time soon. So she was surprised but very excited when the promised entry permit arrived in the post.

Back in Karl-Marx-Stadt, Gast spent as much time with her lover as she did on research. They took long walks in the countryside and in the evening visited restaurants and bars. Their favourite meeting place – 'their bar' – was the Kosmos in the middle of the old city, where Western music was played continuously, making it the 'in-place' for young people to be.

'A Czech band played all those tunes and songs that were seen as examples of Western decadence with unabashed confidence,' Gast said. 'Karl-Heinz knew them all and made no secret of it. We danced and flirted until late into the night and it seemed as if nothing could disturb our togetherness.'

They inevitably went back to his apartment in Karl-Marx-Stadt. He told her he lived in Plauen and had been given the apartment because of his job, which was in fact true. It was a Stasi safe-house. Her attempts to get more out of him about his life in Plauen were unsuccessful but it didn't seem to matter. She did not question too much in her own mind how Karl-Heinz had managed to get her the entry permit in the middle of a major crisis in the Eastern Bloc, or why a mechanic with a home less than an hour's drive away would need an apartment in Karl-Marx-Stadt.

'I was now in such a close personal relationship with him that the way in which it had all come about seemed meaningless,' Gast said. 'Was life not full of coincidences? Didn't things often develop in ways you hadn't planned? I trusted Schmidt in such a way that any small inconsistencies seemed to be nothing to worry about. The question of who he really was and exactly where and how he lived had become irrelevant to me.'

Gast was completely in love with Schmidt and, he with her, or so he claimed. Inevitably, she had to return to the West. She was desperate to see her lover again but, since her research had finished, was unable to get another entry permit. Karl-Heinz suggested they meet up in Berlin. After the Second World War, Berlin was divided into three Western sectors controlled by the US, the UK and France and an Eastern sector controlled by the Soviet Union. Westerners were able to travel to the Eastern sector just for the day. Gast went in via the S-Bahn, the city's local railway system, which had one stop in the Eastern sector at Friedrichstrasse. It was the easiest crossing point for day visitors. She and Karl-Heinz met in the Hotel Unter den Linden, a short walk from the station, and spent the day sightseeing. Karl-Heinz told her that he had discussed the problems they had meeting up with a friend in the Interior Ministry, Gotthold Schiefer, who was happy to have dinner with them that evening in the hotel to see if he could help. Gotthold seemed like a nice man. He was also blond, but taller and slenderer than Karl-Heinz and he had dark, warm eyes. He was understanding about how difficult it was for them not being able to meet up whenever they wished and suggested that there was perhaps a way that they could do so more often. He did not, however, want to talk about it in public. She should come back to East Berlin the following day. He would obtain a permit that would let her stay longer and they could meet up in the Karl-Max-Stadt apartment and discuss it in detail. As Gast digested this unexpected turn of events, she questioned for the first time whether there might not be more to what was happening than a simple love affair. How could Gotthold supply such a permit so quickly? And more to the point, why? Was he a Stasi officer? Should she say no straight away? Despite her doubts, she decided to go ahead and see what was said the next day. She would let Schiefer explain what he meant first.

'Then I would know where I stood, and could justifiably say no,' Gast later wrote. 'If he said he was from the Stasi I would definitely say "No". I would be absolutely determined about that and indignant that he wanted to do some shabby deal with me.'

So she returned to East Berlin the next day and met up with Karl-Heinz, who drove her down to the Karl-Marx-Stadt apartment. That evening, Gotthold joined them for a drink. He and Karl-Heinz were clearly good friends and they joked and laughed together a lot. Some of the jokes were aimed at the GDR, the East German state. The three of them had a lot of fun that night, but eventually Gotthold came to the point. He could arrange for Gabi to see Karl-Heinz on a regular basis, but she had to help them in return. She asked him if he was Stasi and he nodded. Gotthold Schiefer was in fact Schneider's HVA colleague, Gotthold Schramm.

Just as the Russians had only initially asked Vassall for minor details about people working in the British embassy, so Schramm said they just wanted Gast to provide details of who did what at the university. There was no harm in handing over such information; after all, Gast was not working on anything secret. She was stunned, no longer sure what she should do. Schramm kept up the pressure.

'Look, you love Karl-Heinz, and he loves you. You both want to be together. This can only happen if you co-operate with us. Not much. Just from time to time. Then we can make sure you meet up, but if you do not want to do it then you cannot see

Karl-Heinz again. So what is it? Do you want to see him again or will you split up?'

'Of course I want to see him again,' Gast replied. 'But ...'

'Why the but? You don't have to do anything wrong. Just tell us something about your university and your degree, nothing that's forbidden.'

Gast asked Karl-Heinz what he thought and he told her it was up to her to decide. She had heard what Gotthold had said. It was up to her whether their relationship would continue, but any neutral observer could have seen that he and Schramm were clearly working together. Karl-Heinz simply remarked: 'I hope you are not going to say no, because I want to be with you. You know how much I love you.'

Schramm played on his colleague's expressions of love. 'You heard what Karl-Heinz said. It would be awful for him if you two split up. He doesn't want that and I get the feeling you don't either. Come on, say: "Yes." Nothing will happen to you. No one will know that you are working with us, and we will take care of you. You can be sure of that.'

'All right,' Gast replied hesitantly, 'but only on my studies and the university. Anything more than that is out of the question.'

Schramm insisted that it really wouldn't be necessary to tell them anything else (although of course that was never really going to be the case). Now she and Karl-Heinz could meet up in a house rather than in this tiny flat. Everything would be great for them. They could meet up on a regular basis.

Having drawn Gast in, the HVA did not rest on its laurels; the psychological development of the new agent continued, with the first safe house they used for her meetings with Karl-Heinz located in Siegmar to the west of Karl-Marx-Stadt. It was where her father had been born. When Gast first went there, Schramm arrived shortly afterwards to provide her with a genuine West German passport in another name but with her photo in it. She was to use this passport and the new name to travel to the East. Schramm made her sign for it. Now Gast had no way out. If she was caught, she was a spy, and they could prove it, blackmailing her to get what they wanted, although in fact this would never prove necessary. By now she felt more loyalty to her lover, to Schramm and to the politics of the East than she did to West Germany. Gast was given the code name Gisela and trained in the tradecraft of the spy, learning to encode messages and send them by radio or how to hide them in fake deodorant cans and leave them in 'dead drops' or pass them on to couriers. She saw herself as part of a team 'working for peace'.

Having completed her doctorate, Gast initially struggled to find a job, but she was soon recommended for a research post with a right-wing think tank in Munich by someone she had been at university with who was now working for the centre-right Konrad Adenauer Foundation. Although this felt like second-best for both Gast and her friends in the East, the HVA were not the only ones willing to exploit her potential as a spy. Having been recruited by East German intelligence, she had now been talent-spotted by their West German counterparts and was approached directly to work for the BND. It was more of a triumph for her HVA recruiters than for Gast herself. They had achieved their aims.

The love affair with Karl-Heinz continued for some time. He even asked her to marry him. They had a party to which Schramm brought Russian champagne to celebrate their engagement, but although Gast was completely taken in, it was all fake, even Karl-Heinz's birthdays, which Gast observed religiously. To the last she was completely unaware that she was just an agent, being run by them, and was never really one of the team.

As Gast climbed the ranks of the BND, eventually becoming deputy head of the Warsaw Pact section and the highest-placed woman in West German intelligence, the reports she produced became increasingly valuable. It was even suggested that BND reports on the Eastern Bloc reached Markus Wolf, the head of the HVA, before they crossed the desk of the West German chancellor. Wolfe later said:

We left it to her to decide what to deliver to us. Like her own colleagues in the West, we had absolute confidence in our expert. The question then arises in this world of mirrors: Just whose analyst was she? I can say that she offered both us and the BND totally objective analysis. She knew our interests and could sum up the information we needed in crisp sentences in reports of four or five pages.

If we required the original documents, she would microfilm them and conceal them in fake deodorant bottles. We initially instructed her to deposit them in the lavatory tanks of the trains travelling from Munich across the border to the East. Later this was deemed too risky as well as insufficient to accommodate the flow of information she was providing. A female go-between would meet her at a Munich swimming pool and they would pass the information between their changing rooms.

As Gast became ever more valuable as an agent, she met Wolf and his successor, Werner Grossmann, in Yugoslavia. While Karl-Heinz continued as part of the team running her, the love affair that had been used to ensnare her faded over time as she became close to a male colleague within the BND. Nevertheless, she continued spying for the East Germans, believing that she was doing the right thing, helping in a process that would bring peace between East and West.

When the Berlin Wall finally came down in 1990, the HVA destroyed all evidence of her betrayal, but a senior Stasi officer anxious to avoid going to jail for his activities provided the West Germans with details of a female HVA agent in a senior post in the BND who, from his description, could only be Gast. She was arrested as she travelled to a final meeting with her handlers and tried for treason. It was only during the court process that she discovered the real name of her lover and finally grasped that he was simply a Romeo spy who had deliberately entrapped her rather than having, as she had until that moment believed, fallen in love with her. His name, their engagement, even his birthdays, all were lies. As indeed was the idea that she had been an equal member of a team. All the time she was just an agent who was being used. To add insult to injury, Gast was jailed for six years and nine months, although she would only serve three-and-a-half years, while

Karl-Heinz Schneider was given eighteen months' probation. As she was led out of court, Gast walked past Wolf, who was also on trial. She couldn't even bring herself to look at him, so deep was the betrayal she felt. Although a sexual relationship had been the initial motivation for her espionage, it had become so much deeper than that, as she felt she was truly working for a cause in which she believed. That both of these turned out to be a lie, made it doubly wounding.

***

Far from the classic Cold War flashpoint of Berlin, other intelligence services were making equally creative use of sexual compromise to recruit agents. The Chinese, both the communist People's Republic of China and the non-communist Republic of China (which is confined to the island of Taiwan), have always made good use of sex to induce foreigners to provide them with the information they need. The main intelligence agency of the People's Republic of China, the Ministry of State Security, uses students studying in the West and what the Chinese authorities call 'Overseas Chinese', ethnic Chinese communities living outside China, to gather intelligence, usually with the implied threat that, if they refuse to do so, any relatives still living in China will be punished. Women recruited as agents in this way are expected to use sex as a means of obtaining the necessary intelligence. One of the most prominent recent operations, which involved a female Chinese spy seducing a US government official to obtain intelligence, was carried out in 2002 by Isabelle Cheng, a member of Taiwan's intelligence service, the National Security Bureau.

Cheng, who was based in Washington, seduced Donald Willis Keyser, a Principal Deputy Assistant Secretary of State, in order to obtain intelligence on discussions between President George W. Bush and Chinese communist leader Jiang Zemin during the latter's state visit to the United States in October 2002. Keyser had been specifically picked out by the Taiwanese as vulnerable to such an approach, he had been married four times, and, as the deputy head of the East Asia Bureau, he was in an excellent position to provide high-grade intelligence. Fluent in Mandarin, he was widely regarded as the State Department's leading expert on communist China and on Taiwan and he was scheduled to take part in the conversations between President George W. Bush and the Chinese president. Keyser was 59 and shortly due to retire at the time Cheng approached him. She was 32.

Flattered by the attention of a much younger, attractive woman, Keyser became infatuated with Cheng. During the 2002 Zheng visit, he sent her an email detailing the discussions between the Chinese president and President Bush. In another email, he told the Taiwanese intelligence officer: 'Having my arm around your shoulder, your head resting against my shoulder, and then on my chest, your hand in mine for a couple of hours while you were in "Dreamland" was more than ample compensation.' After Cheng thanked him for some information he had provided, Keyser told her, 'your wish is my command'.

The US intelligence official eventually agreed to go to Taiwan to talk to officials at the National Security Bureau headquarters in Taipei. As a result of the improvement in relations between the US and communist China that resulted from the 1972 visit by President Richard Nixon to Beijing, the US had in 1979 broken off relations with Taipei – which, like the People's Republic, claimed to be the sole legitimate government of China – and American officials were not allowed to visit Taiwan. During August 2003, Keyser travelled to Asia on an official trip that took him first to Beijing and then to Japan. At the end of his official itinerary, he took three days leave, purportedly spending it sightseeing in Tokyo. In fact, he flew to Taipei, where he met Cheng and other Taiwanese intelligence officials at the National Security Bureau headquarters.

The assistance he gave to Cheng even extended to advice on a State Department colleague who might be recruited as a spy. With what appears to have been a complete lack of self-awareness, and without any apparent sense of irony, Keyser suggested the man's 'weaknesses and ego gratification needs' made him an ideal target.

'This is the kind of person who is ripe for recruitment by careful, methodical serious intelligence agencies,' Keyser told Cheng. 'In the days of the Cold War, Soviet and East German intelligence offices were quite practised at identifying people like this, people who did not wake up one day and say, "I want to be a traitor", but people whose relatively minor weaknesses and ego gratification needs made them potential targets.'

After discovering Keyser's illegal trip to Taiwan, FBI officers set up a surveillance operation and observed him passing documents to Cheng and Michael Huang, the head of the Taiwanese National Security Bureau station in Washington, in two separate meetings at a restaurant in Alexandria, across the Potomac River from the US capital. On the second occasion, the FBI officers confronted Keyser as he left the restaurant.

A search of his home uncovered 3,559 classified documents, including top-secret reports from the CIA, the National Security Agency (NSA), America's signals intelligence operation, and from the Defence Intelligence Agency (DIA). The FBI officers also found around 100 data devices (including floppy disks) containing yet more secret documents. Keyser was arrested in September 2004 and initially denied ever going to Taiwan or having a sexual relationship with Cheng. Even though he admitted that on at least one occasion when they were together Cheng was in the nude, he insisted that they had only ever kissed and embraced. As part of his attempt to secure a plea bargain that would persuade prosecutors to drop espionage charges, Keyser eventually admitted visiting Taiwan, but denied passing Cheng any classified information or having a sexual relationship with her.

Yet even as the negotiations over the plea bargain were going on, Keyser continued to meet Cheng and was photographed by FBI surveillance teams on a number of occasions having sex with her in his car, including one incident when, despite the carefully prudent description presented by prosecutors to the court, it was clear that she was performing oral sex on him. After one of their meetings, Keyser told her (in a telephone conversation intercepted by the FBI surveillance team): 'The food was good. The wine was good. The champagne was good, and you were good.'

Keyser eventually pleaded guilty to the unlawful removal of classified documents from the State Department and to lying about his visit to Taiwan and the nature of his relationship with Cheng. He insisted that, despite the surreptitious nature of his relationship with both her and her colleagues in the National Security Bureau, he did not give them any information he was not already authorised to pass to the Taiwanese, although the court was told that polygraph tests had revealed he was still concealing the full truth of what had happened. Keyser was sentenced in January 2007 to one year and one day in jail and ordered to pay a $25,000 fine.

★★★

The communist Chinese were just as adept as their adversaries on Taiwan at exploiting sexual weakness for intelligence purposes. They were responsible for what must rank as one of the most bizarre cases where a romantic or sexual relationship was used to recruit an agent. Bernard Boursicot was an accountant in the French embassy in Beijing in the 1960s when he met Shi Pei Pu at a diplomatic party in the Chinese capital. Shi, a Chinese male opera singer – Chinese opera uses all-male casts – was short and slim. His face was almost effeminate and his hands tiny, perfect for playing female roles. They agreed to meet for dinner a few days later and became close friends. Shi was an interesting man, an opera singer, and the writer of several operas and plays. Boursicot had struggled to make friends among the embassy staff, most of whom looked down on him for his working-class background and lack of education. Some of the young women in the embassy, daughters of the well-off and privileged, had nicknamed him *Bourricot* – the donkey.

Shi treated Boursicot as an equal. There was no sexual relationship between them, but they became close, confiding their fears and dreams in each other. One evening, Shi described the plot of an opera in which he had played the star role. *The Butterfly Romance* involved a young girl who wanted to go to imperial school but only boys were allowed to attend. Wearing her brother's clothes, she enrolled in the school as a boy, and did well, but fell in love with one of the other boys, who was unable to understand why he was so attracted to someone he believed to be a boy. When her family found her a husband and she was called home, she told the boy the truth and confessed that she was in love with him. He said he loved her too and asked her to marry him. Unable to go against her family's choice of husband, she returned home. Distraught, her lover killed himself. When the news reached her she rushed to his tomb, threw herself in and died. The opera ended with the souls of the dead lovers leaving their bodies in the form of butterflies.

Shortly before Boursicot went back to France in 1965, Shi reminded him of *The Butterfly Romance*. He held up his hands and said: 'Look at my hands. Look at my face. That story of the butterfly – it is my story, too.' Shi's parents had had two daughters before he was born, he explained. They needed a boy to continue the line and Shi's paternal grandmother had said that if this child was not a boy, her son would have to take a second wife. So his parents were desperately hoping for a boy. But he was born a girl. To avoid the grandmother's threat being carried out, they lied to her and raised the baby as a boy.

The story had a dramatic effect on Boursicot, who determined to save Shi, to get her out of China and allow her to live as a woman. He decided to make love to her, even to marry her. Their lovemaking was difficult and Shi insisted on taking control, but over the next six months they slept together on a number of occasions and in December 1965, shortly before Boursicot was due to leave, Shi announced that she was pregnant with his child.

Desperate to see the child, Boursicot managed to get back to Beijing four years later and was met at Shi's home by two Chinese men. Hoping to get Shi and his son out of China, Boursicot offered to supply them with documents from the embassy, explaining that he had access to the diplomatic pouch and control over the secret documents once they were put on file. He regularly took secret documents to Shi's home where Chinese intelligence officers copied them and, in return, at the end of his posting, Shi and their son were allowed to travel to Paris. Shi became the darling of the Parisian cultural scene, but the fact that she (a national of a communist country) was living in the home of a former French diplomat in Beijing led to an investigation by the French security service, the *Direction de la Surveillance du Territoire* (DST), and both Shi and Boursicot were arrested.

The scandal fascinated the French public, particularly given that Shi appeared to be a man, but claimed to be a woman. The French newspaper Le Monde ran a headline '*Espion ou Espionne?*', asking whether the Chinese spy was male or female. Boursicot had no doubt, he had made love to her on numerous occasions and she had borne him a child. But when the examining magistrate ordered a sex test, Shi admitted that he was in fact male but had the ability to transform his genitals by forcing his testicles and his penis up inside his body, leaving just two small flaps of skin from his scrotum that appeared to form the lips of a vagina. Shi admitted that the son was not his, or Boursicot's, but had been produced by the Chinese intelligence services to provide a continuing reason for the Frenchman to supply them with secrets. Boursicot was ridiculed and, humiliated by the scandal, attempted suicide. Both he and Shi were jailed for six years for espionage, but a year later they were pardoned by President Francois Mitterrand. The story inspired a Broadway play, *M. Butterfly*, which was later made into a movie starring Jeremy Irons. Boursicot's bitterness at his treatment by Shi and the ridicule he had suffered remained with him until the Chinese singer's death in 2009, when he said simply: 'He did so many things against me that he had no pity for, I think it is stupid to play another game now and say I am sad. The plate is clean now. I am free.'

Like many others before him, Boursicot had come to realise that just as he had betrayed his country, so he himself had also been betrayed. The love Shi claimed to offer him was (like the singer's femininity) just an illusion, the most effective and appropriate means of recruiting him as an agent inside the enemy camp.

Chapter 3

MONEY

Unsurprisingly, money represents one of the most convincing motives for an agent. If someone is in a position to provide intelligence, the easiest way of persuading them to part with it is likely to be financial inducement. But even then, money is rarely the sole motive and there are inevitable risks in paying an agent for information. The more important that information is, or the greater the pressure to obtain it, the greater the sum paid is likely to be, creating an incentive for the agent to manufacture false intelligence. Nevertheless, it is the simplest and, in many ways, the most secure of all motivations for both the agent and the intelligence service concerned. The agent knows from the start what he or she is getting, while if the handler obtains signed receipts confirming that the money has been paid this leaves an agent who has betrayed his employers with little choice but to continue providing information. It also makes managing the agent much simpler.

'With an agent whose motivation is purely financial, it is generally easier to terminate the relationship when his intelligence is no longer of value,' one former SIS officer said. 'It is just a business relationship. With other motivational forces, terminating an agent can be far more time consuming and complicated.' But by far the greatest advantage of using money as motivation is that a large amount of it on offer will test the loyalty of many potential agents and tempt them to turn traitor, even if they have no other reason for doing so. 'I recall a particularly key case many years ago when a sum of money was carried and offered that would have kept most people in luxury for the rest of their lives, and that was the only conceivable motivation,' the former SIS officer said. 'All the man had to do was to open a door! There was of course a risk that he would turn the offer down and report back. Not easy for him though as he was sitting in a particularly sleazy nightclub in Hamburg.'

Some agents have no loyalty to anyone, taking money from whoever will pay them, sometimes selling their intelligence to the highest bidder, often selling it to a number of customers at the same time. One such man was a Belgian called Arsène Marie Verrue, who worked as a spy for the British War Office in the period before the First World War. Verrue, also known as Frederic Rue, was the European representative of the prominent British brewery Courage, for whom he spent a lot of time in Germany, which provided him with useful cover for observing and reporting on the German build-up to war. Verrue was one of the War Office agents taken over by Mansfield Cumming when he became head of Britain's newly formed secret service in 1909. But unfortunately the War Office had either not done enough work on his background or had decided that espionage was such a nasty, ungentlemanly business that it could not afford to be too fastidious when selecting its secret agents. Verrue was a convicted criminal, who had served a number of prison sentences for various offences, including fraud, embezzlement and forgery, facts that ought to have provided a useful clue to both his motivation and likely reliability. He was eventually dropped by Cumming after being sacked by Courage for dishonesty but was still used on an occasional basis as a freelance agent. This was a bad mistake, because having realised quite how much money could be made as a spy, Verrue began working for a freelance espionage agency based in Brussels, then the spy capital of Europe. This agency sold information to whoever would pay the best money and, with the British Treasury displaying a rather parsimonious attitude towards funding intelligence, the agency's most generous, and therefore its most important, client was the German Kaiser's secret intelligence service, the *Nachrichten Abteilung*.

When Cumming decided in 1911 that he needed his own representative in Brussels, he sent an Old Etonian lawyer and British Army reservist, Captain Bertrand Stewart, to set it up, telling him to link up with Verrue, who had just produced some 'valuable intelligence', allegedly from a woman in Hamburg. Stewart was the very opposite of Verrue, a patriotic Englishman incensed at the arrogant way in which Germany was behaving on the world stage. He had no need of money and was absolutely determined to do what he could for his country. Cumming told him to pay Verrue for the intelligence from Hamburg and ask to be put in touch with the woman. The Belgian declined to take Stewart to see her, claiming it was too dangerous, although with hindsight it is clear she did not exist. She and the 'valuable intelligence' were the bait for a sting.

The British were paying Verrue to help their new man in Brussels, but the Germans were paying the Belgian even more to expose Stewart as a spy. Verrue took him to Germany, ostensibly to help him gather intelligence on the newly reinforced German defences on Heligoland, and gave him a code book, telling him to keep it in his pocket at all times. Given that Verrue was supposed to be teaching Stewart how to spy, this was a surprising thing to do. It ran counter to the rules of basic tradecraft and the book was rather too conveniently still in Stewart's pocket when he was arrested by German police in a public lavatory in the north-western city of Bremen. At the subsequent trial in Leipzig, Verrue was chief witness for the prosecution and was completely candid in subsequent interviews with the German press that he had only helped entrap Stewart because the Germans paid him more than the British.

Stewart's trial provoked an outcry in England, where he was seen as completely innocent, a view he rather oddly shared, although his protestations may have had more to do with the belief in polite British circles that the work of a spy was not something anyone of good standing would undertake. One of his friends wrote to *The Times* claiming that Stewart – an Old Etonian and a member of a string of London gentleman's clubs, the Athenaeum, the Carlton, Arthur's and White's – was 'absolutely incapable of a mean or dishonourable act and would never stoop to play the miserable role of a spy'. Stewart was sentenced to three-and-a-half-years' imprisonment but was released after only a few months. On his return to Britain, he issued a writ against the government, naming Cumming as the head of the British secret service, denying that he had ever been a spy and insisting that if the government had only explained this to the Germans, he would never have faced trial. The case was settled out of court to keep Cumming's role secret but, unlike Verrue, Stewart received no money. He was killed in the early weeks of the First World War and the compensation was paid to his wife.

★★★

Sometimes it is not the desire for great riches, but the inability of someone entrusted with secret information to manage their own finances that leads to betrayal. This is a frequent motivation for the 'walk-in', an agent who volunteers their services directly (rather than being sought out), and it led to one of the best-known successes for the French intelligence services. In the summer of 1931, a 38-year-old German civil servant approached the French embassy in Berlin with an irresistible offer. Hans-Thilo Schmidt, an official in the cipher department of the German War Office, said he could provide documents that would give the French the ability to break the most up-to-date military codes in the world, the Enigma machine ciphers used by the German armed forces.

Schmidt's motivation was simple. His civil service salary was insufficient to match his philandering lifestyle. Had the French spotted him as a potential agent, Schmidt would undoubtedly have been vulnerable to a sexual approach. He was unable to resist seducing the family's maids, even after his wife began replacing his conquests with increasingly unattractive women in an attempt to put him off. But as 'a walk-in' who was able to provide something the French were keen to obtain, he could make his own demands, and what he wanted was money.

The fact that Schmidt would be using it not just to improve the lives of his family, but also to fund his libertine lifestyle might suggest that a sexual motivation cannot be entirely ruled out, but with the German economy in freefall and hyperinflation causing the value of the Reichsmark to change hour by hour, it was money Schmidt needed and demanded in return for the documents. The embassy put him in touch with the French military intelligence service, the *Deuxième Bureau de l'État-major général*, which not only carried out spying operations abroad but also controlled the French code-breaking operations.

There was a great deal of scepticism at the *Deuxième Bureau* over Schmidt's offer and some concern that the whole thing might be a sting operation by the Germans, or simply a scam by Schmidt. Nevertheless, a weekend meeting was eventually arranged at the Grand Hotel in the Belgian city of Verviers, across the border from Aachen, in Germany. Schmidt was met by Rodolphe Lemoine, the man running French espionage operations in Germany, who was himself originally German, and Gustave Bertrand, the officer in charge of the *Deuxième Bureau's* code-breaking effort. Schmidt handed over a number of documents, including several manuals for the Enigma machine, and Bertrand took these upstairs to his own room to have them photographed while Lemoine talked to Schmidt in an attempt to evaluate how best to run him. The most important question in Lemoine's mind was not the value of the documents; that was for Bertrand to decide. If he was going to have to run Schmidt for any length of time, he would need to know why the German was prepared to betray his country, putting his own life and his family's future at risk. Understanding a walk-in's motivation is an essential prerequisite in determining both how they should be run and how best to keep them under control. With a targeted agent, the motivation is already known and has been proven to work, but with a walk-in, the psychology of betrayal is frequently complex and difficult to pin down. This was not the case with Schmidt. It did not take Lemoine long to determine that his fellow German's weaknesses were money and women, and not necessarily in that order. Bertrand later recalled that Schmidt 'was fond of money', which he needed 'because he was even fonder of women'. Lemoine gave the new agent the code name Asché and paid him 10,000 Reichsmark for the first batch of documents, the equivalent of around £30,000 at today's prices.

The *Deuxième Bureau* sought to allay their costs by selling the documents to the British. They were shown to Wilfred 'Biffy'

Dunderdale, the SIS head of station in Paris. Bertrand gave him photographs of the documents, which he took to London to see if they were of interest to the British. If SIS wanted to see all of the documents, they would have to pay. The British code breakers at the Government Code and Cypher School (GC&CS) were doubtful that the manuals would help them unravel the mysteries of the Enigma machine. With their bosses in SIS starved of cash by the Treasury and sceptical that Enigma would ever be broken, the French offer was turned down.

The Poles did not take the same view. Poland was sandwiched between Germany and the Soviet Union, with both countries posing traditional threats to the homeland, but the Polish code-breaking organisation, the *Biuro Szyfrów*, saw Germany as a continuing menace. It had been trying to break the German army's Enigma ciphers since they were introduced in 1928 but without success. So when Bertrand approached the Polish code breakers with Asché's material, they were very grateful and, while they could not afford to pay him, they promised in return to share with the French any intelligence they obtained as a result of the documents. But even with access to these, by September 1932, the Poles were no further forward, so a young Polish mathematician, Marian Rejewski, was recruited to work on the problem, assisted by two other mathematics graduates, Henryk Zygalsky and Jerzy Rozycki.

Helped by Asché's documents, which included an instruction manual describing precisely how the machine worked, they began to make progress. The British knew how the machine worked, and so quite wrongly had not thought the instruction manual would be any use. But it included an example of an enciphered message that showed the plain text and the enciphered text together with the genuine machine settings used to encipher the message. This allowed Rejewski to begin working out the internal wiring of the Enigma machine. Then in August 1932, Lemoine travelled to Berlin under his standard cover as a businessman. He met Schmidt in the Adlon Hotel, where the new agent handed over the Enigma machine settings for September and October plus another Enigma message in both its original plain text and enciphered forms. These were delivered to the *Biuro Szyfrów* by Bertrand personally in mid-September. At a subsequent meeting with Bertrand at the Hotel d'Angleterre in Liege, Asché produced the settings for November and December. By the end of 1932, in a truly phenomenal feat of code breaking, Rejewski had completely reconstructed the inner workings of the German Army Enigma machine. By early January 1933, the Poles were reading their first Enigma message.

So how vital was Hans-Thilo Schmidt/Asché in the battle to break the Enigma ciphers? A better question would be how important was his Enigma material compared to the other intelligence he produced? The role of Asché, as with the work of the Polish code breakers and its impact on the more famous successes at Bletchley Park, is sometimes understated, but just as frequently overstated. The Poles would not have broken Enigma as quickly as they did without Asché, but they would have broken it in time, and probably not that much later. Similarly, Bletchley Park would not have cracked Enigma as quickly as they did without the Poles, but they would have done so eventually, and probably not that much later. The Poles would subsequently acknowledge that Rejewski's success was in part due to the documents produced by Schmidt.

'We did it partly by mathematics and partly *Verrat* [the German word for betrayal],' one of the Polish code breakers told Alastair Denniston, the head of GC&CS. But he was quick to add that they could have done it all by mathematics and, given the speed with which Rejewski achieved the first break, this seems an entirely reasonable claim. That is not, however, to denigrate Hans-Thilo Schmidt's contribution. His early assistance gave the Poles the start they desperately needed, a great deal of confidence in their mathematical methods, and essential experience of breaking the Enigma ciphers, not to mention producing intelligence from the deciphered Enigma messages that would otherwise not have been available. Schmidt would continue to provide the settings for the main German army machine on a regular basis right up until he left the Cipher Office in October 1938. But since his fame as a spy now rests almost entirely on his work on Enigma, and on the sexual elements of his motivation, it is important to stress that this was far from all he produced, and that money played the key role in prompting him to hand over secrets. Also, for very understandable reasons, not least that the Poles neglected to tell them Enigma had been broken with the help of Schmidt's information, the French valued him far more for the other intelligence he provided.

Hans-Thilo Schmidt owed his position and level of access inside the Cipher Office to his elder brother, Rudolf, who was its head in the 1920s and who had appointed him as his deputy. Rudolf Schmidt, a high-flier in the German Army, the *Reichswehr*, was soon promoted and, by the time Hans-Thilo became a French spy, was in an influential staff job where he had access to all the latest information on German rearmament and the development of military planning. This information was far easier to understand and process than the Enigma documents. It was comparatively straightforward for Schmidt to write reports of intelligence garnered in conversation with his brother in invisible ink and send them by post. This was far safer and quicker than meetings abroad, which would be bound eventually to give rise to suspicion.

Unfortunately, communications with Schmidt were not the only security concerns in terms of running him as an agent. The large sums of money he was being paid for information had transformed the German's fortunes and led to an ostentatious change in his lifestyle. Schmidt and his wife took holidays abroad, bought expensive clothes and extended and updated their house.

The solution to both problems was the creation of a new family business for Schmidt, to supplement his income from his official work for the armed forces. The business, a factory producing animal fat for German soap factories, was a front. The workers had little to do in reality, and very little fat was ever actually produced or sold, but on paper the business was a roaring success as a result of a licence from Schmidt to a French soap company to use his supposedly unique, new method of extracting fat. The French company paid Schmidt's business large sums of money for the rights to use this process. All of this cash was supplied by the *Deuxième Bureau* in return for the intelligence Schmidt was supplying it in invisible writing on the invoices and at his regular meetings with Lemoine in Berlin or with other agent handlers while on holiday abroad. If Schmidt had more urgent material and needed to arrange a 'crash meeting', he was to telephone Georges Blun, the Berlin correspondent of the *Journal de Paris*, who was himself a *Deuxième Bureau* agent, and tell him that 'Uncle Kurt has died'. They were to meet up immediately after the call in the waiting room of Berlin's Charlottenburg railway station. Schmidt would then hand over the intelligence, which Blun was to pass to the French embassy.

As Schmidt's brother Rudolf rose through the upper echelons of the *Wehrmacht* staff, he became privy to a wide range of secret information about Hitler's plans. It was clear these would lead to war, a source of deep concern to Rudolf Schmidt, as it was to other senior army officers. He shared those fears with his brother, both in private conversations and letters. His indiscretion was a boon for the *Deuxième Bureau*, producing a veritable treasure trove of intelligence, including a description of the new *Blitzkrieg* tactic of using rapidly moving tanks supported by air power to punch through the enemy's front line and two months' notice of the German reoccupation of the Rhineland, which took place in March 1936. When Rudolf Schmidt was promoted to the rank of major-general in October 1937, this gave the *Deuxième Bureau* what was equivalent to a spy inside the highest circles of the German military, who provided – via his brother – a large amount of military and political intelligence ranging from discussions with Hitler over his military plans to the concerns among the German general staff about where the Führer's ambitions might lead.

A few weeks after Rudolf Schmidt received his promotion, he told his brother about a secret meeting between the generals and Hitler in which the Führer told them he had decided to occupy a number of neighbouring countries. Austria and Czechoslovakia would be taken into the Reich, by force if necessary. Hitler even provided a rough timetable for the occupations, Austria in the spring of the following year, 1938, with Czechoslovakia to follow in the autumn.

Schmidt called a crash meeting with Blun and handed him details of Hitler's plans, which the journalist took to the French embassy. Determined to take some credit for the scoop, the ambassador decided to send news of the meeting to Paris by secret signal, albeit omitting the more sensitive details of what was discussed. It was an incredibly stupid breach of security. The Germans, who had broken the French codes, intercepted and read the signal and set up an inquiry into how the existence of the meeting had leaked. Fortunately, that investigation led nowhere.

The French improved the security surrounding their communications with Schmidt and he continued reporting on his brother's activities, including the preparations for the invasion of Poland, in which Rudolf Schmidt played a significant part as commander of the 1st Panzer Division, and for the invasion of France, in which his men were also involved. In a final meeting with one of his French controllers in Lugano in Switzerland in March 1940, Schmidt described a lunch with Hitler attended by Rudolf and other key commanders. They were briefed on how the main German invasion force would go straight through the densely forested and hilly Ardennes region. But Schmidt's intelligence was ignored, the French generals dismissed the plan as unlikely and as a result were unprepared to defend against the attack when it came in May 1940.

The German occupation of France ended Hans-Thilo Schmidt's role as a French spy and, it seemed at the time, the risk he was running, but then Rodolphe Lemoine's son was arrested by the Gestapo. In order to obtain his release, Rodolphe offered to help the *Abwehr*. He told his astonished interrogators how the brother of one of Hitler's favourite generals had provided the *Deuxième Bureau* with monthly settings for the Enigma ciphers and the German plans to invade Austria, Czechoslovakia, Poland and France. Lemoine explained that Asché 'always needed money' and even suggested he might now be spying for Russia. Hans-Thilo Schmidt was arrested in April 1943 and six months later committed suicide to avoid execution.

Rudolf Schmidt was relieved of his command a week after his brother's arrest but acquitted of any crime. Unlike his brother, who hawked secrets for money to fund his lavish lifestyle, Rudolf had never suspected his role in betraying German intelligence and was guilty of nothing worse than indiscretion. He was captured by the Russians at the end of the war and held as a prisoner-of-war until 1955. He died peacefully at his home in Krefeld, in north-west Germany, in 1957.

★★★

The Germans were not without their own Second World War intelligence successes where the agent was motivated by money. Probably the most celebrated of these was what became known as the Ciccro Affair. One evening towards the end of October 1943, Ilyas Bazna, a 39-year-old Kosovo Albanian, turned up at the apartment of Albert Jenke, First Secretary at the German embassy in the Turkish capital Ankara. Bazna had singled out Jenke because he knew him, having briefly worked for him previously. He explained that he was now valet to Sir Hughe Knatchbull-Hugessen, the British ambassador, and had photographs of secret documents, which he was prepared to hand over in exchange for a large sum of money. Bazna was dark, short, stocky and very nervous. Jenke was the brother-in-law of Joachim von Ribbentrop, the German Foreign Minister. He was a political appointee placed in the embassy to keep an eye on the ambassador. Espionage was way beyond his area of expertise. Jenke and his wife thought Bazna looked 'desperate and dangerous', so the German diplomat called in Ludwig Moyzisch. To the outside world, the former Austrian journalist was the embassy's assistant commercial attaché. In fact, he was a professional intelligence officer, the representative of the *Sicherheitsdienst*, the Nazi security and intelligence service controlled by SS chief Heinrich Himmler.

When Moyzisch arrived at the apartment, it took no time at all to determine Bazna's motive. He was demanding 10,000 Turkish pounds for two undeveloped rolls of film of secret British documents. This was a substantial sum of money, more than £50,000 sterling at today's prices, and Bazna wanted 5,000 Turkish pounds for each additional roll of film he produced, plus a monthly salary of 15,000 Turkish pounds whether or not he produced any films. Moyzisch's first thought was that the valet must be a confidence trickster. Further questioning revealed what appeared to be an additional motive; Bazna claimed that his father had been killed by an English landowner in a shooting accident. This was a lie, an attempt to give Moyzisch what he seemed to want, a motive more meaningful and less mercenary than money. In fact, Bazna's father had died peacefully in his bed. Ilyas was an inveterate liar, married with four children whom he had left behind in Istanbul. He had one motive, and one motive alone – he wanted money.

Moyzisch agreed to meet Bazna again three days later and give him a decision. In the meantime, he discussed the offer with the ambassador, Franz von Papen, who had been Hitler's predecessor as Chancellor. Papen sent an immediate signal to von Ribbentrop, outlining Bazna's offer and asking for direction on what to do. He was told to proceed with caution. They gave Bazna the code name 'Cicero' and when he returned a few days later with the two rolls of film, Moyzisch told him to wait while he had the photographs developed.

It was soon clear to Moyzisch that Bazna was genuine. He said:

> Here, on my desk, were the most carefully guarded secrets of the enemy, both political and military, and of incalculable value. There was nothing suspect about these documents. These were no plant. There could be no shadow of doubt that these were the real thing. Out of the blue, there had dropped into our laps, the sort of papers a Secret Service agent might dream about for a lifetime without believing that he could ever get hold of them. Even at a glance I could see that the valet's service to the Third Reich was unbelievably important. His price had not been exorbitant.

Numerous myths surround the Cicero story. Bazna claimed to have trained as a classical singer and he told Moyzisch that it was his fine singing voice that had persuaded the British ambassador to employ him as a valet. Knatchbull-Hugessen sometimes even accompanied him on the piano, Bazna said. The romantic element of this story gained credence in Berlin at the time and is a staple of virtually all subsequent accounts, but it is almost certainly nonsense. While Knatchbull-Hugessen was a lover of classical music and did play the piano, the Old Etonian insisted that he had no idea that the Albanian could sing and at any event would certainly never have considered accompanying him on the piano. Unlike other elements of Knatchbull-Hugessen's later testimony – politely and rather too generously described by Foreign Office officials as 'misrememberings' – there is no reason to doubt him on this point.

Bazna was in all probability adding one more elaborate lie to build up his own credibility in the face of sustained pressure from Moyzisch, who needed to be able to reassure Berlin that the source was reliable and the intelligence genuine. Embassy officials told the subsequent investigation that Bazna regarded himself as far smarter than he actually was. 'A clever idiot,' one member of the embassy staff recalled, 'always trying to put a fast one over somebody.'

Knatchbull-Hugessen was a very easy target. In terms of security breaches, he was a serial offender and without his friends in the British establishment would surely have already been out of a job long before Bazna arrived on the scene. Ever since his first posting as an ambassador, in Riga in the early 1930s, he had taken secret documents back to his residence each night, disregarding repeated warnings of the risks. They were locked in document boxes, but he routinely left the keys lying on his dressing table and, from some time in 1941, his butler in Ankara, a locally employed Yugoslav called Andrea Marovic, had been passing details from the ambassador's papers to the *Abwehr*, the *Sicherheitsdienst*'s bitter rival.

These earlier leaks had come to light in October 1941, when British code breakers at Bletchley Park deciphered a message from Viktor Friede, the *Abwehr* station chief in Ankara, to his bosses in Germany reporting that he had two agents inside the British embassy. One of them had supplied a complete courier bag. Friede's message coincided with the disappearance in August 1941 of a diplomatic courier bag en route from Cairo to Ankara that was later discovered discarded in an embassy store cupboard, presumably having been returned after its contents had been copied by the Germans.

The second agent was 'the ambassador's manservant' who was being paid a monthly salary for the information he supplied. A few weeks after Friede's signal, the British ambassador in Moscow, Sir Stafford Cripps, was warned by the Russians that Knatchbull-Hugessen's safe 'was opened every night by somebody inside the house and that the contents were photographed and passed on to the Turkish authorities'. In fact, there was rarely any need to open the ambassador's safe, since Knatchbull-Hugessen left the documents in the boxes in his study or his bedroom, giving Marovic easy access to his papers. Harold Gibson, the SIS head of station in Istanbul, was sent to Ankara to brief the British ambassador, whose subsequent refusal to accept that there was a problem and determination to keep Marovic on his staff was described by one senior British official as 'disturbing and astonishing'.

This was something of an understatement given what we now know. On the morning of Saturday, 30 January 1943, Knatchbull-Hugessen travelled to Adana on the border with Syria to meet Winston Churchill. The British Prime Minister, who had been in Casablanca a few days earlier for a conference with US President Franklin D. Roosevelt, was flying in from Cairo for talks with Turkish President Mustafa İsmet İnönü as part of a long-term British plan to draw Turkey into the war on the side of the Allies. Knatchbull-Hugessen had clearly been unable to keep the fact that he was meeting Churchill to himself. No sooner had he left for the conference than Marovic was on the phone to the German embassy to tell them that Churchill's aircraft was on its way to Adana. Berlin was swiftly informed. The security implications of the German awareness that Churchill was about to arrive in Turkey are staggering. The British Prime Minister flew back to Cairo the following day, while Knatchbull-Hugessen briefed the British, American and Turkish press at the embassy, noting with some satisfaction that news of the meeting had taken the Germans 'completely by surprise'.

This illusion was shattered when British security officials reported the butler's phone call to the German embassy, but even then, the British ambassador insisted that it was 'not practicable for him to dismiss Marovic until he had found a successor'. It was not until mid May, after terse instructions from London that the issue was 'a serious one which admits of no delay', that

Knatchbull-Hugessen finally accepted he must sack Marovic. Two months later, he appointed Bazna as his valet.

Quite why it was that no one seems to have been concerned that even after Marovic's departure the second German agent might still be in place is unclear. Bazna was not slow in realising that the combination of his access to the boxes and the ambassador's keys, and therefore the documents, represented a life-changing opportunity. The question is whether he worked this out by himself. There is some evidence that Bazna was not working alone, raising the possibility that the other German agent had tipped him off to the money-making opportunity represented by the ambassador's lack of security. Moyzisch was surprised by the standard of the photographs Bazna produced; they were taken with a Leica, the type of camera the *Abwehr* routinely provided to its agents. At one point, one of the photographs was clearly being held by someone who was definitely not Bazna. A *Sicherheitsdienst* inquiry concluded that it was highly unlikely that Bazna was operating alone.

Whether or not Bazna had an accomplice, the Cicero case is a classic of spy tradecraft. Knatchbull-Hugessen frequently left his keys on his dressing table. Each morning, while the ambassador took his bath, Bazna would take them, open the dispatch boxes in the ambassador's study, lay the documents out on the desk and photograph them. If for some reason it was not possible to do it in the morning, he had a second opportunity in the afternoon when the ambassador went into town to play the piano. A month after Bazna first started working for the Germans, he took wax impressions of the keys and gave them to Moyzisch, who sent them to Berlin where a second set of keys were cut. Now, even when Knatchbull-Hugessen did not leave his keys lying around, his valet could open the boxes and copy the documents. To signal that he was ready to make a delivery, Bazna would telephone Moyzisch's office to invite him for a game of bridge or poker. The rendezvous for collecting the films was predetermined at the previous drop and changed every time. In order to ensure that Bazna was never seen near the German embassy or meeting any German officials, he would wait in the shadows in one of the many quiet, dark streets in Ankara. A car would draw up along-side him and slow to walking pace. He would jump in, hand over the film, take his money and get out again when the car slowed to walking pace in another dark street.

The Cicero documents were undoubtedly extremely useful to the Germans. They included correspondence between Knatchbull-Hugessen and the Foreign Office, as well as the ambassador's handwritten notes of his conversations with Turkish government officials. These revealed substantial detail of Britain's continuing efforts to draw Turkey into the war and Operation Saturn, a plan to send RAF aircraft to Turkey, from where they would provide air support for an attack on Rhodes. According to Maria Molkenteller, the *Sicherheitsdienst* translator who dealt with the documents, they also included the minutes of the Cairo conference of November 1943, at which Churchill, Roosevelt and Chinese Nationalist leader Chiang Kai-Shek discussed the war against Japan and a second Cairo Conference in December 1943 when Roosevelt, Churchill and İsmet İnönü met, agreeing that Turkey should remain neutral. Given that Knatchbull-Hugessen took the minutes, Molkenteller's claim is entirely credible. The documents revealed that Turkey had agreed to declare war on Germany on 15 February 1944, which presumably allowed von Papen to warn the Turkish government of the likely conse-quences. At any event, Turkey did not enter the war for another year, by which time its involvement had become largely irrelevant.

There were at least two references in the Cicero documents to Overlord, the cover name for the Allied invasion of Western Europe. This was in many ways the most controversial piece of information Cicero provided, since when Moyzisch published his own account of the affair in 1950, the publicity for his book inaccurately suggested that Knatchbull-Hugessen's carelessness had given the Germans the date and other details of the D-Day invasion. In fact, none of the mentions of Overlord actually revealed its meaning. It was clear from the context that it must be an Allied invasion and that it would be launched against France, but this was scarcely revealing; indeed, it was no more than the Germans were already being told by *Abwehr* agents in the UK in reports sent under British control as part of the Double Cross deception operations.

One of the other myths of the Cicero Affair is that the content of the documents was ignored in Berlin as a result of squabbles between SS chief Kaltenbrunner and Ribbentrop over whether it was genuine. The two certainly had arguments over the Cicero product, but not about its veracity. The dispute was rather over who 'owned' the intelligence and should therefore get the credit for it. Ribbentrop unsurprisingly claimed that since his brother-in-law Jenke, a diplomat, had been the first contact, it was Foreign Ministry intelligence who should do so. Kaltenbrunner, on the other hand, pointed out that as the actual intelligence operation was carried out by the *Sicherheitsdienst* and they were the ones who took all the risks, the intelligence should belong to them. Eventually, with the assistance of a piece of subterfuge from one of Kaltenbrunner's aides, the *Sicherheitsdienst* retained control of the dissemination of the Cicero documents.

Claims of attempts by either Kaltenbrunner or Ribbentrop to smother the intelligence are demonstrably false. Indeed, the Cicero product was understandably regarded as so important that one copy went straight to Hitler's headquarters and a second to Obergruppenführer Ernst Fegelein, the senior SS representative on Hitler's staff. The Foreign Ministry received two copies and set up a committee of three ministers to oversee the use of the intelligence. When, a few weeks after delivering his first rolls of film, Bazna doubled the price of each roll of film to 10,000 Turkish pounds, his terms were agreed immediately. When he demanded 50,000 Turkish pounds for the wax impressions, this sum was also paid. The willingness to pay virtually anything Bazna asked did not derive solely from the perceived value of the intelligence. It was funded as part of Operation Bernhard, a *Sicherheitsdienst* operation to destabilise the British economy by flooding the currency markets with fake Sterling banknotes. Cicero's money was sent to Ankara in bundles of forged £5 notes that Moyzisch then exchanged for Turkish pounds. Bazna was ultimately paid between 600,000 and 700,000 Turkish pounds or roughly £80,000 sterling, the equivalent of £3.2 million today.

The security surrounding the operation was understandably tight. The rolls of films were sent to Berlin by air with only occasional oblique references to Cicero appearing in *Sicherheitsdienst* communications between Ankara and Berlin. So closely was the secret protected that the first confirmation of the Cicero leaks came not from intercepted communications, but from the US Office for Strategic Services (OSS), the forerunner of the CIA, which discovered that a German agent inside the British embassy in Ankara had revealed details of a number of agreements between Britain and Turkey, including the plan to send RAF aircraft to Turkey. On 15 January 1944, Roosevelt sent the OSS report direct to Churchill, who ordered an immediate investigation.

Moyzisch ordered Bazna to suspend all attempts to copy the ambassador's papers. By now terrified that he would be discovered, the valet gave six weeks' notice and left the ambassador's service at the end of February 1944. Sir John Dashwood, the Foreign Office investigator, realised the significance of Bazna's decision to quit and identified him as a key suspect, but the inquiry was hampered by the insistence of Knatchbull-Hugessen that the documents could not have been copied in his residence and that they must have been stolen on the train that took him from Ankara to Adana for the flight to Cairo. It would be odd if Knatchbull-Hugessen – given his previous experience with Moravic – had not realised the significance of Bazna's departure, but he must also have realised that acknowledging the likelihood that his valet was the spy would, or at least should, have ended his career. Only the subsequent, indefensible cover-up by the Foreign Office, where Anthony Eden, a university friend of Knatchbull-Hugessen's, was Secretary of State, averted the need for his resignation.

Suggestions that the Cicero documents represented the most damaging intelligence uncovered by a Second World War spy are wide of the mark. It was an excellent operation, which produced reams of valuable secret intelligence, but its likely impact on the war was limited. Indeed, the most dangerous security leak caused by Knatchbull-Hugessen's arrogance and stupidity occurred months before Bazna started working for him, when Marovic warned of the imminent arrival of Winston Churchill at Adana. If the Germans had shot down the British Prime Minister's aircraft over the Mediterranean, either on its way to Turkey or during the return flight to Cairo, that would have had a far greater impact on the war than any of the intelligence which Bazna produced.

★★★

One interesting feature of the Cicero case was the *Sicherheitsdienst*'s use of forged sterling banknotes to fund its operations. This idea was taken a step further by SIS in the immediate post-war period with a smuggling operation based in the British-occupied sector of Berlin, which netted millions of roubles that were then used to pay agents inside the Soviet Union. Operation Junk was controlled from a three-storey mansion at Winklerstrasse 20, in the Grunewald area of West Berlin, which is now the official residence of the UAE ambassador. At the time, in the late 1940s and early '50s, it was the main base from which SIS ran its agents inside the Soviet sector of Berlin and what was to become Soviet-occupied East Germany.

The final Soviet assault on Berlin in May 1945 had flattened much of the German capital, forcing the remaining residents to find shelter where they could among the rubble. The value of the German currency, the Reichsmark, had collapsed. Barter was the only way for many Germans to get hold of the necessities of life. Cigarettes became the most common form of currency, with one cigarette worth the equivalent of ten Reichsmarks.

With the Cold War already under way, the city's main growth industries were the black market and espionage, recalled the former SIS officer who ran the operation. Tony Divall, one of a number of young Royal Marine commandos drafted in to work for SIS in the decade after the war, said that Berliners were prepared to exchange their most treasured possessions for black-market food, alcohol, cigarettes or coffee. As a result, the intelligence agencies of both East and West had little difficulty finding agents willing to undertake the most dangerous of missions in exchange for a small box of food and cigarettes. SIS initially funded its operations by creating a fake army unit and indenting for full rations, using the tinned food, coffee, alcohol and cigarettes issued to the imaginary unit to pay the agents for any information they had either on escaped Nazis or the new enemy, the Russians.

Financing operations inside the Soviet Union itself presented far more formidable problems. The Russians had blocked the movement of roubles abroad, leaving Western intelligence agencies with no way of paying and funding the agents they were sending into the Soviet Union. Then, one of the SIS agents told his handler about a small-scale smuggling operation involving railwaymen on trains transporting industrial equipment to the Soviet Union. The Russians were ripping up everything of any value in their part of Germany and sending it back home by rail as 'war reparations'. Trains would leave Berlin and travel around the Soviet Zone picking up wagons loaded with industrial equipment, and then make their way across Poland to Brest-Litovsk on the Soviet border to be unloaded. Each train was manned by a crew of around a dozen men, who worked in shifts as the train made its way around the eastern sector, across Poland and back, a journey that frequently took several weeks.

The crews were smuggling items that were in short supply in the Soviet Union on to the trains and trading them with the workers at the Brest-Litovsk railway yard. It was a very small-scale operation, not particularly well organised, run by a number of East European Jews who had survived the concentration camps and were now making a living on the black market. They were based around the Bahnhof Zoo, West Berlin's main railway station, flitting between the Eastern and Western sectors of Berlin and led by a Polish Jew who shared the name of one of James Bond's most famous villains. Mandel Goldfinger had progressed from running a black-market stall to owning a small jeweller's shop, buying gold jewellery cheaply from straitened Germans and selling it on to the occupying forces. His main interest in the smuggling ring was in Swiss gold watches, which were in high demand in the Soviet Union, particularly ladies' watches, which were known to the Russians as '*Damskis*'.

Divall, a fluent German speaker who could pass as a native German, suggested to his bosses that they should take over the smuggling ring and exploit it to obtain roubles that could then be used to pay agents inside the Soviet Union. They gave him the go-ahead to take control of Goldfinger's smuggling operation.

The agent who had first reported the smuggling operation was told to put the word out that an associate of his, a Herr Stephan, was interested in acquiring roubles. Within a few weeks, Goldfinger had produced a sample 2,000 roubles, the result of smuggling just two Swiss watches along the rail link. In an operation that demonstrated agents can be employed for other reasons than to gather intelligence, particularly when the motivation is financial, Goldfinger and four other black marketeers were recruited by Divall, operating under the work name of 'Herr Stephan', to run a vastly expanded smuggling ring. Each of the five then enlisted their own railwaymen to smuggle the watches along the line.

Goldfinger and his colleagues, who became known within SIS as the 'Godfathers', bought the men's watches for around £18 each and the *Damskis* for just £4, selling them on to the railwaymen for £24 and £8, respectively. The Russians paid 1,000 roubles per watch and when the railwaymen returned from Brest-Litovsk with their roubles the 'Godfathers' gave them £50 per 1,000 roubles, effectively doubling the smugglers' money. As the official exchange rate was £100 per 1,000 Roubles, but 'Herr Stephan' paid £70 per 1,000 roubles, this left everybody, including SIS, with a handsome profit.

The front-line agents, in this case the railwaymen, were not making easy money. They were running immense risks. The trains were searched regularly by border guards and the railway crews were riddled with informers. Initially the watches and roubles were hidden by concealing them inside condoms suspended inside a water tank, but this severely limited the number that could be smuggled. Attempts to conceal them inside tins of food were too obvious and the watches were soon discovered, but SIS recruited a railway engineer who hollowed out various parts of the train to hide the contraband. There were inevitable setbacks. One railwayman was sentenced to eighteen months' imprisonment for 'sabotage' after a hollowed-out coupling pin broke under stress, spilling twenty *Damski* watches onto the track. But the hollowed-out components allowed up to 100 watches to be smuggled at any one time and SIS's need for roubles was soon more than satisfied.

The operation, which ran from 1946 to 1955, was so successful that both the Americans and the Russians tried to muscle in on it. When the CIA's attempt to set up a rival smuggling network led Goldfinger and his fellow Godfathers to demand more money, SIS cut the Americans in on the existing supply, at a price. An SIS German agent was used as a middleman while the SIS officer then running the operation sat in a car outside 'to make sure the German did not run off with the £1,000 in cash as soon as he completed the deal', one former SIS officer said, in a clear demonstration of the main motivation for those taking part.

The KGB's attempt to establish themselves in this trade was clearly more complex, but it became obvious when one of the Godfathers produced a bundle of mint, consecutively numbered rouble notes (which could not have been obtained without official Soviet involvement). Fortunately, the KGB officers concerned were trying to make money for themselves, rather than using it to track down SIS agents, although the fear that would happen was very real. It was not until 1955, when the officer then overseeing the operation was replaced by George Blake, a KGB agent-in-place inside SIS (who was apparently motivated by ideology), that Operation Junk was blown. By then, it had produced millions of roubles to fund SIS operations inside the Soviet Union. Blake was jailed for forty-two years in 1961 after blowing numerous SIS operations and helping the KGB and the East German Stasi to roll up all of the SIS networks in East Germany, costing the lives of countless agents. He escaped from Wormwood Scrubs prison in 1966 and fled to Moscow.

★★★

The corrupting use of money to recruit spies was not a practice confined to the Second World War or the Cold War tussle between the USSR and the NATO allies. One of the most extraordinary and longest-running cases of espionage carried out for financial gain occurred in India in the 1970s and '80s and had its origins in industrial espionage. Coomar Narain, the Delhi representative of a Mumbai-based engineering and trading company SLM Maneklal, began modestly, using bottles of Johnny Walker Black Label whisky and small-scale payments to persuade government officials to tip him off to opportunities for the company to expand its business. Having been a senior civil servant in the Commerce Ministry, Narain had built up a network of friends and contacts across the Indian Civil Service and set about exploiting it to obtain favourable business opportunities for his boss, Yogesh Maneklal, the company's owner. At the end of their working day, civil servants would drop into the company's Delhi offices in Hailey Road, a tree-lined street in the upmarket embassy area of the Indian capital, where Narain would ply them with glasses of Black Label in exchange for information.

Narain had no plans for his corruption of Indian officialdom to evolve into anything more substantial, but with hindsight it always had the makings of a perfect long-term intelligence operation, starting modestly, with titbits of information passed between friends, and gradually growing into a widespread net of informers who seemed to have such trust in Narain that they happily handed him classified government briefing papers. While they gossiped and sipped whisky with their ebullient host, one of his lackeys would take the documents around the block to the local 'Quick Photostat' shop, have a copy printed off and bring it back to their boss, who would return the originals to the civil servants and send them on their way, usually with a surprisingly small pay-off, a bottle of Black Label, 100 rupees (less than £10), or even on occasion just 50 rupees. Sometimes, the document was sent on ahead of time, delivered by a young Civil Service office boy on a bicycle, so that it could be returned without any interruption to the conversation between Narain and his contact.

It was not until the late 1970s, as SLM Maneklal's business expanded into the Soviet Union and other Eastern Bloc countries that the immense potential of Narain's ability to persuade his former colleagues to hand over secret government documents came to the attention of people with wider interests, in the shape of the KGB. In exchange for favourable status for the company's business operations across the Eastern Bloc, Narain began expanding his network to take in senior civil servants inside the Ministry of Defence and even the offices of the Prime Minister and the President. He also stopped using the local 'Quick Photostat' and acquired his own photocopier.

Using a complex series of cut-outs (or intermediaries), designed to continue the appearance of industrial rather than state espionage, Narain sold copies of literally hundreds of secret and top-secret Indian government documents at £100 apiece to a Commerce Ministry civil servant who then sold them in turn to two Indian businessmen operating in Eastern Europe. It was these businessmen who passed the documents on to Jan Haberka, the Delhi station chief of the Polish intelligence service *Służba Bezpieczeństwa,* his HVA counterpart Otto Wicker, and most importantly of all Gennadiy Afanasyevich Vaumin, the KGB *Rezident* in the Indian capital. The two Indian businessmen were rewarded for their role with lucrative contracts for their companies across the Eastern Bloc.

The material included top-secret papers on India's atomic energy programme, military satellites, government electronics systems and the country's defence planning – including potential purchases of military aircraft, warships and weaponry. They also included top-secret government policy papers and reports from the Indian foreign intelligence service, the Research and Analysis Wing (RAW), and the internal security service, the Intelligence Bureau (IB), on key issues relating to foreign policy, including relations with China and Pakistan, and on sensitive internal issues dealing with India's ethnic divides. Just in case anything was missing, Narain's contacts provided copies of high-level Indian ciphers, which allowed the KGB to read Indian military and diplomatic communications.

By the early 1980s, it was not just the Eastern Bloc intelligence services that had discovered Narain's network of spies across the Indian Civil Service. SLM Maneklal's significant business interests in France led to officials at the French embassy being brought on to Narain's client list. The vastly expanded scale and financial implications – at the time France was vying for Indian defence contracts worth a total of £4 billion – resulted in Narain and his more important government sources receiving substantial sums of money paid into numbered Swiss bank accounts. Narain also held 'lavish parties' where, along with unlimited supplies of his trademark Black Label whisky, he laid on expensive call-girls, ensuring that all those involved were kept happy, no matter how small their role. The woman who provided the prostitutes described Narain as 'one of my best customers'. He always paid promptly and 'courteously' provided her employees with transport home, she said, denying any knowledge of a spy ring. 'I thought that he was engaging the girls to help get contracts awarded to his company.'

In the wake of the Indian intervention in the Pakistan civil war of 1971, which led to the creation of Bangladesh, Indian Prime Minister Indira Gandhi had moved her country closer politically to the Soviet Union. This may have persuaded some within government to adopt an ambivalent attitude towards the KGB role in the Narain espionage operation, but the involvement of the French, with their huge bids for Indian defence contracts, and the realisation that some of their own documents had leaked led the IB to intervene. Mrs Gandhi was told of the investigation in September 1984. The following month she was assassinated by two of her Sikh bodyguards in response to the Indian Army's storming of Amritsar's Golden Temple four months earlier. Her son, Rajiv, took over as Prime Minister, but by the time he was told of the investigation he had called elections for late December and ordered the IB to wait until after the elections before taking action.

Pookat Gopalan left the Prime Minister's office after work on Wednesday, 16 January 1985 and headed down to the office of SLM Manaklal. Gopalan was the senior personal assistant to P.C. Alexander, the Prime Minister's Principal Secretary. He took three secret government documents to Narain's offices to

be copied. Gopalan and Narain were sipping whisky and chat-
ting when the police burst in, arresting them both and sealing off
the building. The IB investigators found the three documents in
Gopalan's briefcase, but it was only as they searched further that
the full scale of the operation became clear. The Press Trust of
India reported that investigators seized 'trunkloads of confidential
documents' including 'a photocopy of almost all the important
files in the Prime Minister's and Defence Ministry secretariats'.
At the same time, a number of other senior civil servants, including three more members of the Prime Minister's office, led by the
deputy head of the unit, T.N. Kher, were being arrested at their
offices or homes.

Next day, Rajiv Gandhi stood up in parliament to announce
the uncovering of a plot involving the sale of government secrets
to a number of foreign countries. As head of the Prime Minister's
office, Alexander was forced to resign immediately, although he
denied any knowledge of the spy ring and was never charged.
Gandhi did not name any of the foreign countries involved,
but the Indian media was clearly being pointed in the direction of France, with Poland and East Germany being painted as
minor players and the KGB getting no mention at all. On the
Saturday after the initial arrests, IB officers arrived at the home
of the French deputy military attaché Lt-Col Alain Bolley and
ordered him to pack and leave immediately. He and his family
were escorted to the airport and they departed on that evening's Air France flight to Paris. Meanwhile, Serge Boidevaix, the
French ambassador, was told that he also was no longer welcome
and, although the Indian authorities would not openly expel
him, he should make plans to leave within a month. Jan Haberka,
the Delhi representative of *Służba Bezpieczeństwa,* and his HVA
equivalent, Otto Wicker, were also expelled. They, though, were
pushed out without the fanfare given to the French departures
and, amid rumours that a KGB officer had also been forced to
leave, investigators said there was considerable pressure from
Moscow to suppress details of the level of Eastern Bloc involvement. It only later emerged that the Soviet Communist Party – at
the request of the KGB – had made payments in US dollars to

'the family of Rajiv Gandhi'. These amounts were included in an audit of the party's accounts for December 1984 and authorised again in December 1985. The Russian government confirmed the payments in 1992, describing them as justified in the 'Soviet ideological interest'.

Meanwhile, Narain was clearly enjoying being thrust into the limelight as the 'kingpin' of the spy scandal, dismissing pleas from his wife to deny the allegations. Geeta Narain complained that a man who was 'afraid even of a lizard' was scarcely a neat fit for James Bond, but to no avail. Her husband insisted, 'I just want to get rid of it all,' and was said by the IB investigators to be 'singing like a canary' about his network of thirty top civil servants and the million dollars he personally had made from his 'supermarket of secrets'. Although he was equally quick to point out that this was nowhere near as much as his boss, Yogesh Manaklal, and the two businessmen dealing with the Poles, East Germans and the KGB had made from the multi-million dollar deals they obtained across Eastern Europe and the Soviet Union in return for the documents.

A five-month investigation led to eighteen people being charged with conspiracy to pass secrets to foreign countries and a lengthy court process, with the trial being held in camera. It was not until July 2002, more than seventeen years after the first arrests, that the hearings finally came to an end. The judge gave Yogesh Manaklal the longest sentence, fourteen years 'rigorous imprisonment', for having 'cajoled and inspired' Narain into 'nefarious activities for the sole object of winning favours from his foreign collaborators'. Twelve former senior civil servants, including four from the Prime Minister's office and another four from the Ministry of Defence, were jailed for ten years. Coomar Narain escaped imprisonment, having died of natural causes in March 2000.

★★★

Although intelligence services routinely exploit the financial weaknesses of others to recruit agents – the Narain case being but a spectacularly large-scale case of this – money represents a means by which they themselves can be penetrated. The ability of intelligence officers to handle their own finances is a key issue in the vetting process and for very good reasons. Many of the best 'walk-ins' are looking for money to pay off their debts. Intelligence officials are government employees and as a result are often poorly paid. If they lose their security clearance, and therefore their job, as a result of a failure to live within the limited means their salary allows them, they will almost certainly feel aggrieved, adding to the risk of betrayal.

The NSA and GCHQ worked very closely together through the so-called UKUSA Accord (the UK, US agreement for signals intelligence sharing that was a direct result of the Bletchley Park successes in the Second World War). The most damaging Cold War intelligence disaster for this co-operation was caused by a former member of staff who lost his security vetting and resigned after being declared bankrupt. Ronald Pelton, who had been a highly experienced member of the NSA's Group A, which covered interception of Soviet and Eastern Bloc communications, subsequently contacted the KGB and offered to provide details of a number of extremely successful US and UK secret signals intelligence (Sigint) operations against the Soviet Union.

After joining the US Air Force in 1960, Pelton was sent to Indiana University to study Russian and was then trained to transcribe, analyse and report on intercepted Soviet communications. His main posting was to Peshawar in northern Pakistan, from where US spy planes flew along the Soviet Union's borders with Afghanistan and Iran intercepting radio communications. After five years in the air force, Pelton joined the NSA as a civilian. By 1979, he had worked himself up to a position where he was in charge of a key unit within A Group and had computer access to all of the secret programmes collecting intelligence on the Soviet Union and on Russian forces based in Eastern Europe.

Well regarded by colleagues within the NSA for his ability and experience, Pelton was deeply immersed in the work of A Group and had acquired an encyclopaedic knowledge of NSA and GCHQ operations against the Soviet Union. But his ability to manage his own personal finances was abysmal, and in April 1979, he went bankrupt, owing $65,000 (now equivalent to

£165,000). Three months later, he was forced to resign having lost his security clearance. By the beginning of 1980, Pelton's life was falling apart and his marriage was in trouble. With no solution to his financial problems on the horizon, he telephoned the Soviet embassy in Washington and said that he had worked for the US government and wanted to talk to someone. The implication was obvious.

Pelton was invited to the embassy the following day and given an initial interview. He proved his authenticity by identifying the locations of NSA offices and their Soviet targets around the US capital. The former NSA analyst had no documents to share, but it was immediately clear that he was a uniquely qualified source with a good memory of his work against Soviet communications over the past two decades. After his first interview with KGB officers in the Washington embassy, a detailed list of questions was put together by the KGB's 14th Directorate, the then Soviet equivalent of the NSA or GCHQ, and Pelton flew to Austria, ostensibly on holiday but in fact to be interviewed again in a more secure environment than the US capital.

From this point on, classic KGB tradecraft kicked in. Pelton was provided with an initially small sum of money for expenses and made to sign a receipt. All contact in the US was to be made via pre-arranged calls to the public phone at a pizza restaurant in Falls Church, Virginia. After arriving in Austria, he would go to the Belvederegarten, a popular park in the centre of Vienna, at a pre-set time. An undercover KGB officer would then approach him and take him to the ambassador's residence, where he was questioned by a team of KGB specialists led by Anatoly Slavnov. The intention was to draw out everything Pelton knew and on the first visit to Vienna, in October 1980, the questioning went on for around eight hours a day over a number of days, for which Pelton was paid a total of $20,000 (around £39,000 at today's prices).

The KGB already had some knowledge of UKUSA operations against the Soviet Union from Geoffrey Prime, an agent inside GCHQ who had resigned from the agency several years earlier. Pelton provided them with a golden opportunity not only to update the information Prime had provided but, since he had far greater access, to add to it significantly. The October 1980 interviews provided substantial intelligence, which led to further questions that were answered by Pelton during a second visit to Vienna in January 1983; for this he was paid an additional $15,000.

Pelton was no ordinary spy. He had written the Group A manual for deciphering a number of complex Soviet encryption systems, all of which the Russians believed – until Pelton told them otherwise – were completely secure. Even though he was working from memory, the level at which he had operated within the NSA meant that the Russians did not need to know the detail of what the various UKUSA operations had revealed to the US and Britain; they could work that out for themselves. The very existence of programmes successfully attacking various electronics systems, communications and ciphers used by the different parts of the Soviet government and military was enough. They had to assume that their systems were all completely compromised and needed to replace them with more secure versions that the NSA and GCHQ would not be able to decipher, which is of course exactly what the Soviets now did.

The damage caused by Pelton was incalculable. His information revealed the seven most important intercept operations carried out by NSA and GCHQ. These included the use of US Vortex spy satellites to capture unencrypted Communist Party and military telephone calls that were carried by a system of microwave towers covering the entire Soviet Union, an operation that yielded an unrivalled picture of what was happening in the Soviet Union and was described by Charles Lord, the then NSA deputy director, as the 'holiest of holies'. But that was not all. Every major success against Soviet codes and ciphers was compromised, as were the means of intercepting the communications, including Broadside, the joint NSA–CIA eavesdropping centre inside the US embassy in Moscow, which within months of Pelton's initial debriefing was jammed by the Russians, rendering it inoperative. Another operation blown by Pelton was a joint NSA–CIA project in which fake tree trunks containing interception and recording devices were placed near Soviet military installations around Moscow.

The KGB also learnt of the joint NSA–US Navy tap on a Soviet Navy undersea cable in the Sea of Okhotsk (which linked the Soviet Pacific Fleet's base at Petropavlovsk with its main headquarters in Vladivostok). In an operation code-named Ivy Bells, the Americans had attached a 6m (20ft) pod containing recording devices to the cable producing top-secret and largely unencrypted communications between naval commanders. This included material not just for the Pacific Fleet, but instructions and plans for the entire navy that were sent to Vladivostok from Moscow and relayed on to Petropavlovsk. As a direct result of Pelton's information, in 1981 the Russians removed the pod, ending a highly successful eight-year operation that had provided details of the location of Soviet nuclear missile submarines in the Pacific and would have given early warning of any Soviet move on to a war footing.

The betrayal could not have come at a worse time for the NSA and GCHQ, with hard-line leaders in charge in Moscow, who were convinced that the administration of US President Ronald Reagan was intent on a pre-emptive nuclear strike against the Soviet Union. At this, one of the tensest, most dangerous periods of the Cold War, the UKUSA partners lost much of their ability to decipher top Soviet codes and ciphers, severely restricting the amount of intelligence they could provide.

Meanwhile, Pelton's life was spiralling out of control. His marriage had broken up. He drifted from job to job. He was living with his mistress, an ex-beauty queen, and the KGB payments had been spent on their joint addiction to alcohol and drugs. In April 1985, he attempted another, desperate attempt to provide more intelligence to the KGB, and although he successfully set up a meeting in the Belvederegarten – borrowing the money from a friend to pay for the flight to Vienna – the KGB failed to show up. Pelton later claimed that his Soviet contacts had probably failed to recognise him because he had lost weight, but in fact they had bled him dry of the intelligence he could offer and there was unlikely to be anything useful left to obtain.

Four months later, a senior KGB officer named Vitaly Yurchenko defected to the CIA. Yurchenko had been one of the KGB officers who had first spoken to Pelton in the Soviet embassy in Washington. He could not remember his name but provided enough information to identify him. The evidence against Pelton was limited, but the FBI invited him to an informal meeting and persuaded him to condemn himself by talking about what he had done without a lawyer present – under the assumption that like most other Soviet spies at the time, he would be debriefed and this case closed rather than pursue a prosecution against him that risked the disclosure of more secrets in court. But Pelton had given far too much away.

The then NSA chief William Odom and Director of Central Intelligence William Casey were determined to prosecute, and while full details of what Pelton had done could not be revealed publicly in case it told the Russians more than they already knew, the Ivy Bells operation was known to have been blown and, since the Russians had recovered the pod, could be talked about openly. Pelton's trial took place largely in camera but so determined were Odom and Casey to ensure that he was convicted as a deterrent to others tempted to follow his lead, that they sent William Crowell, the head of Group A, to brief the jury on the various operations that had been exposed and to explain what their loss meant to national security. Pelton was jailed for life and released on parole in November 2015.

In an interesting footnote, Yurchenko subsequently defected back to the Soviet Union, where he was awarded the Order of the Red Star for 'a successful infiltration operation'. This, and the fact that both of the KGB agents he gave away were no longer of any use to the Russians, led to claims that the original defection was a deception operation designed to divert attention away from the far more important KGB agents, Aldrich Ames and the senior FBI officer Robert Hanssen.

Tennent Bagley, a former CIA officer, was convinced that Yurchenko's defection was deliberately staged:

> Having pursued defectors for the KGB, Yurchenko knew better than anyone else the fate of Soviet intelligence officers who had gone over to the adversary and betrayed state secrets.

They could expect no mercy. Those caught while spying in place were shot. Those who had fled to the West were sentenced to death in absentia and, if possible assassinated. Not Yurchenko. He was restored to duty in the KGB and received a medal.

Nevertheless, other CIA officers involved in the case disputed Bagley's contention, pointing out that the official Agency conclusion was that he was a genuine defector and that the KGB reaction to his return was a cover-up, as Yurchenko was shunted off into an unimportant job and then quietly retired.

★★★

The KGB had got far more than their money's worth with the $37,000 they paid to Ronald Pelton. There is, however, one major flaw in the use of money to motivate agents, namely the risk that an unscrupulous agent who is unable to find genuine intelligence to justify the payments he is receiving may fabricate it in order to ensure that he or she gets paid.

One of the most high-profile examples of this problem came with the now infamous controversy surrounding the intelligence that former Iraqi president Saddam Hussein had tried to obtain uranium ore from Niger. The claim was one of a number made by the US administration in its attempts to justify the invasion of Iraq in 2003. In a highly controversial sixteen-word section of his State of the Union address that year, President George W. Bush said: 'The British government has learned that Saddam Hussein recently sought significant quantities of uranium from Africa.'

This statement was bitterly labelled by many in the US intelligence community as nonsense and ultimately did more to discredit the administration's attempts to justify the war in Iraq than any other single piece of intelligence. The irony was that, amid a plethora of exaggerated claims that were given far more credence than they deserved, the British intelligence underlying Bush's much criticised 'sixteen words' was in fact entirely accurate and matched a wide range of well-sourced intelligence reporting already available to the CIA. The problem was that it had become tangled up with fake documents forged to satisfy the demand for intelligence that Saddam was trying to restart his nuclear weapons programme.

The background to those concerns lay in the aftermath of the 1991 Gulf War. When that war broke out, Western intelligence agencies were aware of the existence of an Iraqi nuclear programme but believed it to be so basic that it would be incapable of producing a nuclear weapon without significant assistance from an existing nuclear power. They were wrong. The International Atomic Energy Agency (IAEA) weapons inspectors who entered Iraq at the end of the war uncovered a nuclear weapons programme that was far more sophisticated than anyone had thought. They estimated that if the war had not intervened, Iraq could have had the capability to produce a nuclear weapon by 1993. The IAEA inspectors supervised the dismantling of Iraq's nuclear facilities and took control of its remaining stock of more than 500 tons of uranium. If Saddam wanted to restart his nuclear weapons programme, he would now have to obtain uranium illicitly.

Iraq's main supplier of uranium in the past had been Niger. The former French colony is also the main source of the uranium for both the French nuclear energy industry and its nuclear weapons programme. As a result, Niger's uranium industry is seen as a key part of France's critical national infrastructure and is strictly protected through a French company, Cogema, whose security was at the time overseen by the French security service, the *Direction de la Surveillance du Territoire* (DST). France was determined to ensure that Iraq never obtained uranium from Niger again.

As a result, the French were very receptive to intelligence produced by a freelance Italian intelligence tipster called Rocco Martino, who in the spring of 2000 suddenly developed a very productive source on Iraqi attempts to obtain uranium from Niger. Martino, who operated under the code name Giacomo, was a latter-day equivalent of Arsène Marie

Verrue, selling intelligence to anyone who would buy it. His main sources of income were originally SISMI, the Italian secret service, and Italian businesses and newspapers. But by the late 1990s, his relationship with the Italian intelligence service was on the wane. His handler, Antonio Nucera, had quit SISMI, leaving Martino with no sponsor inside the agency, and his most important customer was now the French foreign intelligence service *Direction Genérale de la Sécurité Extérieure*. He was run by the DGSE's Brussels station on a retainer of around £1,200 a month.

The French would hardly have expected Martino to become an important source of intelligence on Niger, but in early 2000 all that changed. Nucera introduced Martino to another of his former agents, Laura Montini, an Italian secretary inside Niger's embassy in Rome, in the hope that they might be able to help each other. 'Nucera asked if I was interested in meeting a person who worked in an African embassy and who had been able to supply documents and information, including the embassy's cipher,' Martino told the Italian investigating magistrate who headed an inquiry into the affair.

Martino swiftly replied that yes, of course he was interested, and so Nucera introduced him to Montini. As a DGSE stringer, Martino knew that the French were very interested in any intelligence suggesting that Saddam was trying to buy uranium from Niger. So he was not slow to recognise Montini's potential. Without disclosing that he was working for the French, he agreed to pay her £350 a month to provide anything she could get on Iraqi relations with Niger. A few months later, Montini handed him a copy of what appears to have been a genuine letter relating to a visit to Niger by Wissam al-Zahawi, the Iraqi ambassador to the Vatican, in February 1999. Martino passed it to his DGSE controller, who unsurprisingly was very interested in anything further he could get.

Martino told Montini that his friends were very interested in the letter and were prepared to pay good money for more information on al-Zahawi's visit and in particular on any agreement by Niger to sell uranium to Iraq. 'He told me that if he was able to obtain a copy of a contract then he would have earned a lot of money from an unspecified "intelligence" organisation,' Montini said. There was no contract and there were no other documents, but the lure of the money was too great. Working with one of the diplomats inside Niger's embassy, she produced a number of documents that, taken at face value, were evidence of a successful attempt by Saddam to persuade Niger to supply him with uranium. Martino was ecstatic; this was worth real money.

The interest shown by his DGSE controller in the original, genuine piece of intelligence had created a market that Martino was happy to feed and is probably the clearest demonstration in recent time of the weakness of money as a motivating force. 'It can lead to fabrication, or more generally, embellishment,' one former SIS officer said:

> Certainly whenever there is an agent whose motivation appears to be only money; a good case officer will always try to check out the intelligence with collateral. It is generally dangerous to accept as accurate, key intelligence that comes only from one source whose motivation is simply money. The case officer should always try too to widen the motivation by searching for other factors that could motivate him or her and also double checking that the access that the source appears to have is valid.

Fortunately for the DGSE, although not for the Americans, Martino's hapless collaborators in the Niger embassy had made validation simple. The documents were swiftly recognised as forgeries and Martino's DGSE controller told the Italian they were worthless. There was no way he was prepared to pay the £140,000 that the Italian was demanding for them. There the matter should have rested, but Martino was determined to find a buyer for the documents.

In the months following the 9/11 attacks against the United States, some within the administration of George Bush were already pointing a finger at Iraq. In this atmosphere of suspicion,

SISMI received a number of uncorroborated reports suggesting that the al-Zahawi visit had led to an agreement to supply Iraq with 500 tons of uranium. There was even an alleged text of the contract. All of this was passed on to the CIA, but none of it came from the Martino documents, which SISMI had not seen. Martino was no longer working for them. At this point, only the DGSE had seen those documents and they had recognised them immediately as fakes. There was no other intelligence of an actual agreement, but what made the SISMI intelligence interesting was that it fitted perfectly with what was known to be sound reporting on the al-Zahawi visit to Niger by the CIA, SIS, the DGSE and, crucially, by GCHQ. The visit, which took place in February 1999, was part of a tour of African countries that also took in Somalia and the Democratic Republic of the Congo, where SIS reporting likewise showed al-Zahawi asking about the availability of uranium. There was no significant doubt that Iraq wanted to obtain uranium; the intelligence on the visits to Niger, Somalia and the Democratic Republic of the Congo was sound, but the SISMI description of a 'contract' went much further than any of the other intelligence and, amid concerns that the administration was hell-bent on finding any evidence that would back removing Saddam from power, the CIA was anxious to try to find out for certain whether an actual agreement to supply uranium existed or not.

At this point, Valerie Plame, an officer in the CIA's Counterproliferation Division, suggested sending her husband to check out the report. Joe Wilson was a former State Department African specialist who had served in the US embassy in Niger before going on to become ambassador to Gabon. He knew the prime minister and the minister of mines and energy, 'both of whom could possibly shed light on this sort of activity', Plame said.

There was some cynicism within the CIA that Wilson would be able to determine the truth. One CIA officer later recalled that the general view was – not unreasonably – that 'the Nigeriens would be unlikely to admit to a uranium sales agreement with Iraq, even if one had been negotiated'. Nevertheless, it was agreed to send Wilson to Niger. The concern among some within the

CIA over how the administration might use the intelligence was already apparent, with Plame telling her husband about the SIS report of Iraq trying to obtain uranium ore from Niger with the words: 'There's this crazy report ...'

That statement – making it very clear what answer Plame and her colleagues were expecting – would not be most intelligence officers' idea of how to brief anyone on a mission, but she took no part in her husband's official briefing, during which he was told what he could and could not say to the Nigerien officials. Wilson came back from Niger with denials of any deal, but confirmation that Iraqi officials had tried to discuss 'expanding commercial relations' with Niger's Prime Minister Ibrahim Mayaki. Given that Niger exported very little else, Mayaki had taken this to mean that they wanted to discuss uranium sales. Although the meeting took place, he insisted there was no discussion of trade since this would have breached UN sanctions against Iraq. Wilson's findings were not seen as particularly important by either the CIA or the Defense Intelligence Agency (DIA). He had confirmed the previous reports that Iraq was trying to obtain uranium but, as expected, had not produced any reliable information one way or the other as to whether a contract or its supply existed.

Then, in June 2002, SIS reported what it believed to be incontrovertible evidence that the Iraqis had expressed interest in purchasing uranium from Niger. They could not show it to the Americans because it came from a third party, a foreign intelligence service that SIS rightly believed to be an impeccable source. The identity of the foreign country, although not precisely which of its intelligence services, would later become known to the CIA and the world at large as France. What was never revealed, and under the terms of the liaison agreement between the French and the British could not be revealed, was that it came not from the DGSE but from the DST. This was the organisation which under the French system was in charge of all security surrounding Niger's uranium industry. Under the terms of the liaison arrangement between the DST and SIS, the British were not allowed to say where the intelligence came from unless the French agreed. Fully aware that anything it might say would be seized on by the US administration as a justification for war against Iraq, the DST allowed SIS to transmit the basic intelligence to the Americans but refused permission for the document that confirmed the intelligence to be passed on. The French government was understandably concerned that the Americans would risk the source of the document by using it as evidence to support their case for a war in Iraq, an operation that France was not prepared to back (and ultimately would not back). So tight were the DST restrictions on sharing the intelligence that SIS was told that it could not even tell its sister organisation, the British security service MI5, where it came from.

In September 2002, just as the British government was about to publish a dossier outlining the case for war against Iraq, SIS obtained further intelligence that included additional confirmation of the Iraqi attempts to buy uranium, but still showed no firm evidence of a contract. The DST was reluctant to see its intelligence used in the dossier, but eventually agreed so long as it went no further than its own assessment that Saddam had 'sought' uranium from Africa. In order to describe what was known as accurately as possible, and in accordance with the DST demands, both SIS and the British government dossier used the words: 'Iraq has sought the supply of significant quantities of uranium from Africa.'

Meanwhile, Rocco Martino had yet to find a market for the documents produced from Niger's Rome embassy by Laura Montini. In October 2002, he offered them to Elisabetta Burba, a journalist with the Italian news magazine *Panorama*, for a cut-price £10,000. Suspicious of their veracity, Burba took them to the US embassy in Rome to ask for their assessment. She then flew to Niger and decided it was not possible that Iraq had obtained uranium there. Burba and her editor at *Panorama* decided to drop the story. Yet again, Martino received no money. By then, the US embassy in Rome had sent the Martino documents to Washington, where analysts had realised they were fake.

In October 2002, the French Ministry of Foreign Affairs Director for Non-Proliferation visited the State Department and told US officials that France had intelligence showing that

Iraq had tried unsuccessfully to obtain uranium from Niger. Two months later, the State Department issued a factsheet that talked about Iraqi 'efforts to procure uranium from Niger'. As a direct result, the IAEA asked for sight of the evidence behind that claim. The CIA was not prepared to share any of its intelligence, but in a bizarre move the State Department sent the IAEA the Martino documents provided by Burba, which the department's own intelligence analysts had concluded were forgeries.

Meanwhile, President Bush had decided to use his State of the Union address in January 2003 to refer to Iraqi efforts to obtain uranium from Niger, and so his speechwriters tried to devise a way of mentioning it without compromising either the CIA's or SISMI's sources. Since the British had already gone public with their intelligence, it was decided that the safest thing would be for Bush to identify them as the source, which is why the US President used that precise form of sixteen words: 'The British government has learned that Saddam Hussein recently sought significant quantities of uranium from Africa.'

At the beginning of March 2003, with war only a few weeks away, the IAEA declared the documents the State Department had passed it (in other words, the Martino documents) to be fakes. At this point, Joe Wilson spoke to the *Washington Post*, which published an article, quoting him without naming him, in which he appeared to suggest that he had seen the documents before he went to Niger. As a Senate Intelligence Committee investigation later pointed out, he could not have seen them, since the CIA did not have them when Wilson was sent to Niger in March 2002. They only came into US hands when Burba took them to the US embassy in Rome in October of that year. But Wilson was not alone in assuming that the intelligence he was sent to investigate came from the fake Martino documents.

By now the situation surrounding the President's 'sixteen words' had become toxic as a direct result of Martino's documents and, in what has to have been much more of a political decision than an analytical one, the CIA withdrew all of its intelligence, not just the questionable material suggesting a contract had been signed, but also on the Iraqi attempts to obtain uranium from Niger. The DST did not follow the CIA's lead in withdrawing its intelligence and neither did SIS, both judging that the document from which it derived was very clear evidence that Iraq had attempted to obtain uranium from Niger.

As controversy over all aspects of the intelligence used to justify the war continued and with clear evidence that some of this had, at best, been manipulated to create a false picture, the British government announced a Review of Intelligence on Weapons of Mass Destruction to be carried out by Lord Butler, a former head of the British civil service, and four other senior former British officials. The Butler Review saw all of the documentation and was fully briefed on all aspects, including the DST intelligence. Although their report, published in July 2004, was highly damning of much of the intelligence produced by SIS and others, they concluded that the intelligence that Iraq was trying to obtain uranium from Niger was 'credible' and that the President's sixteen-word claim that 'the British government has learned that Saddam Hussein recently sought significant quantities of uranium from Africa' was 'well-founded'. They added that 'the evidence was not conclusive that Iraq actually purchased … uranium and the British government did not claim this'.

Nor, of course, did President Bush, but the attempt by Rocco Martino, an agent motivated purely by money, to obtain intelligence from a sub-agent also motivated by money, and the forged documents produced as a result, had completely discredited genuine information from multiple sources including the DST, the intelligence agency that was best placed to know what was going on inside Niger.

Money, as so often, was a very effective way of recruiting agents, but – from the intelligence agencies' point of view – a very ineffective way of obtaining reliable ones.

Chapter 4

PATRIOTISM

E.M. Forster's declaration that 'If I had to choose between betraying my country and betraying my friend, I hope I should have the guts to betray my country,' is frequently cited as an argument in favour of the traitor, not least in the case of the KGB's infamous Cambridge spies. Nevertheless, the patriot's willingness to put his or her country first can be a very powerful motivation for espionage. Just like ideologues, patriots are more likely to be willing to do anything 'for the good of the cause', although it is important to add one caveat. Patriotism is often accompanied by a highly moralistic attitude that can severely restrict the missions in which an agent is prepared to take part.

One of the greatest advantages of patriotism as an agent motivation – apart from the not entirely unimportant factor that it is relatively inexpensive – is that it allows the intelligence services to recruit people who have good reason for entering the target country and have already established 'natural cover', often built up over years, before their recruitment. The prime example is the businessman who sells legitimate goods into a country where access is otherwise very difficult. Initially, he might have been suspect, but over time he is accepted. His presence is of assistance to a country that may have limited links to the outside world. He is seen as a friend, not an enemy.

Mansfield Cumming, the founder of SIS, realised this very early in his tenure as 'C'. In a report on his first six months in charge of what was then the foreign section of the Secret Service Bureau, Cumming said that 'voluntary help' from Britons 'whose business or profession gives them special facilities for finding out what is going on abroad' was a valuable source of intelligence. One of those businessmen was Frederick Fairholme, a director of the Sheffield steel firm Davy Brothers. His Scottish father had married a Bavarian baroness and he had spent his childhood in Austria. As a result, he spoke fluent German and the directors of the German steelmaker Krupp, with whom he dealt on his company's behalf, treated him as one of their own.

Fairholme had a first meeting with Cumming in January 1910 and was immediately able to supply important new intelligence on the German navy's latest guns and their newly developed armour-piercing shells. The report subsequently issued by Cumming was extremely detailed, but given the destruction wrought by the German shells on Royal Navy ships during the First World War seems to have been ignored by its recipients at the Admiralty.

Another patriotic Briton employed by Cumming in pre-war Germany was the 27-year-old journalist Hector Bywater, who lived in the German city of Dresden and who had made his reputation by writing on the superior capability of the German navy long before he began working for the British secret service. His credentials had therefore already been checked out by the German naval authorities, who were flattered by his complimentary coverage of their capabilities. As a result, he was given much more extensive access than if he had simply been a British journalist writing for a Fleet Street newspaper.

Bywater was given the typically Cumming-esque code name of H2O and travelled around northern Germany mapping out defences and using his role as naval correspondent of the *New York Herald* to talk his way into the dockyards and naval installations. One of his earliest missions was a visit to survey the defences on the North Sea island of Borkum and check out a report supplied by 'R', the money-motivated Brussels-based agent Arsène Marie Verrue. Bywater reproduced his report from that mission in a 1930 article in the *Daily Telegraph* on the work of a secret service agent:

On island, three hours, with crowd of trippers, but large part of it *Sperrgebiet* [prohibited zone], sentries with fixed bayonets and plenty of barbed wire. Persistent reports have been current that Emden is being developed as a naval base but am unable to find any sign of this. Barracks are being enlarged, however. Borkum defended by twenty guns of various calibres, from 24cm downward, and including several 15cm high-velocity pieces on field carriages. I find in Emden a general impression that, in the event of war, Borkum will be one of the first objectives of the British Fleet. The *Ausflüge* [excursions] from Emden provide one with an opportunity to cross to Borkum as one of the crowd, and in comparative safety, so long as German-made clothes are worn. Next to Norderney, by Norddeutscher Lloyd Seebaderdienst steamer from Bremen. Make a careful survey of the island and find no traces of the fortifications which had been reported as being in progress. This report came from R. This is not the first fairy tale he has told, and henceforth his reports will be suspect.

Bywater also included a vivid description of how he successfully managed to get on board the *Von der Tann*, a German navy battle-cruiser anchored off Hamburg. 'I determined to visit her, though the risk was considerable,' he wrote, with no attempt to under-play his role in the affair:

> By a stroke of luck, I found that a local shipping man, to whom I had a letter from a mutual friend in Berlin, knew several offic-ers of the ship, and had visited them on board. He was going again and, by very tactful manoeuvring, I got him to invite me to accompany him. We went across in a launch, but on arriving at the ship's ladder I remarked to my companion that, being a foreigner, I might not be welcome on board. He then spoke to the officer of the watch, who was one of his friends, explained who I was (or, more strictly speaking, who he thought I was), and I was promptly invited to come up. We spent two hours in the ship, and saw nearly everything, except the inside of the gun-turrets and the engine-room. I memorised all the impor-tant details, and subsequently wrote an elaborate report on the ship. This was the first German battle cruiser to be personally inspected by a British Secret Service man.

Expatriate Britons were also a good source of intelligence for Cumming: one of his more unusual patriotic agents was a former government fisheries expert who, with the assistance of his son, set up a coast-watching service along the Norwegian coast to report on passing German warships. Walter Archer was a pioneering expert on the sex life of the salmon who had carried out much of his research in Norway, where in his twenties he secured control over fishing rights on a major salmon river, the Suldalslågen. By his late thirties, Archer's extensive expertise and espousal of what were then ground-breaking views on the control of salmon fishing – by banning the salmon companies from netting the fish in confined waters to ensure a good proportion of fish reached the upper reaches of the river to spawn – had led to his appointment as Inspector of Salmon Fisheries for Scotland and then Chief Inspector of Fisheries for England and Wales.

When ill-health forced his retirement in 1912, Archer decided on a once-in-a-lifetime sailing tour around the Norwegian and Danish coasts in his yacht, the *Edirene*, accompanied by his son Hugh, a former Royal Navy officer. For Cumming, this seemed an opportunity too good to miss and he recruited the pair to set up a ship-watching network, giving Walter Archer the code name Sage, while Hugh Archer became Sagette. Their motivation was the kind of patriotism that prompted Charles Carruthers and Arthur Davies, the fictional heroes of the classic Erskine Childers novel *The Riddle of the Sands*, to tour the north German coastline mapping naval defences and installations. It was simply the right and proper thing for an Englishman to do (although Cumming's funding of their tour provided an added incentive). Unfortunately, the motivation of the lighthouse keepers, ships' pilots and coast guards they recruited to report on German naval movements was purely financial and the allowance Cumming made for their payments overly optimistic. Sage and Sagette ran substantially over budget and refused to hand over their agents until Cumming promised to pay them an additional £2,000, the modern equivalent of some £200,000. Eventually, a deal was done and the extensive coast-watching service Sage and Sagette had created subsequently proved very successful in tracking German battleships.

The use of Britons who work abroad to report on the countries they visit or live in became, and remains, standard practice for SIS, although only in rare circumstances are they as valuable as Fairholme and only *in extremis* are they asked to do anything that might appear in any way suspicious. A number have been arrested over the years and jailed or killed in the countries in which they operated, along with a number of completely innocent Britons who were in the wrong place at the wrong time and incorrectly assumed to be spies. The risks were very clear to Cumming even in those very early days of the British secret service. 'I am afraid that it will always be difficult to get voluntary help from people living abroad – even those of British birth. The risk they run is so great, and the consequence of detection so serious, that it is only in rare cases that they are likely to be of any use.'

One of Cumming's patriot agents who paid the ultimate price was Edith Cavell, the British nurse shot by the Germans during the First World War. Cavell, the matron of a Brussels hospital, was recruited shortly before the Germans took over the city to collect intelligence from German soldiers treated in her hospital. This she did, but she also assisted some 600 British servicemen trapped behind enemy lines to escape to the Netherlands (which was neutral), and it was this work that led in August 1915 to her arrest. Herman Capiau, a member of her network, wrote that 'whenever it was possible to send interesting intelligence on military operations, this information was forwarded to the English intelligence service punctually and rapidly'.

When Cavell was detained, she was initially charged with espionage, but it was for her role in helping British soldiers escape that she was put on trial and executed. The death of a good agent as a result of her own decision to help British soldiers escape coloured the SIS view of such work right up to the Second World War. During that conflict, it insisted that MI9, the official War Office section running escape operations from occupied territory, should come under its control to ensure that agents providing intelligence never put important espionage operations at risk in the same way.

While these cases demonstrate how SIS used patriotic Britons to provide it with intelligence, the British secret service was also ready to make full use of nationals of other countries who, for patriotic reasons, were prepared to provide intelligence that might damage potential enemies or even help bring down their own governments. One of these was the Danish naval officer Walter Christmas, who, although he took full advantage of the money and sex that Cumming's service provided for him, also saw himself as working for the good of Denmark in helping to defeat Germany and even said that part of his motivation for helping the British lay in the fact that, 'I have always looked upon myself as at least half English.'

One of the most extensive operations run by SIS that involved agents spying for their own patriotic reasons was the more than 1,000-strong Belgian and French network known as *La Dame Blanche*, named after the legendary ghost of a white lady whose appearance was supposed to signal the downfall of the Hohenzollerns, the German royal family. It was formed from the remnants of the *Service Michelin* train-watching network originally run by the French and rescued by Henry Landau, an SIS officer based in the neutral Netherlands, after the Germans arrested a number of the group's leaders and broke up the organisation.

Left without any contacts with the allies by the German arrests, the two surviving Michelin leaders, Walthère Dewé and Herman Chauvin, contacted Landau and offered him the services of their agent network. He quickly accepted but was then knocked back by their demand that they be recruited as members of the British armed forces, something he knew the British War Office would never allow. Facing a make-or-break moment, Landau played for time, saying he would contact his bosses in London, but that it would take a day or two to get a reply. Realising that there was no way the demands could be met, he did not even bother to contact Cumming. He simply waited a few days and then told the Michelin leaders that the deal was done. One of the first things

Dewé and Chauvin did was to change the network's name to *La Dame Blanche*, hoping that the disappearance of any reference to the *Service Michelin* would convince the Germans they had been successful in closing it down.

The train-watchers were able to provide indispensable intelligence on German troop movements. Divisions moved en masse to and from the front along the main Belgian railway lines, with each type of unit using a mix of different coaches and trucks, which made them easy to identify. An infantry battalion would have twenty-five covered wagons containing the men, eight covered wagons for the horses, a single standard railway carriage for the officers and ten open-topped wagons for vehicles. The other main units in the divisions were the artillery and cavalry regiments, with each artillery battery having a train of its own made up of six covered wagons for the men, twenty-five for the horses, four open-topped wagons for the guns and a single standard carriage for the officers. A cavalry squadron would have four covered wagons for the men, around twenty-five for the horses, four open-topped wagons for the vehicles and one carriage for the officers. The train-watchers were even able on occasion to identify the precise unit being transported from the regimental insignia on the sides of the artillery pieces and vehicles. The intelligence they produced told the allies which areas of the front were being reinforced, or weakened by withdrawals, and which units were based where.

Having been assured by Landau that they were now part of the British armed forces, the leaders of *La Dame Blanche* formed the network into a military structure comprising three separate 'battalions' of agents, based on the cities of Liege, Namur and Charleroi. The battalions were in turn subdivided into three 'companies' each, whose bases were situated in different areas of their respective cities. The fourth platoon was tasked with collecting the reports from the other three and taking them to a transmission point, which was usually the residence of an agent or a shop owned by a member of the network. Each of the battalions had a separate section that ran these letter boxes and gathered together all the reports for carrying to the three principal letter boxes in Liege, one allocated to each battalion.

The cellular structure of the network of letter boxes, with each separate from the others and unknown to any of the links in the chain, provided *La Dame Blanche* with far greater security than its predecessor (or most other networks). Special secretariat units operating within each of the battalions examined the reports obtained from the central letter box before having them typed and transmitted on to one of the networks leaders, either Dewé or Chauvin.

Once the leadership had approved them, the reports were encoded using a piece of easily remembered text. The first text selected was the *Pater Noster* (the Lord's Prayer in Latin). Each of the letters to be encoded was replaced with two numbers divided by a comma. The first of these derived by finding a word in the prayer with the original letter and giving the number of that word's position, while the second number was taken from the position of the letter within that word; hence the 'q' in '*Pater Noster qui es in caelis*' (the first six words of the prayer) would be encoded as 3,1. The cipher had the very great merit of being hard to crack without first discovering what text it was based on.

The encoded messages were then sent on to a final letter box close to the frontier and where they were then smuggled through the *tuyaux*, the individual smugglers' crossing points that dotted the electric fence built by the Germans along the border between Belgium and Holland. Many of the *passeurs*, the couriers who passed the reports through the wire, were smugglers. Landau said:

> Border characters of every type were used at these frontier passages. Guides who frequented the scrub and bush of the Campine, the area to the north of Liege, bordering on the Dutch frontier. Strong, fleet of foot, fearless, quick with the knife and the use of the guns, they were the terror of the German sentries and Secret Police detailed to watch them. Smugglers and poachers in peacetime, they knew every inch of the frontier and the passing of refugees, soldiers' letters and finally spy reports came natural to them.

But others were ordinary people with 'natural cover' that allowed them to go back and forth across the border on a routine basis, such as a midwife who wrapped the reports around the whale bones in her girdle and delivered messages while on her way to deliver babies. Another of the daring female agents was a *chocolatier*, who smuggled the messages in one of the boxes of Belgian chocolates she was taking into the Netherlands to sell. She always carried a number of boxes of chocolates, only one of which had a false bottom, and would flirt with the German guards, giving them free chocolates in order to distract them. Other hiding places for the reports included hollow keys, false bottoms of food tins, the handles of baskets, on silk paper that was then sewn into the courier's clothes, and the inside of a hollow tooth. One especially innovative means of getting the messages through the wire was via the women who laundered the uniforms of the German border guards. They wrapped the guards' clean clothes in brown paper on which the reports were written in secret ink. The discarded wrapping was then taken away by Dutch rubbish collectors who were themselves British agents.

The train-watching reports were far from the only intelligence the Belgians provided. When the nuns of the Sisters of the Doctrine Chrétienne were forced out of their convent in Beauraing so that it could be used as a German field hospital, two of them volunteered their services to Anatole Gobeaux, commander of the 'Chimay Company' of *La Dame Blanche*, offering to collect intelligence from the German troops being treated there. They gathered a substantial amount of this from the soldiers in their care, all of which they passed on to Gobeaux. One of the nuns, Sister Marie-Melanie, spent a lot of time talking to a young German artilleryman who had boasted to her about a big new gun, the *Kaiser-Wilhelm-Geschütz*, which was so powerful it could land shells in Paris, more than 120km (75 miles) away. A few weeks earlier, a French refugee who came to the convent in search of food and shelter had told her that at his village, Crépy-en-Laon, many people had been evicted from their houses to allow the Germans to construct concrete gun platforms there. She passed the details of both conversations on to Gobeaux, who sent one of his agents to Crépy, where he saw an enormous gun with a barrel more than 30m (100ft) long. A report was sent back via courier to Landau, which helped corroborate a recent report from a spy inside Germany of trials of a high-trajectory gun. The *Kaiser-Wilhelm-Geschütz*, which would become better known as the Paris Gun, could fire a 106kg (234lb) shell more than 42km (26 miles) high, the first human-made projectile to reach the stratosphere, and had a range of more than 130km (80 miles), which allowed it to hit Paris from behind the German lines. Landau was ecstatic both at the confirmation of the weapon's existence and its precise location. The nuns also correctly predicted the timing and main point of attack of the final great German offensive, the *Kaiserschlacht*, launched in the spring of 1918 in a failed attempt to win the war before the Americans were able to deploy their vastly superior forces. Shortly before the end of the war, in a message to the agents of *La Dame Blanche*, Cumming told them that they had been indispensable to the impending allied victory:

> The work of your organisation accounts for 70 per cent of the intelligence obtained by all the allied armies not merely through the Netherlands but through other neutral states as well. It is on you alone that the allies depend to obtain intelligence on enemy movements in areas near the front. The intelligence obtained by you is worth thousands of lives to the allied armies.

In order to confirm their military status, most of the agents were awarded honours. Unfortunately, this meant that their names were published in the *Official Gazette*, so when the Germans invaded Belgium in May 1940 they knew who to arrest. Nevertheless, Walthère Dewé had already gone underground, having formed the Clarence agent network that reported to SIS for the most part by clandestine radio transmissions and which by the end of the war numbered around 1,500 agents. In January 1944, as he arrived at the home of another Clarence organiser for a meeting, Dewé found the Gestapo raiding the house. He ran off and might well have escaped but for a Luftwaffe officer who, seeing a civilian running away from the authorities, drew his pistol and shot him dead. Ironically, the Gestapo, who had no idea that the man they had been chasing was the leader of the Clarence network, admonished the Luftwaffe officer for shooting someone who might have had vital information or might have been completely innocent and just scared of being arrested. Claude Dansey, who controlled SIS operations in occupied Europe for most of the war, later said that, in terms of the quality and quantity of its reports, the *Service Clarence* occupied first place among the military intelligence networks operating in occupied Europe.

★★★

Towards the end of the First World War, the British intelligence services turned their eyes eastwards. The Bolshevik Revolution in 1917 and the subsequent break in relations between Britain and Russia soon provided the British secret service with a number of new recruits from among the patriotic Russians and Ukrainians who opposed the new regime. It is impossible to prove beyond a shadow of a doubt that Boris Bazhanov, a Ukrainian patriot and opponent of the Bolsheviks who infiltrated the Soviet Communist Party to become secretary to both Stalin and the Politburo, was a British spy. However, there is a great deal of evidence to suggest that, from the very moment he joined the Communist Party in October 1919, he was a British agent-in-place, attempting to climb as high in the Soviet communist hierarchy as possible, and doing so with spectacular success.

The evidence includes a series of extraordinarily detailed SIS reports from inside the Kremlin's most important governing bodies during the early 1920s, a time when Bazhanov was at the very heart of power. They were passed out of Russia via Ernest Boyce, the SIS head of station in the Finnish capital Helsingfors (now Helsinki), and included a ground-breaking report of a meeting of the Politburo on 19 May 1923 that not only confirmed for the first time it was the body that controlled the Soviet Union, but also provided a detailed analysis of the relative importance of its individual members at a time when Lenin was ailing. The report was graded A1, the highest rating SIS could give to its intelligence, and noted that 'in Lenin's absence, Trotsky is the chairman of the Politburo, and as such is the most influential personage in Russia' – and therefore the man Stalin would need to defeat in order to take control; that the Soviet Union was reaching out to Turkey, Afghanistan and Persia in order to undermine Britain's position in the region; and that, critically, the Soviet leadership was desperate to keep the trade links with Britain open at virtually any cost.

Boris Georgievich Bazhanov was born in 1900 in the Ukrainian city of Mogilev-Podolsky, close to the border with Moldova. During the Russian Civil War that followed the 1917 revolution, fighting between the Bolsheviks and the Ukrainian nationalist forces saw the city repeatedly change hands. There were a number of SIS Russian specialists operating in the area around this time, taking advantage of the opposition to the Bolsheviks to recruit agents. They included George Hill and Harold Gibson, both experienced in undercover operations against the Bolsheviks – Hill had known Trotsky personally – and Wilfred Dunderdale, then in naval intelligence but soon to transfer to SIS, who was mounting secret service operations into the Ukraine from Constantinople. These three are the most likely candidates for the man who recruited Bazhanov.

Whether it was a result of a British plan or on his own initiative, Bazhanov decided that fighting communism from outside the system was doomed to failure. 'It had to be undermined from within,' he said. So he switched sides, joined the local communist party network and adopted the character of its most fervent advocate of Bolshevism. As the front line between the Bolsheviks and the Ukrainian nationalists moved backwards and forward, Bazhanov helped form new revolutionary committees, using his literacy to become the local party secretary, establishing a history and base within the party that seemed impeccable. In his own words, he was a 'Trojan horse' inside 'the communist fortress', using 'a mask of communist ideology' to disguise his real intentions. 'The game was very risky, but I could not allow myself to be deterred by the thought of risk,' he said. 'I had to keep constantly on my guard. I had to watch my every word, every move I made, every step I took.'

In late 1920, Bazhanov moved to Moscow to study engineering at the Moscow Higher Technical School, the country's leading technical university. Like all Soviet universities, it had a communist party cell, but since this was poorly supported by the students, Bazhanov had no problem getting himself elected party secretary. His leadership roles in various party organisations were to be invaluable to him when, in late 1921, he eventually obtained a job working for the Central Committee in Moscow. Here, he began ingratiating himself with top party officials, including Lazar Kaganovich, a close ally of Joseph Stalin. Impressed by Bazhanov's assistance, Kaganovich promoted him to a post checking the Central Committee minutes to ensure they made sense. Acting on his own initiative, Bazhanov then redrew the party statutes, deliberately wording them so that they could be misused to assist an unscrupulous politician to take control of the party apparatus. He showed the new version to Kaganovich, who took them in turn to Vyacheslav Molotov, another prominent Soviet politician and protégé of Stalin. Molotov took Bazhanov and his proposed new statutes to Stalin. 'Stalin looked at me long and hard,' Bazhanov later recalled. 'He understood, as I did, that my statutes represented an important instrument for using the Party apparatus to gain power.'

Stalin put the proposals to Lenin, who agreed they should be discussed by the Politburo, which then sent them to be examined by a commission headed by Molotov, with Bazhanov as its secretary. He was now on good terms with a number of future senior Soviet politicians who appointed him to various posts where he was careful to press their interests, and by extension those of Stalin. Bazhanov had access to all the reports crossing the desks of the top Soviet leaders, including the top-secret minutes of the Politburo, all of which SIS managed to obtain. At the end of 1922, he became secretary to the *Orgburo*, the Central Committee's main administrative body, which dealt with all the documents emanating from the various bodies and commissions associated with the Soviet Communist Party Central

Committee, including the Politburo. He immediately instigated a complete reorganisation of the files, ensuring that he could obtain any document he wanted at any time. But despite the access this gave him to intelligence, his extraordinary career as an agent-in-place was not done. In August 1923, Bazhanov was appointed secretary of the Politburo itself, at the same time becoming Stalin's principal secretary. Five months later, Lenin died and, using the statutes drawn up by his new secretary, Stalin outwitted Trotsky to become Soviet leader. It was the pinnacle of Bazhanov's career as 'an anti-Bolshevik soldier' inside the enemy camp. 'I had imposed upon myself the difficult and perilous task of penetrating right into the heart of the enemy headquarters. I had succeeded.' He had access to every level of the Kremlin. 'The Politburo was the principal repository of power in the USSR,' he said. 'It was responsible for all major decisions respecting government of the country, as well as all questions of world revolution. All segments of the government which had matters to submit to the Politburo sent them to me.'

Bazhanov's ability to obtain intelligence was not at its peak for long. Genrikh Yagoda, the head of the OGPU (a predecessor to the KGB), had become suspicious of him and it was clear that he was under surveillance. Bazhanov made a brief visit to Finland in December 1924, ostensibly to buy skates for the Soviet national ice-skating team, although, given subsequent events, it may well have been to tell Boyce that he could no longer continue. It is probable that he was followed during his time in Helsingfors and on his return Yagoda went directly to Stalin, accusing Bazhanov of being a 'hidden counter-revolutionary'. Bazhanov managed to persuade the Soviet leader that the accusation was the result of his having won an argument with Yagoda during a party meeting, but it was clear that the time had come to get out.

To take the heat off himself, he stepped down as secretary of the Politburo and managed to get himself sent to Norway as the captain of the Soviet skating team. He also arranged for his girlfriend to be sent to Finland at the same time, which allowed them to defect together. Yagoda attempted to stop Bazhanov going, without success, but he had little difficulty blocking the girlfriend's trip to Finland. If Bazhanov defected now, it would have been obvious that his girlfriend was going with him and she would have been in serious trouble, so he had no choice but to return home at the end of his Norwegian trip. When Bazhanov subsequently broke off the relationship with the girl, she denounced him to the OGPU. He had enough friends at the top to survive an investigation, but was now under suspicion from Stalin as well as Yagoda, and the Soviet leader blocked him from going abroad.

Any attempt to escape through Europe was now impossible but Bazhanov managed to manoeuvre himself into a senior party post in Ashkhabad, the capital of the Central Asian republic of Turkmenistan. It was an unpopular post, and so easy to obtain, and was also, importantly, only about 50km (30 miles) from the border with Persia. Yagoda insisted that Bazhanov must be accompanied at all times by an OGPU minder, Arkadi Maksimov. In the early hours of New Year's Day 1928, with Maksimov drunk from the night's celebrations, Bazhanov told him they were going on a hunting expedition. He kept all the bullets for the hunting rifles, leaving Maksimov unable to prevent him crossing the border into Persia and with little choice but to defect with him or face the firing squad.

Bazhanov's time in Persia contained all the elements of a classic spy movie, including car chases involving armed OGPU agents, who at one point were even forced to share the same taxi as him but were unable to act because an armed Persian guard was separating them. With the Russians claiming the pair were murderers and thieves, Bazhanov and Maksimov were held in jail in Meshed for their own safety but asked their guards to inform the British consul in the city that 'they were enemies of Bolshevism and had extremely valuable political secrets which they wish to impart to His Majesty's Government'.

The consul was informed and Major Leo Steveni, a British intelligence officer, was dispatched to Meshed to get them out of jail and spirit them to India and safety. Steveni was given firm instructions that he should extract as much intelligence out of them as possible before they left, just in case they never made it to the border. With the OGPU in hot pursuit, the best of the British consul's agents, a Persian merchant, escorted them south to the Indian border, negotiating and bribing local officials to prevent their being handed over to the Russians. The group drove for miles over rocky mountain tracks, while Bazhanov sat in the back of the car writing intelligence reports for Steveni. Eventually, they managed to reach the Indian frontier, where the Viceroy's personal train was sitting waiting to take them to the British intelligence base at Simla for a lengthy debriefing.

The reports written by Bazhanov were understandably regarded as gold dust in London, where SIS tried for several months to persuade the Labour Prime Minister Ramsay Macdonald that the defector should be brought back to London. When that plan was blocked for fear of making relations between Britain and the Soviet Union worse than they already were, SIS did a deal with the *Deuxième Bureau* by which Bazhanov was given asylum in France in return for a share in the intelligence bonanza. Wilfred Dunderdale, now SIS head of station in Paris, used him to monitor the substantial Russian expatriate community in Paris, spotting Soviet agents, analysing Russian newspapers and in general advising on all things Soviet. Valentine Vivian, the head of the SIS counter-espionage section that monitored Soviet intelligence operations, was also a frequent visitor. Bazhanov continued providing both the British and the French with reports until at least 1936 when, with the amount of useful information he could supply dwindling, he was allowed to start working for the Poles as well to make up his money. He died in Paris in 1982.

The case of Boris Bazhanov epitomises the complex issue of agent motivation. His reasons for doing what he did clearly changed over time. So what parts did the twin motivations of patriotism and ideology play from the start? Like many of those who defected from the Soviet Union, the answer is not simple. There have been very few defectors from the Soviet Union who did not insist that their reason for leaving was opposition to Soviet-style communism, and Bazhanov's subsequent claim to have adopted a 'mask of ideology' to fight the Bolsheviks needs to be examined from that perspective. He was recruited by the British during a civil war fought between Ukrainian nationalists and the Bolsheviks. From the Ukrainian side this was very much a patriotic war. If Bazhanov hated the communist ideology so much from the start, he did very little to destroy communism from within. The intelligence he passed to London came from the highest levels within the Kremlin and certainly assisted British policy-making, hardly acts that were supportive of the Soviet Union, but his changes to the party rules played a key role in helping Stalin to power, and thereby entrenching Stalinism.

Of one thing we can be absolutely certain, his motive for fleeing had little to do with ideology and everything to do with saving his skin. But was his hatred of communism his central motivation from the very start, as he later claimed, or was it, like many of those who defected to the West simply something he adopted at a later stage to give respectability his actions?

★★★

The British practice of using patriotic businessmen as spies resulted in an embarrassing scandal in December 1925, when John Leather, the Paris representative of the British Burndept Wireless Company, and two of his colleagues were arrested by French police for espionage. They had employed two young Frenchwomen to seduce French officers and obtain intelligence on French military aircraft and bases. The French press revelled in the sensational story of British spies and their French Mata Haris. The Foreign Office in London denied that they were British spies, but it soon emerged that Leather was a serving army officer and the cousin of a senior SIS officer. He was jailed for three years, his colleagues for two and the 'Mata Haris' for six months. Hugh Sinclair, the new 'C', was curtly informed by the Foreign Office that it had made 'a gentlemen's agreement' with its French counterpart that neither country would spy on the other again.

★★★

During the 1930s, the British Treasury reacted to economic depression by making deep cuts in public funding and SIS was forced to patch up its resulting lack of coverage across large swathes of the world by persuading the employees of a number of companies working abroad to use this 'natural cover' to mount espionage operations. SIS relied heavily on 'exchange relationships' with British firms, such as Vickers, Shell, British American Tobacco, the Hudson's Bay Company and the Anglo–Persian Oil Company, under which their employees would collect intelligence and in return the companies would be given economic intelligence that would help them. The difficulties of operating in the Soviet Union led to the use of Metropolitan–Vickers Electrical Company, which provided equipment and maintenance for a number of Soviet power stations and was part owned by Vickers. It was an obvious vehicle for such 'natural cover' operations, but in 1933 the OGPU uncovered the company's intelligence-gathering operations and six of its British staff plus a dozen of its Russian employees were put on trial.

The case made headlines around the world and the court was packed with hundreds of journalists, including a young Reuters reporter, Ian Fleming, who would subsequently make the father of his espionage hero, James Bond, an employee of Vickers who spied for SIS. As in the Bond books, the main female character at the trial was a beautiful young Russian blonde, Anna Sergeevna Kutuzova, who told the court that she had overheard the company's Managing Director, Charles Richards, a British intelligence officer in Russia in the immediate aftermath of the Bolshevik Revolution, giving two senior managers instructions on what information to collect.

Given the Soviet propensity for conducting show trials of 'Western spies' who were in reality nothing of the sort, the world's press understandably looked on the case with a jaundiced eye, accepting the insistence of John Simon, the British Foreign Secretary, that Richards had not been in contact with British intelligence for years. The arrested Russians admitted accepting money for intelligence ranging from the descriptions of the state of other Soviet factories to details of rail movements of troops and munitions and the quality of shells produced in a factory close to one of the company's power stations in the Urals, but none of the watching news media believed them. They assumed that the Russian employees had been tortured into making false admissions of guilt, when in fact they were in large parts simply telling the truth. All of the British defendants were eventually allowed to go free, while all of the Russians, bar one who was almost certainly an OGPU agent, were jailed.

★★★

Recruiting agents inside occupied territory during a war is a complex business, as Britain found in 1940, when Czechoslovakia, Poland, Belgium, the Netherlands, France, Denmark and Norway had been invaded by Nazi Germany. At the time, the United States was not willing to go to war – and had no intelligence service to speak of – and the Soviet Union was a Nazi ally.

Fortunately, when a country is occupied by enemy forces, there is rarely a shortage of patriotic members of the local population who are prepared to provide intelligence to a potential liberator, but there is equally no shortage of attempts by the occupying power to infiltrate agent networks. Distinguishing the genuine agents from those put forward by the German security and intelligence services, the Gestapo, the *Sicherheitsdienst* and the *Abwehr* was a major problem, compounding the inherent difficulty of recruiting agents in hostile territory.

Good preparation, with a large number of agents recruited beforehand, good co-operation with the intelligence services of the occupied countries, and the willingness of patriots like the Belgian Walthère Dewé, the organiser of *La Dame Blanche* and the Clarence Network, to set up intelligence networks themselves and get in contact with the British, ensured that there was a substantial number of agents providing SIS with intelligence, far more than its detractors ever gave the service credit for.

Many of those working for the intelligence services of the occupied countries' governments-in-exile, based in London, were themselves intelligence officers, members of their own intelligence services or armed forces, and do not therefore qualify as agents, but all of the occupied countries mentioned above provided a substantial level of intelligence to the Allied cause throughout the war.

Norwegian agents recruited in the months before the German invasion by Frank Foley, the SIS head of station in Oslo, and his deputy Leslie Mitchell, formed the skeleton of a coast-watching service that was steadily built up after the German invasion of Norway as more and more patriotic Norwegians determined to help to defeat the Germans made their way to Britain. Mitchell was sent to the Shetland Isles to control the Shetland Bus, a fleet of Norwegian fishing boats, ferrying agents in and out of Norway from Cat Firth, a secluded inlet 16km (10 miles) north of the main Shetland town of Lerwick.

French agents were also ferried to and from France by a flotilla of small boats controlled by the Royal Navy out of the Helford estuary in Cornwall and the Scilly Isles. The French networks produced extremely useful order of battle intelligence in the run-up to D-Day in 1944. French agents stole the plans for the Atlantic Wall (the German system of coastal defences) and drew detailed sketches of the beaches where the landings were to take place. Some of the best of this intelligence came from Source K, a telephone engineer called Robert Keller, who managed to tap into the long-distance telephone line between the German command centre in Paris and Hitler's headquarters in East Prussia. French and Polish agents also provided intelligence that allowed the RAF to pre-empt a number of V-1 rocket attacks on England. Polish agents from the Monika network, a special operations mission whose intelligence material was handled by SIS, identified 103 V-weapon sites in northern France and Belgium between June and August 1944. A single French agent identified the location of thirty-seven separate V-1 launch sites, allowing the RAF to bomb them and preventing an unknown number of British civilian casualties.

Polish intelligence was extremely well organised, and its officers and agents provided a vast amount of intelligence, with a number of Polish agents being controlled directly by SIS. The service's best Polish agent, and the source of some of its most authoritative reporting from inside Germany, was Madame

Halina Szymańska, code-named Warlock, much of whose information came directly from the head of the *Abwehr*, Admiral Wilhelm Canaris. Intelligence chiefs in London regarded her reports as the 'most valuable and amongst the best received from any quarter'.

As the wife of the Polish military attaché in pre-war Berlin, she was one of the most popular hostesses on the diplomatic circuit – one SIS officer who knew Szymańska described her as 'a very attractive and formidable personality'. Canaris was a personal friend of her husband and a regular guest at her parties. When the Germans invaded Poland in September 1939, Szymańska, then still only 33, was staying with family in Lublin. Fearing the Russians who were invading from the east more than she did the Germans (who were advancing from the west), Szymańska took her children in the direction of Berlin in an attempt to contact her husband. Stopped near Poznan by German troops, she claimed diplomatic immunity. The Germans demanded the name of a senior officer or politician who could vouch for her and were taken aback when she named Canaris, who by coincidence happened to be visiting their headquarters at the time. When they took Szymańska to see him, her children huddled in front of her, she burst into tears. The German intelligence chief calmed her down and resolved to help her, almost certainly seeing her arrival as an opportunity to continue previous attempts to reach out to the Allies.

One former wartime SIS officer said:

> Canaris was violently anti-Nazi. He took a very dim view of what the Nazis were up to. He had a penchant for attractive ladies. He is supposed to have placed four at various posts overseas. He was able to arrange for Madame Szymańska and her children to travel in a sealed railway carriage across Germany from Poland to Switzerland, where he maintained contact with her. Indeed, he himself visited her in Berne a number of times.

On arrival in Berne, Szymańska moved into the apartment Canaris had arranged for her and, as a patriotic Pole eager to do what she could for her country, reported her links to the German intelligence chief to the Polish embassy. The Poles passed her case on to SIS and, although for purposes of her diplomatic immunity she was nominally employed as a secretary at the Polish embassy, her salary was paid by SIS.

Andrew King, who was based at the SIS station in Switzerland and was one of the SIS officers involved in running the Szymańska case, recalled that Frederick van den Heuvel, a highly experienced officer who had been in the service since the First World War, was sent out to Geneva as SIS head of station and told: 'Your number one mission in life is to handle this woman. Everything else is second class.' Subsequently, with Switzerland running a number of other sources providing reports from inside Germany, King himself was posted in Berne to concentrate entirely on handling Szymańska.

Canaris, code-named Theodor by SIS, first visited her in Berne in the winter of 1939 and made a number of subsequent visits, during which he authorised her to pass information on to the British and ensured that she also had access to his representative at the German embassy in Zurich, the *Abwehr* head of station Hans-Bernd Gisevius. 'I don't suppose you could call Admiral Canaris an indiscreet man or he would not have held that high position in Germany for so long,' Szymańska later recalled. 'But he could be very outspoken. I was asked to relate our conversations to the British only.'

The production of Source Warlock, as Szymańska's material was known, began with a visit in late 1940 when Canaris spent some days in her apartment. He provided her with the detailed German plans to invade Greece via Bulgaria and Yugoslavia, which was to be occupied 'with or without' its government's permission. But as important as that intelligence was, it was a less detailed but even more important bit of news that cemented her role as one of the best British sources on Germany. 'He told me that winter of 1940 that Germany would certainly make war on her treaty partner sooner or later,' Szymańska said. When she reported this back to King, he pressed her for more detail and Canaris explained that Hitler was planning to invade the Soviet Union in May 1941.

'She was able to tell us that an irrevocable decision had been made by Hitler, against the advice of his staff, to attack Russia in May of that year,' another wartime SIS officer said. 'At this time, the main German military effort appeared to be preparing the invasion of England in the spring. This valuable nugget of intelligence foretold a relaxation of the pressures on England and a future sharing of the war burden with Russia.'

Although Canaris's prediction that it would begin in May 1941 was to be a month out, it was the first report the British received from any source that Hitler was preparing to turn on his erstwhile ally Stalin. 'The date was wrong only because the Germans were held up in Yugoslavia which delayed the operation by a month,' the wartime SIS officer recalled. 'So yes I reckon you can give her credit for that. She was a very significant contact.'

The *Abwehr* chief was back in Berne in the spring of 1941, confirming that withdrawals of German troops from the Balkans that had been detected by the British code breakers at Bletchley Park were part of preparations for Operation Barbarossa, the invasion of the Soviet Union. In late September, fresh from a tour of the Eastern Front, he made a fourth visit to Berne to report on the problems the Germans were facing, Szymańska recalled. 'He said that the German front had run fast and bogged down in Russia and that it would never reach its objectives.'

There was good news for the British in that fierce resistance from the Russians had tied down far more troops than expected, ending any hope of mounting an invasion of the United Kingdom that year, although plans were still in place to do so once Russia had been defeated. Canaris stayed for some weeks in Switzerland, telling Szymańska the problems were due to fierce fighting by the Russians and the effects of a severe winter. He also revealed that, with many families having lost relatives, the serious losses in the east had hit morale hard in Germany. The general German population was only expected to remain passive through the winter if there was sufficient food, but cuts to meat and fat rations were already planned.

Canaris returned to Berne to visit Szymańska in late March of 1942, bringing so much intelligence that King had to put out a series of running reports over the space of a couple of weeks, during which Szymańska shuttled between Canaris and King. The *Abwehr* chief reported that the invasion of the United Kingdom had been definitely postponed until the conclusion of the Russian campaign, which the Germans hoped to win by the end of the year. But serious losses on the Eastern Front had led to a considerable loss of morale among German troops there, and in France the resistance movement was causing great difficulties. Szymańska said that by now Canaris was 'talking about the tension within German and the conspiracy that was gathering against Hitler'.

The 'delicate nature' of the 'Most Secret' Warlock material led to strict limitations on its use. It was not to be included in general intelligence summaries and those customers who were on the distribution list were told to treat it 'with great respect'. As the war progressed, Canaris was a less frequent visitor and Szymańska's main source of information became the *Abwehr* head of station in Zurich, Hans-Bernd Gisevius. But by early 1944, with Canaris and the *Abwehr* rapidly losing influence within Germany, Gisevius was no longer in a position to provide much useful intelligence.

Stewart Menzies, the wartime SIS chief, believed to his deathbed that more might have been made of Szymańska's links to Berlin, telling a colleague that Canaris had made an offer of talks that he had been ready to accept on the basis that even if it came to nothing the intelligence gained from them would have been priceless. 'But this biggest intelligence coup of all time,' Menzies said, 'was thwarted in certain Foreign Office quarters for fear of offending Russia.'

The SIS station in Stockholm also ran a number of agents in Germany. The most extensive description available of these networks comes from the German interrogation of SIS agent R34. Carl Aage Andreasson, a Danish businessman who was able to travel in and out of Germany, was captured by German intelligence in January 1944. He told his interrogators that there were four separate British networks in Berlin alone, while in Hamburg, SIS had some eighty agents, patriotic Germans working to end the war and save their country. The so-called CX reports from this period produced by SIS include good intelligence from inside Hitler's personal circle about the Führer's increasingly idiosyncratic behaviour. Reports were sent in microfilm concealed inside crates of goods exported to Sweden. In what constitutes a major breach of security, particularly given that he was run from Stockholm, Andreasson clearly knew the bare details of the Szymańska case. He told his interrogators that the most important British agent was a woman who had a relationship with a senior German and who had provided the British with continuous information from inside Berlin, including advance warning of Operation Barbarossa, the invasion of the Soviet Union. Whether this was enough to reveal the role of Canaris is unclear, but it was on 12 February 1944, shortly after Andreasson's arrest, that the *Abwehr* chief fell out of favour and Hitler ordered him to stay out of Berlin.

Canaris's and Szymańska's activities represented the highest level of 'patriotic' spying that SIS operated, but almost certainly the most glamorous mission run by a patriotic foreign national working for SIS was carried out by the Dutch agent Pieter Tazelaar. He was put ashore by a Royal Navy motor boat at Scheveningen in Holland wearing a specially designed rubber suit to protect his civilian clothes. Tazelaar was tasked to exfiltrate two Dutch politicians, who would be attending a party at a local hotel and get them to London. In a scene replicated in the 1964 James Bond movie *Goldfinger*, Tazelaar emerged from the water on to the beach and removed his rubber suit to reveal a dinner jacket and full evening suit complete with bow tie. A fellow agent then tipped some Hennessy XO brandy over him to give him an air of authenticity and Tazelaar staggered past German guards into the hotel as if he were one of the guests at the party. His mission was a failure, but Ian Fleming, who as the officer in charge of liaison between the Royal Navy and SIS, oversaw its execution, never forgot it. Although the scene did not appear in the original book – almost certainly for security reasons – Fleming ensured it made its way into the film.

★★★

Although SIS was intensively involved in the espionage struggle against Germany, long before the Second World War ended the agency was drawing up plans to use British businessmen travelling to a post-war Soviet Union to collect intelligence. The Russians were suspicious of any Westerners, imagining them all to be spies. Before the war, the Foreign Office had refused to allow SIS officers to have diplomatic immunity, but those rules had been relaxed during the conflict and it was now time to allow SIS officers posing as diplomats to make full use of this 'official cover'. Genuine businessmen working in Russia, though, would have the sort of 'natural cover' that would also make them very useful as agents, said Rodney Dennys, the deputy head of the Russian section.

'To the Russian, there is nothing more natural than British nationals engaged in commerce, industry and financial dealings, which are the basis of the existence of the imperialist bourgeoisie,' Dennys said. Using businessmen agents would be inexpensive, since they would be spying for patriotic reasons not for money, and there was total deniability. 'Even if suspicion should fall on any company or individual, HMG can simply say that it is not always able to control private commercial intelligence activity,' Dennys explained. Companies that were already preparing to operate in post-war Russia included a number that had already worked with SIS before the war. The Hudson's Bay Company and the two main travel agencies Thomas Cook and the Sir Henry Lunn company (now TUI), were among them.

'Travel is a sure thing,' Dennys said. 'Sir Henry Lunn Ltd is even now making approaches to the Russian Trade Mission about organising tours on a grand scale. A worm placed in this apple would soon grow fat.'

Johnson Matthey, the precious metals company, saw Russia as a good source of platinum; the Harland and Wolff shipyards were seeking contracts to build ships for the Soviet Union; and the Price Forbes Insurance company was also building up its portfolio in the USSR. Dennys pointed out that one of the Price Forbes directors, Carl Duvier, had spent the war in SIS and would be extremely useful as an agent. Duvier, who like the fictional James Bond had been an officer on the Royal Naval Reserve during the war, remained a serving naval reserve officer until the late 1960s.

Nor were businessmen the only people with the sort of 'natural cover' provided by a genuine reason to be in Russia, Dennys added. Musicians, ballet dancers, actors and sportsmen would also have privileged access to the Soviet Union. 'A start should be made now, by preparing the ground with the Football Association to get them to start work immediately the right moment comes along.'

Unfortunately, the plans worked out by Dennys were leaked to the KGB. His boss in the Russian section was Kim Philby, who had been working for Soviet intelligence since the mid 1930s, and who passed the plans straight to Moscow Centre, thus ensuring that the companies concerned, and more importantly their employees who had been recruited as SIS agents, had absolutely no cover whatsoever.

As well as using British businessmen and companies, SIS tried to insert Eastern European émigrés back into their home countries. They, it was reasoned, would have even better 'cover', with their familiarity with local culture and often contacts with surviving anti-Soviet nationalist groups. Philby was given credit for having betrayed several such attempts to set up networks of intelligence agents and saboteurs across Eastern Europe and the Soviet Union, although the conception and planning of many of those he is blamed for having destroyed, like the ill-fated Operation Valuable, which saw numerous Albanian patriots sent back into their homeland only to be arrested and shot, were hopelessly over-optimistic.

SIS also set up a number of agent networks across the Baltic republics, but they were swiftly compromised and played back against the British. 'We had to know the SIS plans and the only way we could do that was by successfully infiltrating our men into the SIS networks,' said Major Janis Lukasevics, the officer who controlled the Latvian KGB's counter-espionage operation. Once the networks were infiltrated, they were to be left in place, feeding back false information to London and providing Soviet intelligence with details of what the British were trying to do.

'There was a decision not to touch them, to continue finding out what their specific tasks were. Well, we quite quickly found out that their job was not just spying but also to prepare the way for other spies, to set up a link and new points of support and to establish contact with resistance groups.'

More than thirty British agents, most of them émigrés, were dispatched to Lithuania, Estonia and Latvia over a period spanning a total of ten years. The Estonian resistance group 'the Forest Brothers', which had worked through the war first against the Russians, then in opposition to the Germans and then again as the tide of the war turned against the Russians again, continued operating into the 1950s. However, Anthony Cavendish, who as an SIS officer based in Germany helped to ferry some of the British agents into Latvia, recalled that for the most part the missions ended in failure, as did similar attempts to link up with the Ukrainian and Byelorussian nationalist movements.

'At suitable phases of the moon, teams of two or three highly trained agents were dropped into the Ukraine or Byelorussia,' Cavendish said. Several missions were sent in 'and after arrival the dropped agents made radio contact with their base station in Western Germany. However, several of the agents were captured, tried – some in show trials – and then shot.' In an attempt to undermine the Soviet dominance of Eastern Europe, both SIS and the CIA used agents recruited during the war.

The Eisenhower administration had been elected on a platform of liberating the Soviet satellites – the so-called 'Rollback' policy – but in the ten years since the war ended, the Russians had in fact considerably strengthened their hold over Eastern Europe. All reports from inside the Soviet-occupied states spoke of high levels of dissatisfaction, but the presence of 100,000 Russian troops held out little hope that any revolt might succeed.

Nevertheless, in the mid 1950s both SIS and the CIA had stepped up their covert operations across Eastern Europe, recruiting agents and training teams of Polish, Hungarian, Czech and Romanian émigrés for covert action before sending them into their home countries. Allen Dulles, the head of the CIA, told the US National Security Council that 'developments in the satellites present the greatest opportunity for the last ten years both covertly and overtly to exploit the situation.'

SIS and CIA operations inside Hungary were stepped up in advance of the 1956 uprising there, actions that were carefully co-ordinated with the Hungarian opposition. SIS had been in close contact with dissident elements inside Hungary for some time, spiriting them across the border into the British-controlled zone of Austria for resistance training in preparation for a future uprising. The SIS head of station in Budapest buried packs of weapons and communications equipment, including instructions on how to contact SIS, at points in the woods around the Hungarian capital that were agreed with the organisers of the Hungarian opposition.

Paul Gorka was one of a group of Hungarian students who were recruited to gather intelligence on Soviet activity inside Hungary and equipped with 'enough weapons to shoot our way across the border'. They were sent 'coded messages from Vienna asking us for information about Russian troop movements, index numbers of military vehicles, so that a picture could be built up of details of Russian occupation units,' Gorka said. 'We replied with information written in invisible ink in innocuous letters to special addresses.' But Gorka and his fellow students developed the unfortunate habit of meeting in a popular Budapest coffee bar to discuss their activities and were swiftly rounded up. 'I was interrogated for seven weeks, sometimes in the presence of a Soviet major,' Gorka recalled. 'I was tortured several times. Sometimes I was left in my cell with both feet immersed in icy water, other times I was hung from a beam by my arms handcuffed together. When I was cut down after several hours, my hands were black and so swollen that it was impossible to remove the handcuffs. Under torture, I confessed and after a brief trial was sent to prison for 15 years.'

Some Hungarian dissidents were smuggled across the border into Austria to be given weapons training and lessons in how to organise an armed resistance. They rendezvoused with their contacts in true Cold War fashion, often quite literally under a certain lamp-post in a back street of a border town. Michael Giles was one of the SIS officers training the dissidents for resistance work:

> I had this battered old Volkswagen and I was picking up agents on the Hungarian border. We were taking them up into the mountains and giving them a sort of three-or four-day crash course. I would be told to pick somebody up from a street corner at a certain time of night in the pouring rain. Graz was our staging point. Then, after we'd trained them – explosives, weapons training – I used to take them back. This was in 1954, two years before the uprising. But we knew it was going to come. We were training agents for the uprising.

The stage for the Hungarian uprising was set by the forced resignation in April 1955 of the country's reformist Prime Minister Imre Nagy and by Nikita Khrushchev's so-called 'secret speech' in February 1956 in which the new Soviet leader denounced Stalin for his brutality (and which by condemning his hard-line policies gave heart to reform-minded communists throughout the Eastern Bloc). A Polish journalist whose family were Israeli was visiting his girlfriend, a secretary in the Polish Communist Party headquarters, when he saw the speech lying on her desk. He persuaded her to let him borrow it and took it to the Israeli embassy, where a copy was made and passed to the Americans. Thousands of copies of the speech were distributed clandestinely throughout Eastern Europe. As details of the speech became more widely known, the clamour for reforms began to grow, particularly in Poland and Hungary.

On 23 October 1956, students marching in Budapest to demand democratic elections, the withdrawal of Soviet troops and the return of Nagy were joined by a quarter of a million people on the streets of Budapest. Large numbers of weapons began to appear in the crowd, many of them from British and American arms caches in Austria and Hungary. Fighting broke out with the security forces. In an attempt to placate the demonstrators, Nagy was reappointed Prime Minister. There was sporadic fighting for several days, followed by a series of reforms that Nagy introduced, including the abandonment of the one-party system and the disbandment of the *Államvédelmi Hatóság* (ÁVH), the Hungarian equivalent of the KGB. Khrushchev's reaction was brutal. He sent in Soviet and other Warsaw Pact forces to suppress the uprising and arrest Nagy, who was subsequently put on trial for treason and executed.

SIS agents inside Poland, some of whose involvement went back to the networks run by the British Special Operations Executive during the Second World War, were also involved in opposition riots that took place in Poland at the same time, while SIS provided training support and weapons caches for opposition groups in both Poland and Czechoslovakia, just as it had in Hungary. Despite all this activity, however, the Eastern European communist regimes remained immovable.

★★★

There is an understandable belief that the most productive Western Cold War agents were Russian, but the spy who produced the most important intelligence on Soviet military intentions during the 1970s and early '80s – one of the most dangerous periods of the post-war era – was a Polish army officer. Ryszard Kukliński's family were deeply patriotic. His father was a wartime hero who had fought the Nazi occupation as a member of the Home Army, the Polish resistance. Captured by the Gestapo, he was incarcerated and murdered in the Sachsenhausen concentration camp. The family were both staunch Catholics and committed socialists, and after the war Ryszard adapted to the new communist rule, joining the Polish People's Army and rapidly climbing up the promotion ladder to reach a high-flying post on the Polish General Staff.

Kukliński became disillusioned with communism after taking part in preparations for the Warsaw Pact's 1968 invasion of Czechoslovakia. Like many of the young communists inspired by Krushchev's 1956 denunciation of Stalin, Kukliński was appalled by the Kremlin's reaction to the Prague Spring reform movement in Czechoslovakia. By now, he was a senior staff officer, working with Soviet colleagues on plans for the invasion of Western Europe. These 'unambiguously offensive' plans involved the use of tactical nuclear missiles and accepted without any apparent concern that the inevitable response in kind by NATO would lay waste to his homeland. When an outbreak of protests in the 1970s in Poland was brutally crushed – with around forty people shot dead by troops and militia – Kukliński decided to act.

He proposed taking a sailing trip by yacht along the German, Danish, Dutch and Belgian coasts that would look like a holiday but was in fact a spying trip. So far as his bosses were concerned, Kukliński was mounting an intelligence operation. He and a number of Polish army colleagues would be collecting intelligence and photographing naval bases and NATO warships. But Kukliński's main aim was to use the trip to make contact with the US military and offer his services as a spy.

When they docked in Wilhelmshaven, Kukliński posted a letter written in halting English to the 'USA Ambassy Bonn' in which he said he was a serviceman 'from Communistische Kantry'. He wanted 'to meet (secretly) with US Army Officer' who had to be able to speak Russian or Polish. Kukliński gave a number of days when the yacht would be in Holland and said he would telephone the US embassy. When he rang the embassy in The Hague, a meeting was arranged with two CIA officers at the main railway station in the Dutch capital. The officers had no idea who they would be meeting – the most likely person was thought to be a low-ranking sailor – but it was deemed worth an initial meeting at least. After checking for surveillance, they took Kukliński to the nearby Central Hotel where they were stunned to learn that he was a colonel on the Polish army's General Staff, liaising with senior Soviet staff officers and privy to top-secret Warsaw Pact war plans. Kukliński laid out his motives. He was no traitor. He would take no money for what he was doing. He was, rather, a patriotic Pole fighting for his country's freedom from Soviet rule. Everything he did over the next nine years seemed to those working with him, the majority of them experts in the handling of agents, to confirm those motives.

The case was controlled from CIA headquarters at Langley by David Forden, a former head of station in Poland who spoke Polish well enough to hold regular meetings with Kukliński at safe houses in West Germany. Kukliński would know him only as Daniel, but the closeness that developed between them was a model of the kind of relationship based on trust that is essential to the running of a long-term agent operating in a dangerous situation. The routine exchanges, often several times a week, would be carried out by the CIA's Warsaw station using techniques very similar to those used by the Germans in wartime Ankara to make contact with the British ambassador's valet 'Cicero'.

Kukliński's code name was Gull, an allusion to his love of the sea. Using Minox cameras supplied by the CIA, he photographed every major document that came across his desk, more than 30,000 of them over the nine years during which he was in play. A car driven by a CIA officer would meet him on a backstreet of Warsaw at night so he could hand over the unprocessed film and his reports, which he always signed as Jack Strong. There were numerous fallback plans to avoid surveillance and even if 'casuals' – civilians with no link to the Polish authorities – were spotted, the car would drive around the area and make repeated passes of the location until the officer was absolutely certain no one could see the drop take place.

On one occasion, Kukliński was noticed by two secret policemen in a Polski Fiat 125. They gave chase but he managed to evade them by running down a series of back alleys to the main station, taking a train into the suburbs and then a bus back to Warsaw city centre, from where he rang his son pretending to be drunk and asked him to come and pick him up. The incident led to contact being broken off for several months to avoid any possible follow-up surveillance by the authorities, but throughout that period Kukliński continued to photograph more documents, which he would hand over once contact resumed.

Kukliński delivered regular updates of the latest Soviet plans for the invasion of Western Europe, details of Soviet deception operations designed to fool the US spy satellites and the specifications and photographs of every new piece of Soviet military equipment as it was introduced – including the T-72 tank and new medium-range missiles aimed at NATO countries. He also provided details of the times it would take each military unit to move into its forward location ready for war – information that included the fact that Scud missiles would be ready to fire within forty minutes, a piece of intelligence later misused by the Blair government in the run-up to the Iraq War to suggest a threat to British bases in Cyprus.

The breakdown of how each Warsaw Pact unit would be deployed in an attack on the West, which included details down to individual regiments, was invaluable in the planning of NATO defences. Kukliński also provided the locations, layouts and details of the communication systems of the three secret Soviet military headquarters hidden deep underground in Poland, Bulgaria and near Moscow, from where a war against the West would be controlled, information that allowed the US to develop plans to destroy them.

For one of the most dangerous decades of the Cold War, the US – and therefore NATO – had unprecedented detail of Soviet military capabilities and plans, intelligence that led to major changes in the locations, size and operational plans for NATO forces in Germany and Western Europe. Had a war been fought, NATO commanders would have known precisely what Warsaw Pact forces were going to do at every turn, allowing them to preempt or counter their plans easily.

Kukliński's role as a long-term CIA agent-in-place was brought to an end by the internal Polish crisis created by unofficial opposition groups that had been calling for reform throughout the spring and early summer of 1980. At the beginning of July, the Polish government introduced dramatic increases in the price of food – meat prices went up by between 60 and 90 per cent. This sparked a wave of industrial unrest across the country, leading to the creation of *Solidarność* ('Solidarity'), an independent (and therefore illegal) trade union. In an attempt to defuse the situation, Polish Communist Party leader Edward Gierek sanctioned a deal that allowed the formation of independent trade unions, the right to strike without repercussions and 'freedom of expression'.

The Russians reacted predictably, ousting Gierek and replacing him with the more hard-line Stanisław Kania.

But even before the agreement had been put in place, the Polish Ministry of Defence and the Internal Affairs Ministry had begun planning for martial law. In late October, Kukliński reported that he was part of a small five-man team of staff officers, led by the Chief of the Polish General Staff General Florian Siwicki, who were drafting up plans to introduce martial law.

Meanwhile, the agreement permitting free trade unions had failed to take the sting out of the industrial unrest in Poland, and decisions to give various groups of workers wage increases only led to more strikes by other workers demanding pay rises. In late November, Polish railway workers threatened to call a general strike. A rail strike would leave Soviet forces unable to move in the event of war. It was a step too far for Moscow. On 29 November, a temporary restricted area was set up all along the East German–Polish border preventing Western observers from monitoring troop movements in what was widely seen as a precursor to Soviet intervention.

Two days later, Warsaw Pact defence ministers met in Bucharest, raising further concern about the likelihood of a Soviet military invasion. Kukliński sent a 'very urgent' report revealing that the Polish delegation had backed a plan to allow Soviet, East German and Czechoslovak forces to intervene under cover of carrying out military manoeuvres. They had to be ready to invade on 8 December, he said, adding: 'I very much regret to say that although everyone who has seen the plans (a very restricted group of people) is very depressed and crestfallen, no one is even contemplating putting up active resistance against the Warsaw Pact action.'

In the event, following a personal letter from US President Jimmy Carter to Soviet leader Leonid Brezhnev warning against intervention, condemnation from a number of Western leaders, and an emergency meeting of Warsaw Pact leaders in Moscow, the Russians decided to give the Poles more time to end the unrest, albeit with the continued threat of Soviet 'military assistance' hanging over them if they did not deal 'decisively' with the problem.

The pressure from Western leaders, and the certainty that it was no longer possible to mount a surprise invasion to which the West would struggle to respond – as had happened in Czechoslovakia in 1968, Hungary in 1956 and most recently in Afghanistan in 1979 – led Moscow to push Polish leaders to deal with the situation themselves. By late January, Kukliński was reporting that contingency plans for the introduction of martial law were being drawn up. This did not stop him also supplying fresh plans for a future invasion of Western Europe, giving the full details for two alternative options, one using a combination of conventional forces nuclear strikes from the first, the second initially using conventional weapons prior to a staged transition to the use of nuclear weapons. The plans described which Warsaw Pact units would be allocated to attack particular NATO forces and how they would carry out those attacks.

In mid-February 1981, with no end in sight to the industrial unrest, Moscow ordered the appointment of Polish Defence Minister Wojciech Jaruzelski as Prime Minister and Kukliński reported hurried preparations for the introduction of martial law and the arrests of key *Solidarność* activists. Although martial law was not yet introduced, police harassment of trade unionists was stepped up, and in late March the trade union staged a strike in protest. It was a major show of strength at a time when large numbers of Soviet troops were carrying out a joint exercise with Polish troops on Polish soil. In a clear threat to the strikers, Jaruzelski announced that, at his request, the manoeuvres were being extended by a week.

In a personal letter to 'Daniel', Kukliński lamented the 'hopeless' situation in which he and his colleagues now found themselves. 'In this extremely gloomy atmosphere, one of the most committed officers openly said that Poland had to undertake far-reaching political reforms,' Kukliński said. 'We Poles realise that we must fight for our own freedom, if necessary, making the ultimate sacrifice. I remain convinced that the support your country has been giving to all who are fighting for that freedom will bring us closer to our goal.'

A few days later, Kukliński was reporting that Kania and Jaruzelski had been called to Moscow for discussions with Brezhnev and other members of the Soviet Politburo on the 'preparations with the assistance of Soviet consultants for introducing martial law'. Kukliński, who had been present in discussions following the talks, said Jaruzelski was opposed to martial law. 'In the darkest recesses of his mind he could find no place for the thought that they could introduce such a thing in Poland,' Kukliński said, adding that the talks had only increased the risk of Soviet intervention.

The unrest continued through the summer, with a million *Solidarność* members taking to the streets in August to protest against the combination of rising prices and low wages. In early September, Kukliński reported that he and his team had been ordered to draw up a new decree that would allow the rapid introduction of martial law.

A few days later, *Solidarność* passed a resolution in support of 'free and independent trade unions' in the Soviet Union and across Eastern Europe. The response from the Soviet leadership was swift. Describing the resolution as 'an outrageous provocation', it ordered the Polish leadership to take 'immediate, determined, radical steps' to end the union's 'actions hostile to the Soviet Union'.

Even before the furious reaction from Moscow, Kukliński was reporting precisely how the crackdown was to take place: 'In brief, martial law will be introduced at night, either between Friday and a work-free Saturday or between Saturday and Sunday, when industrial plants will be closed,' he said. 'Arrests will begin about midnight, six hours before an announcement of martial law will be broadcast over the radio and television. Roughly 600 people will be arrested in Warsaw, which will require the use of around 1,000 police in unmarked cars. That same night, the army will seal off the most important areas of Warsaw and other major cities.'

Then he dropped a bombshell: somehow *Solidarność* had acquired details of the plans for martial law, including the secret code name *Wiosna* (Spring), which was known to only a small group of people. An investigation was under way, and although Kukliński was not responsible for passing it to *Solidarność*, he was rightly concerned that his own contacts with the CIA might be uncovered. He had already been visited by a counter-espionage officer investigating the leak and had decided to temporarily suspend all drops. He signed off his report with a defiant message:

> It appears that my mission is coming to an end. The nature of the information makes it quite easy to detect the source. I do not object to, and indeed welcome, having the information I have conveyed serve those who fight for the freedom of Poland with their heads raised high. I am prepared to make the ultimate sacrifice, but the best way to achieve something is with our actions and not with our sacrifices.
>
> Long live free Poland!
> Long live Solidarity, which brings freedom to all oppressed nations!
> JACK STRONG

In early October, disregarding the obvious risks, Kukliński reported that he was one of those in charge of co-ordinating martial law and produced an official document, most of which he had drafted himself, detailing all the measures to be taken after its introduction. At the end of October, Kukliński was told that a decision had been made. The introduction of martial law was imminent. Two days later, he and three colleagues were called to an urgent meeting. The KGB had found out from an agent inside the Vatican that the CIA had a copy of the martial law plans. The four of them were the only ones with access to it and an urgent investigation was taking place. There were only two copies of the plans and one of them was always kept in Kukliński's safe. On his way home, he spotted surveillance. It was time to get out.

Using a short-burst transmitter designed to go undetected by Polish security systems, Kukliński sent a message to the CIA Warsaw station warning them that he had been compromised. 'Everything is pointing to the end of my mission,' he said. 'I have a choice of taking my life, early arrest, or the help which was once offered to me.' The response was swift. Forden ordered the immediate exfiltration of Kukliński and his family. The Pole then told his shocked wife, Hanka, and their two sons that he had been working for the Americans and that they had no choice but to flee.

On three consecutive nights, CIA officers drove to a predetermined location to collect them but spotted surveillance and called off the pick-up. After the third failed attempt, a fallback operation was put in place. Tom Ryan, the CIA Head of Station, and his wife, Lucille, had been in West Berlin and David Forden had told them to stay there in case having someone on the East German side of the border could help the Kuklińskis get out. It was a good decision. The Ryans were told to drive back to Warsaw and pick the family up because, unlike a car coming from the US embassy in Poland, they would not be under surveillance. The Ryans successfully picked up the Kuklińskis and had them duck down out of sight as they drove to the embassy compound in Warsaw. Then, hidden in boxes in an embassy van protected by diplomatic plates, they were driven across the border into East Germany and then to West Berlin, from where they were flown to the United States and freedom.

In May 1984, after a secret court martial in absentia, the Warsaw Military District Court sentenced Kukliński to death on charges of high treason. It was not until March 1995 that the Polish Supreme Court finally absolved him of treason, ruling that 'the security of the [Polish] state unquestionably takes precedence over the disclosure of a secret, especially if the disclosure is intended to serve a higher cause'.

Ryszard Kukliński and his family settled in the United States. He died in Tampa, Florida, in February 2004. George Tenet, the then Director of the CIA, described him as 'a true hero'. 'This passionate and courageous man helped keep the Cold War from becoming hot,' Tenet said. 'And he did so for the noblest of reasons – to advance the sacred causes of liberty and peace in his homeland and throughout the world.'

Kukliński's remains were taken to Poland and he is buried in the Honour Row at Warsaw's Powązki Military Cemetery.

★★★

Both SIS and the CIA continue to work with patriotic agents around the world, particularly in troubled countries in the Middle East such as Iran, Syria and Libya. During the run-up to the 2003 Iraq War, Iraqis living abroad were persuaded by SIS officers to go back into the southern city of Basra, which the British Army was tasked to take. The agents merged back into Iraqi society and were soon reporting to SIS officers based with the British military headquarters just south of Basra.

The agents were supplied with very short-range data transmission devices. When they had something to report, they uploaded it on to their device, went to a pre-agreed location on the edge of the city and surreptitiously pressed the transmit button. A fake rock planted among the rubble containing a data transceiver stored the report and then re-sent it to the SIS team.

When intelligence was needed more urgently, SIS officers, wearing local dress and accompanied by Special Boat Service (SBS) minders, moved in and out of the city, running the agents in the same way that their predecessors had done on the streets of Cold War Prague or Budapest. Sometimes they met them in safe houses, at other times the agents were simply 'snatched' off the street as if they were being arrested by the Iraqi al-Amn al-'Amm secret police. The SBS commandos, driving 4×4 vehicles, bundled the agent into the back seat, where an SIS officer was waiting to debrief him, and then dropped him off somewhere else in the city.

★★★

Although the CIA and SIS have experienced notable successes with patriot spies, no single intelligence agency has been more effective in exploiting patriotism than the main Chinese intelligence service, the Ministry for State Security (MSS). The authorities in Beijing rely heavily on agents recruited from among the 'Overseas Chinese', the term they use for anyone of Chinese origin living abroad, whether or not they have taken fresh nationality.

Regardless of whether or not they support the Communist authorities in Beijing, the 'Overseas Chinese' generally feel an extraordinary attachment to China, one former Western intelligence officer who worked in the Far East said. 'The Chinese have always exploited the "love of the motherland", felt by the majority of Chinese wherever they live.'

When China began to modernise in the late 1970s, intent on becoming a world economic power by the early twenty-first century, it focused on the so-called 'Four Modernisations'. One of the most important of these was in science and technology, and one of the key means of obtaining the relevant knowledge – alongside collaboration deals with Western technological companies and the sending thousands of young Chinese nationals abroad to study in Western universities – was espionage. Anyone travelling abroad was routinely expected to collect intelligence.

When British universities first began charging students to photocopy information in university libraries in the late 1980s and early '90s, it was not as a result of budget cuts, but because the increasing number of Chinese students studying in Britain were routinely working their way through the libraries' science books and journals, copying any information at all on scientific developments in general and nuclear physics in particular.

Chinese intelligence officers based in embassies and consulates abroad began recruiting any 'Overseas Chinese' who might be able either to provide technological assistance or recruit other members of the Chinese community to assist. The recruitment technique played very heavily on a sense of shared national and cultural identity and China's desperate need to modernise in order to catch up with the rest of the world and restore itself to its historic position as a world leader in scientific and cultural innovation. It was a direct appeal to their pride in their country of origin.

Money was unlikely to be offered as an incentive, although the possibility of business opportunities inside China often was. The more likely inducement would be through improvements in the situation of relatives still living in China, and by extension the notion that the position of family members under Beijing's control might be worsened if the potential agent declined to assist.

Although ethnic Chinese were routinely targeted as agents in many countries around the world, the main target, due to the large number of companies and institutes dealing in a wide range of technologies including nuclear, aeronautics and computer science, was and remains the United States. The close to five million ethnic Chinese living in America represent a large pool of potential agents from which to recruit.

Dongfan Chung was born in the north-eastern Chinese province of Liaoning in 1936. He was 10 years old when his parents fled to Taiwan to escape the civil war between the Nationalist and Communist forces. Chung studied engineering in Taiwan, and in the early 1960s moved to the US, taking a master's degree in civil engineering and then working for the American aircraft manufacturer Boeing. In 1972, he joined Rockwell, which had just won the contract to build the first Space Shuttle.

By now, he had changed his first name to Greg, and he and his wife had become US citizens. During the assessment process, he was asked if he would be willing to 'bear arms' for his adopted country if there was ever a war between the United States and China. His response was in the affirmative, but not in the way the interviewer was expecting. 'If this happens,' he said. 'I will grab a gun and shoot myself.'

It was the moment that China began opening up to the West and seeking to modernise that provided the tipping point for the Chungs. 'Suddenly, the doors opened to China,' Chung's wife Ling said. 'We were curious and searching for self-identity.' After attending a concert by visiting Chinese musicians, Chung bought an *erhu*, a two-stringed Chinese violin, and taught himself to play it. He also began attending events by visiting Chinese academics, at one of which he met an engineering professor from the Harbin Institute of Technology, Chen Len Ku, who asked him about aeronautical stress analysis, Chung's speciality in the Space Shuttle programme. China did not have enough information on this subject, Chen said. Anything Chung could do to help would be welcome.

Chung sent Chen some information accompanied by a letter in which he suggested that he was open to helping in other ways if he could. 'I don't know what I can do for the country,' Chung said. 'Being proud of the achievements by the people's efforts in the Motherland, I am regretful for not contributing anything.'

A second meeting, this time with a senior official from China's state-owned Aviation Industry Corporation of China at a talk in Los Angeles, led to an exchange of letters and invitation to China for an unofficial 'technical exchange' on airframe design, including stress analysis and testing for fatigue. 'I would like to make an effort to contribute to the Four Modernisations of China,' Chung said in one letter. 'It is a great honour and I am excited if I can make some contributions to the modernisations of the Motherland.'

Chung's betrayal of the secrets of the Space Shuttle programme lasted more than thirty years and was only finally uncovered in 2006 as a result of an investigation into another Chinese spy ring. He was convicted in July 2009 of economic espionage and being a Chinese agent. The prosecution presented no evidence of any money changing hands. Chung had acted purely out of love of 'the motherland'. A former FBI counterintelligence officer told the court that it was classic Chinese exploitation of a member of the 'Overseas Chinese' community. 'What they try to do is work on the China aspect,' he said. '"You are not so much hurting the United States; you are helping China." You tell them they're doing it for the good of the Motherland or the good of their country.'

Chung was sentenced to fifteen years and eight months' imprisonment. He was 73. The judge said he had imposed a long sentence because he wanted to send out a message to the Chinese: 'Stop sending your spies here.'

★★★

One of the most prominent cases of 'Overseas Chinese' being used to spy on the United States was that of the double agent Katrina Leung. Born Chen Wen Ying in 1954 in Canton (now Guangzhou) in south-east China, she moved to New York in 1970, where she changed her first name to Katrina, and five years later married a fellow Chinese, Kam Leung. After moving to Los Angeles, Katrina Leung lived in an apartment block known to the FBI as 'a nest of Chinese spies' and became involved with companies carrying out illegal technology transfer to China.

This led to her recruitment in December 1982 as an informant by FBI Special Agent James Smith, an intelligence officer tasked to send agents into China to collect intelligence. Smith gave Leung the code name Parlor Maid and sent her into China on a difficult mission, making contact with her old friend Hanson Huang, who had been imprisoned in China for espionage. Huang was a key figure in a Chinese nuclear weapons spy ring in the US, code-named Tiger Trap by the FBI, who hoped that Huang's imprisonment might make him willing to deal with them. Leung managed to carry the mission off against the odds, getting into the jail and speaking to him, albeit not managing to do anything other than prepare the ground for future contacts. She was an impressive woman in many ways and less than a year after recruiting her, Smith began an affair with her, in contravention both of FBI rules and all sensible tradecraft.

The aim of the Parlor Maid operation was to 'dangle' Leung in front of Chinese intelligence officers operating out of the Chinese consulate-general in San Francisco and in Beijing as a potential agent, in the hope that the Chinese would attempt to recruit her as well so she could be run as a 'double', ostensibly supplying intelligence to the Chinese, but in fact limiting her reports to them to relatively unimportant data and using them to gain access to far more important intelligence on Chinese espionage operations against the United States. She was a very successful agent, using her growing reputation as a prominent member of the Los Angeles Chinese community to entertain Chinese diplomats and visiting Chinese officials, including then Chinese President Yang Shangkun.

Her close links to officials at the San Francisco consulate-general and in Beijing gave Leung access to a great deal of useful intelligence and, despite initial concerns that she might have already been spying for the Chinese before Smith recruited her, she successfully passed polygraph lie detector tests in 1984 and 1986 that confirmed her reliability. The FBI was particularly pleased with her access when, only a few months after the Tiananmen Square demonstrations were put down in June 1989, she travelled to Beijing to provide valuable information on the political situation, which was virtually impossible to obtain by other means.

But sometime in the late 1980s, Leung appears to have been turned by the Chinese. The balance of usefulness between what she provided to the FBI and what she gave the Chinese had switched in Beijing's favour, while the affair with Smith severely constrained his ability to act. If he launched an investigation, the affair between them would leak out and he would lose his job.

Unknown to Smith, and almost certainly at the instigation of her new bosses in Beijing, Leung began a second affair with Special Agent Bill Cleveland, who ran the FBI's San Francisco counter-espionage operations against the Chinese. She also began opening Smith's briefcase and photocopying official documents, which she passed to her new Chinese controller. The first clear sign that Leung had been 'doubled back' against the FBI came in June 1990, when the top-secret US electronic surveillance systems that transmitted everything photocopied on the Xerox machines in the Chinese consulate in Los Angeles, including the cheques paid to Chinese agents (which were routinely copied for the records), suddenly stopped working. Leung had given away the Americans' top-secret surveillance systems. The Chinese responded by replacing the photocopiers and transporting all the old machines to Beijing, where the systems were reverse engineered, allowing them to be used back against the Americans and other nations.

The second clear indication was even more worrying, particularly for Cleveland. In April 1991, he was sent an NSA tape of a female agent talking to her Chinese controller, Mao Guohua, the head of the MSS America Department. Cleveland immediately recognised the voice of the female agent. It was Leung, his mistress, and she was telling Mao about a number of current FBI operations and investigations against the Chinese. He telephoned Smith immediately and, while for security reasons he used guarded language, his message was clear. Leung could no longer be trusted. Her loyalties were with the Chinese not the FBI.

At that point, the Parlor Maid operation ought to have been brought to an immediate halt. The problem was that both Cleveland and Smith were stymied by their sexual relationships with Leung. Although neither knew that the other was compromised, both of them knew that if they brought the house down, they would lose their jobs. Smith confronted Leung. She claimed that the Chinese had told her they knew she was working for the FBI. She had no choice but to supply them with intelligence if she were to remain in a position to obtain the intelligence the FBI needed in return.

Leung admitted to Smith that she had disclosed highly sensitive intelligence about FBI investigations and operations but claimed that she was still favouring the FBI. She refused to take a fresh polygraph text, but even so Smith continued to describe her as a 'reliable' agent in reports to his bosses, who were so in awe of his depth of knowledge and reputation that, despite reports that ought to have suggested the operation had gone disastrously wrong, they did not question his judgement at any point. When a very reliable FBI source reported that an agent called 'Katrina' was a Chinese intelligence agent with an extremely productive source inside the FBI, Smith's bosses simply informed him and left him to deal with the issue, even though the 'extremely productive source' was clearly likely to be him. When the same source reported that Leung was 'in bed with' the FBI's Los Angeles division, again Smith's bosses informed him and asked him to investigate. Unsurprisingly, he did nothing. He retired from the FBI in November 2000, by which stage Leung had been paid $1.7 million by the FBI for her work as an agent.

An investigation against Leung did not commence until May 2001 and the investigation of Smith was not opened until January 2002. Even then the incompetence continued. Prosecutors did a deal with Smith under which he came clean about everything that had taken place in return for a limited sentence of three years' probation and a $10,000 fine. As a part of the deal, Smith was not allowed to provide evidence on behalf of Leung, which led the judge in her case to throw it out on the basis that, without Smith's evidence, she could not possibly obtain a fair trial. Leung ultimately pleaded guilty to two minor charges of lying to the FBI and failing to report taxable income and spent just three months in jail and eighteen months in home detention, together with three years' probation, 100 hours of community service and a $10,000 fine.

Chapter 5

ADVENTURERS, FANTASISTS AND PSYCHOPATHS

The 'second oldest profession' attracts more than its fair share of people with personality traits that would be considered a dangerous liability in any job, yet alone one where lives – including very often the lives of the agents themselves – depend on people getting it right. Espionage appeals to myriad adventurers, risk-takers, fantasists and egotists. Most intelligence services use psychologists in the recruitment process to try to weed out these types, not least because intelligence officers with those traits are much more likely to become dissatisfied with their own role and vulnerable to recruitment by the other side's spies. But while most intelligence services avoid recruiting them as officers, what seems at first to be flaws in their personality can sometimes make them surprisingly successful as agents.

The most famous risk-taking adventurer in the history of modern espionage was undoubtedly Sidney Reilly, the so-called 'Ace of Spies' who worked for Mansfield Cumming in Russia in the wake of the 1917 Bolshevik Revolution. The Irish name was part of the spy's 'legend'. Reilly claimed to be the son of an Irish father and Russian mother. In fact, he was a Russian, born to a Jewish family in Odessa, southern Russia, in March 1874 and his real name was Sigmund Georgievich Rosenblum. He went to Britain in his twenties, acquired a wife there and, through her, a British passport. By the early 1900s, Reilly was combining extremely dubious business activities with even more dubious espionage activities on behalf of a variety of governments.

There have been suggestions that at one time or another between 1903 and 1917 he worked for the Japanese, Russian,

German and British governments – in some cases simultaneously. There is some evidence that he was working undercover for the British in Port Arthur in the Russian Far East in 1902 and 1903. By 1915, Reilly was in the then Russian capital Petrograd, where he had acquired a young Russian wife – in a bigamous marriage, given that he was still married to the British woman.

He moved to New York in the summer of 1915 to procure weapons for the Russian armed forces and according to Norman Thwaites, the deputy head of Cumming's New York station, made $2 million from the contracts by being 'entirely unscrupulous', so much so in fact that Thwaites initially suspected him of being a German agent.

Reilly approached Thwaites in October 1917 and told him he felt he should be doing 'his bit' in the war. Thwaites said:

> His appearance was remarkable. Complexion swarthy, a long straight nose, piercing eyes, black hair brushed back from a forehead suggesting keen intelligence, a large mouth, figure slight, of medium height, always clothed immaculately, he was a man that impressed one with a good deal of power. When later I knew him better, I discovered intellectual qualities of an unusual kind. He was a gambler by nature, whether in hazardous occupations or in games of chance.

Thwaites despatched Reilly to Canada, where he was commissioned into the Royal Flying Corps and sent to London. Whether this was part of his recruitment into the British secret service is unclear, but Cumming's diary records that he first met Reilly on 15 March 1918. The new man was brought into the Secret Service headquarters in Whitehall Court by John Scale, Cumming's new head of station in Stockholm. Scale had appointed Reilly as the first of his agents, giving him the designation ST1, the S standing for Sweden and the T for travelling, since Reilly was expected to operate not in Sweden, but in Russia.

Even at this first meeting, it was clear that Reilly was full of himself. 'Major Scale introduced Mr Reilly who is willing to go to Russia for us,' Cumming wrote. 'Very clever – very doubtful – has been everywhere and done everything.' Reilly demanded £500 cash (around £30,000 at today's prices) and £750 worth of diamonds. The British secret service chief decided that handing that much money over to Reilly on trust was 'a great gamble', but he needed someone to go into Russia immediately. Twelve days earlier, the Russians had signed the Treaty of Brest-Litovsk, making peace with Germany and freeing up German troops to reinforce the Western Front, but a number of Russian generals were deeply unhappy with the move, which they felt had sold them out.

'I was instructed to proceed to Russia without delay,' Reilly said. 'The process of affairs in that part of the world was filling the allies with consternation. My superiors clung to the opinion that Russia might still be brought to her right mind in the matter of her obligations to her allies. Agents from France and the United States were already in Moscow and Petrograd working to that end.'

Reilly went first to Petrograd where, under cover as a Turkish businessman, Konstantin Markovich Massino, he renewed contacts with a number of former associates who could be trusted to help his mission and arranged to go to Moscow to meet one of the dissenting generals.

What happened next became part of the legend of the audacious British 'master spy'. He went to meet the general in the Kremlin wearing his Royal Flying Corps uniform. The Bolsheviks made hay with the British meddling, using it to drive a wedge between Reilly and Robert Bruce Lockhart, the official British representative in Moscow.

The Bolsheviks told Lockhart that Reilly had marched up to the door of the Kremlin in full dress uniform and demanded to see Lenin. 'Asked for his credentials, he declared that he had been sent specially by Mr Lloyd George to obtain first-hand news of the aims and ideals of the Bolsheviks,' Lockhart wrote. When the Bolsheviks complained about the incident, Lockhart at first thought it must be a madman masquerading as a British agent. When he found out that Reilly really was a British secret service agent, he was initially furious, but once the two met they got along well.

'My experiences of the war and of the Russian revolution have left me with a very poor opinion of secret service work,' Lockhart said. 'The methods of Sidney Reilly, however, were on a grand scale which compelled my admiration. He was a man of great energy and personal charm, very attractive to women and very ambitious. I had not a high opinion of his intelligence. His knowledge covered many subjects, from politics to art, but it was superficial. On the other hand, his courage and indifference to danger were superb.'

The close relationship between Lockhart and Reilly led to one of the greatest spy scandals of all time – the so-called Lockhart Plot. By mid 1918 most of the Allied representatives in Russia had given up all hope of persuading the Bolsheviks to re-join the fight against Germany, and a number of plans were being made to try to subvert the new government. Two members of the Latvian regiment who the Bolsheviks were using to police Moscow contacted the British, asking for support for the anti-Bolshevik underground. They were sent to Lockhart, who asked to meet Colonel Edouard Berzin, their commanding officer, to confirm the proposal had his backing. Lockhart then passed Berzin on to Reilly, who offered him and his men large sums of money if they would help overthrow Lenin and install a provisional government.

Once Reilly had sounded Berzin out to see if he was genuine, he explained his plans to the Latvian officer. 'I stressed the money side of the question, promising large sums to the commandants and proportionate rewards to the lower ranks,' Reilly recalled. 'Berzin assured me that the task I had set was easy, that the Letts [Latvians] were full of disgusted loathing for their masters, whom they served only as a *pis aller* [last resort]. In consideration of my princely proposals he could positively guarantee the future loyalty of his men to me.'

Whether the plan was, as the Bolsheviks later claimed, to kill Lenin and the other members of the Bolshevik leadership, or simply as one of Reilly's colleagues said, to have them 'marching them through the streets of Moscow bereft of their lower garments in order to kill them by ridicule' and then intern them, is unclear. The Bolshevik claim cannot be easily dismissed, given the need to get Russia back in the war. Prior to the Revolution, the British secret service had been involved in the torture and murder of Rasputin (the charismatic monk who had exercised an unhealthy influence on the Tsar's wife and so on government policy), largely because he was thought to be persuading the Tsar to stay out of the war, while one SIS officer later claimed to have had orders from London to murder Stalin.

Reilly's own account suggests that the murder of Lenin and Trotsky, if not of the entire Bolshevik leadership, was very much on the agenda. 'Lenin and Trotsky were Bolshevism,' Reilly wrote. 'Once they were removed the whole foul institution would crumble to dust, but while they lived there could be no peace in Russia.'

Lockhart brought in the French and Americans to help finance the plan, which involved an armed attack on a session of the All-Russian Congress of Soviets due to be held at the Bolshoi Theatre, at which the whole Russian leadership would be in attendance. The attackers, armed with pistols and hand grenades, would hide behind the stage curtains waiting for a signal from Reilly, at which point the Latvian troops would close all exits and cover the audience with their rifles, while Reilly leaped on the stage and seized Lenin, Trotsky and the other leaders.

Unfortunately, the Bolsheviks found out about the plans, postponed the congress and used the party newspaper *Pravda* to announce the discovery of 'The Lockhart Plot', an Anglo–French conspiracy to overthrow the Bolsheviks, shoot Lenin and Trotsky, and set up a military government allied to the West and hostile to Germany. Lockhart had paid out a million roubles to fund a counter-revolution, *Pravda* said. 'The intention of the allies as soon as they had established their dictatorship in Moscow was to declare war on Germany and force Russia to fight again.'

The Russians later said the Latvian soldiers were part of a sting operation, a story that has since become widely accepted. But the claim that Reilly and Lockhart were duped was not made until the 1960s, by which time the KGB was involved in a full-scale propaganda war designed to use the Cambridge Spy Ring, and Kim Philby in particular, to build up its own reputation at the expense of SIS. The actual evidence strongly suggests that the plot was given away by a Bolshevik spy.

The subsequent post-mortems within SIS concluded that the plot began to unravel after Lockhart brought the French and US consul-generals into the British plans. One of the advisers to the French Consul-General was René Marchand, the Moscow correspondent of *Le Figaro*. Reilly admitted to a strange feeling of concern ahead of a meeting with the French. 'I had an uneasy feeling such as one frequently gets in dangerous situations, when one's nerves are constantly on the *qui vive*.'

The French Consul-General introduced Reilly to Marchand, 'whom he described as a confidential agent of the French government and here it was that the uneasy feeling, which had haunted me all along, became acute.'

Reilly was right to feel anxious; Marchand was a double agent and was passing on all the intelligence he garnered from the French to Felix Dzerzhinsky, head of the *Cheka*, the Bolshevik secret service. The SIS post-mortem held Reilly largely to blame for the collapse of the scheme. 'He very quickly involved the French and there seems little doubt that the French then brought in a French correspondent who was actually in touch with the *Cheka*,' a former SIS officer who had studied the files said:

> In a sense, he [Reilly] was landed in it by Lockhart. I think Lockhart was very glad to have got away and not get tarred with Reilly's brush as it were. There is a slight smell around that whole period. The French were probably the culprits in that they were very slack about security and they produced this correspondent who was supposedly working for them but was also working for the Russians. It all came unstuck then.

The Bolsheviks responded to the Lockhart Plot by launching the 'Red Terror', raiding the British embassy, shooting the naval attaché Captain Francis Cromie when he tried to resist, and arresting half-a-dozen British spies. Thousands of Russians suspected of involvement in the opposition networks were swept up in a series of mass arrests. Hundreds were executed. Reilly

went underground, gathering intelligence and setting up networks of agent and couriers. Both he and Lockhart, who had got
out, were sentenced to death in absentia and when Reilly did
eventually make his way back to London, he was awarded the
Military Cross.

Reilly applied for a full-time post with SIS, saying, 'I venture to think that the state should not lose my services. I would
devote the rest of my life to this wicked work.' But his fame, his
tendency to exaggerate his exploits and his womanising embar-
rassed Britain's spymasters, while his maverick tendencies and
rabid anti-Bolshevism gave them genuine concern that he was a
prime candidate to go rogue. He was not helped by the fact that
during his time in Russia, his discarded wives had become 'tire-
some' with their constant telephone calls to the office demanding
to know the whereabouts of their errant husband and, by 1923,
when a further bigamous marriage to Pepita Bobadilla, an actress,
hit the headlines, he had already been discarded by SIS. But he
was not done with the 'wicked work' of espionage.

Seven years after the Lockhart Plot, Ernest Boyce, the SIS station chief in Helsinki, recruited Reilly, now 51, to go back into
Russia to check out a supposed anti-Bolshevik opposition group
called the Trust. Was it a genuine émigré organisation or was it an
OGPU front? Reilly never returned. The Trust had been created
by the OGPU in order to penetrate the pro-monarchist émigré
groups, to control their activities and to uncover remaining opposition contacts inside Russia. The famous British 'master spy' was
arrested and taken to the Lubyanka, the OGPU's Moscow headquarters. He was interrogated there under torture and eventually,
on Stalin's orders, murdered. Four OGPU officers took him to
woods north-east of Moscow on the evening of 5 November
1925. On their way they stopped, claiming that the car had
broken down. All four OGPU officers, together with Reilly, got
out of the car to stretch their legs. According to a report from
an SIS agent in Russia, one of the OGPU officers, named only
as Ibrahim, lagged behind the party and then, 'put several bullets
into Reilly'. He fell but was still alive and another officer fired the
shot that killed him.

SIS was pursued by a number of his wives, including Pepita, for compensation. But the agency insisted, disingenuously given that he had been working with Boyce, that 'all Reilly's activities after 1921 were his own private affair' and – perhaps more understandably considering Reilly's 'somewhat complicated matrimonial tangles' – that it had no intention of paying up.

Nevertheless, despite his reputation as a dangerous maverick, and his undoubted sleight of hand where money was involved, Reilly's usefulness and his ability as a spy are not in doubt, according to one former SIS officer who made a detailed study of Reilly's files:

> He's been written off by historians by and large, but he has been greatly under-rated. He was very, very good – a very able agent and a far more serious operator than the impression given by the myth. Historians do have this tendency to write off something that has been made to appear glamorous. He was unusual but I don't think he was glamorous. He was a bit of a crook, you could almost say, certainly [guilty of] sharp practice. But as an agent he was superb.

★★★

Fantasists are clearly a potential problem for any intelligence service. During the Second World War, the German military intelligence service, the *Abwehr*, was desperate to recruit agents inside Britain and therefore particularly vulnerable to fantasists. In a sense the greatest of them all was the Spaniard Juan Pujol Garcia, now better known by his British code name Garbo.

Pujol initially offered to spy on Germany for the British, using his wife as a go-between to contact the SIS head of station in the Spanish capital Madrid. When the British turned him down, on the grounds that he was clearly a fantasist, he approached the *Abwehr* instead, offering to go to London to spy for them. The Germans snapped him up, but instead of heading for London, Garbo went to the Portuguese capital Lisbon where, armed only with a Blue Guide to Britain, a Portuguese book on the Royal

Navy and an Anglo–French vocabulary of military terms, he produced a series of highly imaginative reports built around a colourful network of agents in the United Kingdom. They included a Swiss businessman based in Bootle, who reported 'drunken orgies and slack morals in amusement centres' in Liverpool, and an enthusiastic Venezuelan living in Glasgow who obtained details of naval movements from Clydeside dockers apparently willing to 'do anything for a litre of wine'.

Garbo's messages to the *Abwehr* were intercepted and deciphered at Bletchley Park, where they caused some consternation. Intelligence officers were already running captured German agents to feed fabricated information back against the *Abwehr* in order to give them a completely false picture of Allied plans in a scheme known as the Double Cross System. The British brought Garbo to the United Kingdom, took control of his intelligence networks and expanded them in a highly imaginative fashion.

Disruptions to Garbo's flow of intelligence that might have been occasioned by the tragic death from cancer of the Swiss businessman in autumn 1942, were avoided by his dutiful widow's decision to continue working for the fictional cause. So dedicated was she that she became, in effect, Garbo's personal assistant. The Venezuelan agent also became more important to Garbo's fantasy network, acting as his de facto deputy, and cultivating his own equally fictitious agents in Scotland, among whom was a deluded communist who firmly believed that the secrets he passed over were destined for Soviet intelligence. Garbo was even canny in his choice of mistress (naturally), having seduced a secretary whose sensitive position in the War Cabinet offices provided him with ample opportunities to prise a stream of sensitive material from her. She felt secure in her indiscretion, believing that her lover's true identity was a Spanish Republican, a deception that Garbo also practised on the network's imaginary wireless operator.

Garbo set up a large network of agents in Wales, mostly Welsh Nationalists, but led by an ex-seaman, 'a thoroughly undesirable character,' working for purely mercenary reasons. None of these agents with their wonderfully colourful personalities and extensive back-stories ever existed, but they helped to ensure that

Garbo became the most important of the double agents used to fool the Germans into believing that the D-Day landings would take place in Calais rather than Normandy. Without the deception operation in which he took such a large part, the Germans would have had far more troops in Normandy and might well have succeeded in defeating the Allied invasion.

But while Garbo would become by far the most famous of the fantasist spies who worked for the Germans during the Second World War, he was by no means the only one, and one of the many others, an *Abwehr* agent code-named Ostro, presented the committee that ran the Double Cross System with so many problems that they repeatedly called for him to be 'liquidated'.

Paul Fidrmuc was born in June 1898 in Jägerndorf in Moravia, in what was then part of the Austro–Hungarian Empire. As a young lieutenant in the Austrian Imperial Royal Army during the First World War, he fought on the Russian and Italian fronts. After the war ended, he studied in Vienna, but was forced to give up his studies after the collapse of the family business and moved to Lübeck in north-west Germany. There, he worked in the iron and steel export business and married Rigmor Hvale, the daughter of a Danish politician, before moving to Hamburg, where he began writing articles for trade magazines in Britain, America, Canada, Italy and France. Fidrmuc moved to Hamburg and in 1934 began combining journalism with work as a freelance *Abwehr* agent. Still working for the *Abwehr*, he moved to Denmark in September 1938 under cover of the Copenhagen correspondent of the *Deutsche Allgemeine Zeitung*. He travelled widely in Britain and America, collecting military intelligence under the guise of journalism and, after war broke out in September 1939, the Danes arrested him as a German spy. He was sentenced to eighteen months' imprisonment, but in February 1940 was released in a prisoner exchange.

Fidrmuc went first to Rome and then, in August 1940, to Portugal, where he based himself in Estoril, the old summer residence of the Portuguese royal family on the Atlantic coast west of Lisbon. Fidrmuc set up in the Hotel do Parque and spent much of his time in the English Bar overlooking the bay. It was a notorious meeting place for the Axis and Allied spies who made Lisbon the wartime espionage capital of the world. He also spent a lot of time gambling with his blonde wife at the Casino Estoril, the inspiration for James Bond's *Casino Royale*.

They rented a villa in an expensive area and Fidrmuc set up an import–export business that attempted to evade the Allied blockade of Germany. The SIS station in Lisbon was soon reporting his close links to two Nazi sympathisers, Francis Lestrade-Brown, the European representative of US Export Airlines, an air freight company, and Francis van der Vliet, a former member of the Dutch Nazi party, who ran the flights by the Dutch KLM airline from Lisbon to the UK.

Lestrade-Brown and van der Vliet were the sources of much of the information Fidrmuc used to construct his reports, which routinely took a factual basis and built up a complex and entirely imaginary intelligence picture around it. Lestrade-Brown's knowledge of exports to and from the US provided Fidrmuc with the basic material around which to construct his fantastical reports on convoy movements. Van der Vliet supplied his friend with gossip garnered from the KLM pilots travelling to and from the United Kingdom and many of Fidrmuc's reports from Britain centred on something spotted by an agent on a KLM flight from the UK. Fidrmuc also sent in fake aircraft production reports, based on genuine official reports published before the war, and gave accounts of mine-laying operations garnered from foreign sailors docking in Lisbon.

Fidrmuc was in his early forties but had kept himself fit. He was tanned, with a mop of fair hair, was around 6ft tall and went swimming every day. He was also a keen rower, having taken part in the German rowing championships in his youth. Questioned by British intelligence, Lestrade-Brown's mistress pretended not to know Fidrmuc, even though they had been seen together in the English Bar and the Casino. She described him as the most suspicious man in Estoril, which, given the presence there of so many foreign spies, was something of an achievement. He was always 'snooping around', strutting across the beach showing off his muscles, regarding himself as 'a fine physical specimen'.

It was not until the beginning of 1942, after Bletchley Park broke the *Abwehr* Enigma machine cipher, that the British first saw the reports Fidrmuc was sending to Berlin under his *Abwehr* code name 'Ostro'. One of the first to be deciphered gave entirely accurate details of a convoy of troop ships leaving the United Kingdom. At the time, it was far from clear that this would be just one among many, many more that were complete fantasy, and it caused a good deal of concern.

Even once it was clear that more than 99 per cent of his reports were purely imaginary, his remarkable ability to weave fantastic stories around a single, often innocuous, fact to create what one MI5 officer described as 'a welter of nonsense' remained a major problem for the Double Cross Committee.

Fidrmuc was completely unscrupulous and 'possessed of a quite phenomenal fertility of imagination', one member of the committee recalled. 'He maintained a troupe of quite imaginary agents in England, the United States and South Africa, with occasional news from the Near East and India ... The detail was always wrong; his named ships were never in the place mentioned and had frequently been sunk long before. His convoy reports and dates were equally fantastic.'

There was anxiety that, as with the early report, his scattergun approach might lead to another inspired guess that was completely accurate, but what was far more worrying, given that the British were just beginning to build up the Double Cross System, carefully co-ordinating the fake information each of the double agents was sending to his or her controller, was the fact that Berlin seemed to have absolute faith in the accuracy of Fidrmuc and his extensive and fantastical reports, most of which contradicted the carefully constructed picture the British were using the double agents to create in order to deceive the Germans about the Allied plans.

The British-controlled double agents, led by Garbo, were producing one story, while Fidrmuc was producing another. Despite being in Lisbon, Fidrmuc continued to be controlled by Berlin, whereas Garbo and Tricycle, the two other main *Abwehr* agents based in the UK, were run by the *Abwehr*'s Madrid and

Lisbon stations respectively, although of course both of them were actually controlled by the British. Bizarrely, Fidrmuc's controller in Berlin frequently sought his opinion on reports from Garbo and Tricycle. His response epitomised his unscrupulous nature. He brazenly filched details from their reports to give credibility to his next fantasy, with every fact that repeated something said by Garbo or Tricycle seen as authenticating Fidrmuc as a master spy.

John Masterman, the Oxford academic who headed the Double Cross Committee, declared Fidrmuc to be 'in the highest degree dangerous' and the SIS head of station in Lisbon worked out a plan to kidnap him. Fidrmuc often went off on his own in his canoe to find a quiet cove and go swimming. 'His wife and friends regard this as a foolhardy and hazardous undertaking and expect that he will come to grief on one of these journeys,' one SIS officer said.

If he could be abducted during one of these trips and incarcerated for the rest of the war, the committee's problems would be solved. The plan never came off and eventually the Double Cross Committee began to press for his 'liquidation'. But Stewart Menzies, the wartime 'C', the chief of SIS, refused to sanction his murder, arguing that the British only knew how important Fidrmuc was to the Germans from the messages deciphered at Bletchley Park. If they killed him, the *Abwehr* might realise that their ciphers had been broken.

In the run-up to the D-Day landings, the concern that Fidrmuc might make a lucky guess with the potential to compromise the entire deception operation was proved right. With Garbo and the other Double Cross agents directing their fake intelligence to point to the main landings being against the Pas de Calais, Fidrmuc said they would be in Normandy. Fortunately, although the *Abwehr* believed wholeheartedly in Fidrmuc, by this stage even Hitler was beginning to see through him. Garbo was regarded as far more reliable and Fidrmuc was ignored.

Still the calls for Fidrmuc to be 'liquidated' continued and in an attempt to stall the lust for murder, SIS devised a plan to compromise Fidrmuc by feeding him obviously fake information via a female SIS agent based in Lisbon, a beautiful 22-year-old Czech, code-named Ecclesiastic. She had already used her ample charms to seduce one of the *Abwehr* officers based in Lisbon, becoming his mistress and providing a large amount of inside information via pillow talk, but she had aroused the suspicions of some of her lover's fellow *Abwehr* officers and was concerned that her real role might be uncovered if she fed fake material to an agent run from Berlin. Repeated attempts to recruit Fidrmuc as an agent who could be controlled by the Double Cross committee ended in failure but fearing Portugal might enter the war on the Allied side, he moved to Barcelona. Although a third accurate report that Canadian troops were being moved from Italy to France prompted more calls for his 'liquidation', there were more important issues facing all concerned and, despite the best efforts of a substantial number of British intelligence officers, Fidrmuc survived the war.

He was eventually repatriated to Germany, where he was interrogated by the US military who had no access to his decrypted, nonsensical reports and therefore accepted his claims to have been 'one of the most successful and potentially dangerous German agents of the war'.

MI5 begged to differ. Klop Ustinov, a veteran MI5 agent who had spent the last fifteen months of the war in Lisbon, and Joan Chenhalls, a female MI5 officer, went over to Germany to challenge him on the veracity of his reports and check if any of his 'sources' had been real. But their investigation was frustrated by the way in which even at this point, with everything to gain from admitting he had made up his reports, Fidrmuc appeared hurt that they should imagine this to be the case. Rather than admit the lie, he had constructed a complete fantasy life, in which everyone he had ever met, and a number of people who turned out never to have existed, were agents, providing an amazing variety of information that even those people who did exist could never have known. Even the simpler aspects of his pre-war life were reimagined as fantasy. His minor role in the Lübeck Rowing Club was transformed into a position as famous rower with a highly impressive forty-nine victories in international races.

Klop Ustinov's ironic response betrayed the utter contempt with which British intelligence officers regarded their German counterparts. 'Even admitting that the *Abwehr* was the most gullible organisation of its kind in existence,' he said. 'It seems inconceivable that Fidrmuc was able to fool some of the *Abwehr* officers some of the time and all of the *Abwehr* officers all of the time.'

Chenhalls was more succinct, concluding that Fidrmuc was 'a pathological liar' incapable of telling the truth. Tying up the loose ends of the investigation, she and another MI5 officer visited the offices of *The Ironmonger*, one of the British trade magazines for which Fidrmuc had written before the war. They spoke to the advertising manager, Mr Harman, who remembered Fidrmuc and described him as 'something of a liar', Miss Chenhalls said. 'Mr Harman's parting remark to us, in a thoroughly jovial manner, was:"I hope they hang him."'

But in fact, as a loyal German who did his duty, and could scarcely have been described as revealing secrets, Fidrmuc was released. He went back to Barcelona, where he indulged his passion for fantastic espionage schemes by writing a series of spy books, while at the same time acting as a correspondent for the normally authoritative German journals *Die Zeit* and *Der Spiegel*. He died of cancer in 1958, but even so his memory lived on.

Graham Greene, who as the SIS Portuguese expert in London had dealt with the case, based the protagonist of his novel *Our Man in Havana* on Fidrmuc. James Wormold, a vacuum cleaner salesman recruited by SIS, creates a network of supposed spies, based on real people (most of whom he has never met), to provide the plans of a secret Cuban military base, the buildings of which are shaped like the various parts of a vacuum cleaner.

If that were not enough to demonstrate that the reputation of one of the greatest fantasists in espionage history retains an irresistible staying power, one prominent hotel complex on the Spanish Costa Brava was still at the time of writing offering guests the opportunity to kayak around the coast, searching out private coves and following in the path taken in the 1950s by 'the famous rowing champion Paul Fidrmuc'.

★★★

Not all psychological motivations for espionage concern risk-takers, fantasists, or egotists. Sometimes, simpler human emotions are at play. People who have something missing in their life and who have access to top-secret information are often vulnerable to exploitation by a skilled intelligence officer. This was, of course, the case with Vassall but, while sex played a key role in his recruitment, often more subtle methods can persuade an emotionally vulnerable person to provide intelligence.

Joseph S. Petersen was born in New Orleans in 1914. He studied physics at Loyola University and St Louis University, where he received a master's degree in science before becoming a university lecturer. A tall, gangly young man, he was not deemed fit enough to serve in the forces and in 1941 became a civilian code breaker with the US Army Signals Intelligence Service code-breaking operation at Arlington Hall, just west of Washington DC, where he worked on Japanese codes and ciphers.

It was there that he met Colonel Jacobus Verkuijl, a leading Dutch code breaker who had served in the Dutch cryptanalytical operation at Batavia in what was then the Dutch East Indies (now Indonesia) until the eve of the Japanese occupation in March 1942. Verkuijl went to America, taking with him details of Japanese diplomatic ciphers which the Dutch had photographed after breaking into the Japanese consulate in Batavia. William Friedman, the top code breaker at Arlington Hall, welcomed him with open arms and invited him to help the US Army break Japanese codes and ciphers. Verkuijl was allocated an office and an assistant, Joe Petersen. The two got on extremely well and the veteran Dutch code breaker taught the American a great deal about cryptography, and in particular about how to break the sophisticated Japanese codes and ciphers.

Verkuijl had been marked out as the head of the post-war Dutch code-breaking organisation and was intent on taking the opportunity of his time at Arlington to collect as much information as he could on what codes and ciphers the Americans were breaking and the methods they used. Given that the Dutch and the Americans were allies and that, in his work on Japanese codes and ciphers, Verkuijl was helping the US war effort, it is not unreasonable to question why this should be seen as a problem.

However, there were understandable limitations on what Verkuijl would be allowed to see. The secrets of what could and could not be done by the American code breakers and their British allies had to be protected at all costs. Verkuijl knew a great deal about Japanese code breaking, but for very sensible security reasons he could not, for example, be permitted to know that the Allies were breaking the German Enigma ciphers. Nevertheless, he was clearly very interested in how the Americans broke other countries' codes and ciphers and which ones they were capable of breaking, leading to suspicion among some of the US code breakers.

'In my mind's eye, I can still see him,' one later recalled. 'His weather-beaten face, rather narrow jaw, quiet, unassuming manner, low, soft-spoken voice, albeit a little guttural English. I see him and Petersen in the cafeteria at Arlington Hall. These were the only times I ever saw Verkuijl. I never saw him at work. Or was this a mask?'

Verkuijl might not have been allowed into the other main code-breaking sections at Arlington, but Petersen was, and he was prepared to help the Dutchman find out what he wanted to know. Operation Piet, as the Dutch dubbed it, relied heavily on the young Petersen's over-dependent friendship with the older Verkuijl, and although subsequent investigations would look at the possibility of a homosexual attraction, there was another, much more likely possibility.

One former colleague had the clear impression that Petersen saw Verkuijl very much as a father figure. The American's mother had died and his father, a naval captain, was often away at sea. Verkuijl, an older mentor, acted as a substitute father, someone Petersen looked up to and wanted to please. He provided the

Dutchman with so much intelligence and data on code-breaking techniques that Verkuijl complained that he could not handle the huge amount of material on his own and needed a separate team in the Dutch embassy to assist him.

At this point, the Americans ruled that Verkuijl had found out too much and would have to go. One of the reasons he was so restricted in what he could see at Arlington Hall was that the US and British code breakers had broken the Hagelin machine ciphers used by the Dutch government-in-exile. The British had opened the Dutch diplomatic bag to obtain the cipher keys and from that point on both they and the Americans had been able to read everything the Dutch embassy in Washington sent back to its government in London.

The US military told the Dutch ambassador that Verkuijl had seen 'everything he could see' at Arlington Hall and demanded that he be transferred out. Friedman protested, but to no avail. Eventually Verkuijl left, but before he did so he ensured Operation Piet would continue by introducing Petersen to a colleague at the embassy, Giacomo Constantin Stuijt, and asking the American to give his new Dutch friend the same assistance he had provided to him. Petersen did what he was asked, handing over to Stuijt any top-secret documents that might be useful to Verkuijl in setting up a post-war code-breaking organisation, material that included manuals on how to break the codes and ciphers of numerous different countries. He provided top-secret intelligence assessments that were of interest to the Dutch.

After the war, Verkuijl was put in charge of Dutch code-breaking operations. Petersen continued to pass Stuijt material he thought might be useful to his old mentor, including documents on how to break the Hagelin machine ciphers (which the Dutch government was still using, despite Verkuijl's warnings that the messages were easily read). Petersen also handed over top-secret intelligence the Americans had obtained by breaking the diplomatic ciphers of Belgium, Britain, France, Norway, Germany, Italy and Indonesia, the main targets for the Dutch code breakers in the immediate post-war era.

When Stuijt was posted back to The Hague in 1947, Verkuijl visited Washington to hand Petersen over to his new contact at the Dutch embassy, Andre Elsakkers. By this stage, there was also an arrangement under which Petersen was paid $5,000 a year (more than his NSA salary) to continue passing material to the Dutch. A year later, that sum was increased to $7,500. It was not just one-way traffic. The Dutch code-breaking operation provided Petersen with monthly progress reports on their own efforts to assist him in working out what might be useful to them. Some elements of the co-operation became known to senior NSA officials and as a result, Petersen was ordered to break off all contact with the Dutch code breakers, but he never did so.

He only stopped passing documents to the Dutch in May 1953, after Verkuijl retired. Four months later, as a result of a completely unconnected investigation, Petersen was named as a possible homosexual. Although there is no doubt he had homosexual friends, this was not unusual for people who had served as wartime code breakers. A number of people in the wartime US code-breaking organisations had been homosexual, but by the time the NSA was set up in 1952, this was thought to leave those working in sensitive posts vulnerable to blackmail and was therefore seen as an unacceptable security threat.

The FBI was asked to look into Petersen and, although it found no evidence of homosexuality – he was by now married – the enquiry stumbled across his relationship with the Dutch. Investigators soon discovered that he had taken top-secret documents home and passed them to his Dutch handlers, who copied them and returned them. The clumsy way in which they carried out the copying made it easy to trace the hundreds of documents Petersen had handed over. Stuijt and his successor Elsakkers removed the silver, US round-pin staples from the documents to copy them and then stapled them back together with the distinctive, copper-coloured square-pin staples used by the Dutch diplomatic service.

Petersen was charged with three counts, the most serious of which was making secret documents available to a foreign nation.

His lawyer, David Kinney, who had served alongside Petersen as a wartime code breaker, negotiated a plea bargain under which his client admitted just one count of using classified material in a manner prejudicial to the safety and interests of the United States; effectively he was simply admitting taking documents home with him. This prevented the prosecution from having to produce classified material in open court. Petersen was sentenced to seven years in a state penitentiary but in fact served his sentence in a federal prison hospital, where he worked on research for a polio vaccine. He was released after four years.

The NSA remained concerned that Petersen might still be in contact with the Dutch. It had bugs installed in his apartment and even broke in to ensure there were no documents there, but his betrayal had ended with Verkuijl's departure from the scene.

Petersen subsequently worked for the Intelligence Machines Research Corporation (IMR), which was run by a former NSA colleague who had testified as to his character at his trial. IMR did pioneering work in the field of optical-character recognition and invented the box-shaped font still used on credit cards. After retiring, Petersen and his wife devoted their time to breeding dogs. He died in 1992.

***

Although in many ways Joseph Petersen was a very ordinary personality, the popular image of a spy as epitomised by James Bond has led to some extraordinary actions by agents who seemed to think this was what the espionage world was really like. Typical of this tendency were FBI Special Agent Richard W. Miller and Svetlana Ogorodnikova, the slim, pretty, blonde Russian he recruited to try to infiltrate the KGB.

Ogorodnikova and her husband, Nikolai, had emigrated from the Soviet Union in the early 1970s, moving to Hollywood where she worked as a nurse while dreaming of an exciting future in the movies. She built up a reputation in the Russian émigré community for showing cult Russian films at her local church and as a result had routine links with officials at the

Soviet Consulate-General in San Francisco. Such ties were not unusual in the Russian émigré community, particularly among those who still had relatives in the Soviet Union, but the Consulate-General housed a KGB *Rezidentura* tasked with recruiting agents from among the high-technology defence companies and military bases in the California region. It often used Russian émigrés for low-level jobs and in 1982 Special Agent John Hunt, the head of the double-agent programme at the FBI's Soviet Foreign Counter-Intelligence Unit in Los Angeles, singled out Ogorodnikova as a potential informant and double agent.

Hunt cultivated her as a source, intending to send her to the KGB with a story that she had a 'boyfriend' in the FBI who might be tempted into providing them with intelligence. They would think he was working for them, protecting their spying operations from the FBI, while in reality what they asked him to do would tell him and his bosses what operations the KGB were mounting. They could then close them down or keep them running to feed the Russians false information, just as the Double Cross Committee had with the *Abwehr* during the Second World War. Hunt put the idea to Ogorodnikova. Bored with a life in America that had never lived up to its promise and unhappy in her marriage, the pretty, young Russian was over the moon. The FBI 'Special Agent' with his plan to use her as a spy and his talk of her being his 'Mata Hari' seemed to offer the excitement that was missing from her life. She was extremely enthusiastic to take part and approached the Russians, who were predictably less keen on the idea. They were rightly suspicious of what appeared to be an obvious 'dangle', an attempt to compromise the KGB *Rezidentura* with a potentially valuable agent who would, in fact, be penetrating their organisation to obtain intelligence. They rejected Ogorodnikova's approach.

Hunt must at that point have realised that Ogorodnikova was herself now compromised and effectively useless to him. Yet he continued to see her, holding a total of fifty-five meetings with her in the space of one eight-month period and continuing to tell his bosses that she had great potential as an informant, until late 1983 when he decided to drop her. He subsequently denied Ogorodnikova's claims of an affair, which would have been against regulations and could have seen him sacked. He justified his move by saying he had simply decided she would never make the grade. Ogorodnikova was distraught at the rejection and took to drink. Not only had she fallen in love with being a spy, she had fallen in love with Hunt.

On the rebound, Ogorodinkova came into contact with a man who was a prime candidate for the title of world's worst-ever spy. Moscow Centre had decided that the KGB *Rezidentura* should try to recruit the 'boyfriend' as an agent-in-place inside the Bureau. Ogorodnikova was called back into the Consulate-General and told to set it up. She phoned Hunt to tell him the good news, but he refused to talk to her. He had handed her over to Special Agent Richard William Miller.

Miller was by his own admission a serial failure. He was 48, married with eight children and constant money problems, and was addicted to sex and chocolate bars. Miller and his wife were Mormons, but he had been excommunicated from the church over his philandering with other women. He had also been disciplined by the FBI for numerous minor offences, including leaving the keys in the front door of the office overnight, losing a Bureau fuel card, selling Amway household products from the back of his FBI car in government time, and stealing a Mars bar from a local store.

Miller was also overweight, so much so that shortly before he took control of Ogorodnikova his lack of fitness had led to his being suspended for two weeks without pay. He knew his bosses at the Bureau were looking for a way to sack him. If he could cling on to his job for another two years, he would be eligible to retire with a pension. He saw Ogorodnikova as one last chance for redemption, an opportunity to make good for his past failures. If he could get her to go back to the Russians and dangle him in front of them, then maybe he could do the job that Hunt had failed to do, perhaps he could persuade the KGB to take him on as their plant inside the FBI. They would think he was their man, when all the time he was the Bureau's agent uncovering the secret spying operations the

Russians were running out of the San Francisco Consulate-General. 'If I could pull this off,' Miller said, 'I would come out a hero.' Finally, his bosses would have to accept he was good at his job.

Miller spoke to the head of his unit and was given permission to have just two meetings with Ogorodnikova. At the first, on 24 May 1984, she told him that the KGB was still showing interest. At the second, a week later, they made love. He was now having an affair with an informant in breach of FBI regulations. 'It was just something that happened,' Miller said. 'She was a very attractive woman. It just sort of came with the territory. I had a James Bond kind of fantasy.'

That fantasy was spiralling out of control. Breaching regulations by having sex with her was relatively minor compared to what Miller had in mind. He knew his bosses would never allow him to take on a double-agent role himself. They would put Hunt there in his place. So he was going rogue. Like the maverick hero of a spy thriller, he was going to do the job his bosses would never have allowed him to perform. He was going single-handedly to penetrate the KGB.

The Consulate-General had arranged for Ogorodnikova to go to Moscow to be briefed by Moscow Centre on what to do next. When she returned, she told Miller that the KGB had told her to get him to work for them. They had told her they were going to pay her $25,000 if she could get him to spy for them. The 'dangle' had worked. Everything seemed to be going to plan. What would it take for him to do it? Miller said he wanted a meeting with the KGB in Mexico. He would supply the Russians with secret documents in return for $50,000 in gold Krugerrands lodged in safety deposit boxes at three separate banks, a move designed to create a clear evidential trail, and $15,000 in cash. It seemed to Miller that his maverick plan was about to succeed. The Russians were almost on the hook.

He went to see an old friend, Larry Grayson, a private detective who owed him a favour, and asked him if he could set up an audio-visual surveillance operation in Mexico. Who was the target? Grayson asked. 'Me,' Miller replied. 'Shake hands with James Bond.' He told the astonished Grayson that he was planning to meet the KGB in Mexico and set himself up as a double agent. He needed the surveillance tapes as evidence for his bosses that the Russians were on the hook. 'His plan was crazy,' Grayson said later. 'I told him so. I doubted he would have the nerve to go through with it. It was dangerous. It wasn't authorised. The chances of success – setting up an effective double-agent scam to stiff the Russians – were pretty slim.'

Grayson was right. Miller's chances were extremely slim. A week later, Ogorodnikova took Miller to the Consulate-General for a meeting with Aleksander Grishin, the KGB *Rezident*. The normally teetotal FBI officer was so nervous that he had a few drinks to calm his nerves, becoming so drunk that Ogorodnikova decided it was not wise to take him into the Consulate-General. An inebriated Miller got out of the car in the full view of the FBI surveillance team watching the building and was photographed with Ogorodnikova; she went inside on her own, taking with her a photocopy of eleven pages from a secret FBI document detailing what information on the Soviet Union was of interest to US policymakers. It was a sample document to show the Russians he was genuine. In reality, it would have told the KGB very little they had not previously known but, as Miller had already told Grayson, he was trying to sell the Russians 'the illusion' that he was more important than he was.

The FBI team watching the Consulate-General soon discovered the identity of the man they had spotted with Ogorodnikova, and Miller's bosses set up a surveillance operation that they code-named Operation Whipworm – she was Whip, he was Worm. They bugged Miller's and Ogorodnikova's phones and cars, recording not only their conversations but also their love-making, and followed them everywhere. They recorded Grishin telephoning Ogorodnikova and telling her Mexico was no good. She was to take Miller to Warsaw, all expenses paid. They also recorded Miller refusing to go to Warsaw and finally agreeing on Vienna. Once the location and date of the meeting was set, Miller went to his bosses and told them what he had done, asking for permission to fly to Vienna and for back-up for his mission.

Unsurprisingly, they were stunned. They had assumed that Miller was about to betray his country to the KGB, when in fact he claimed to have been doing precisely what Hunt had tried to do and failed. His story stood up. Somehow, despite his ineptitude, he had put himself in a position where the KGB seemed willing to take him on as an agent. Certainly, he had broken the rules and had run a black operation without informing his bosses, but there was no doubting his argument that, if he had told them what he was doing, they would not have allowed him to take it forward. The Justice Department official overseeing the operation decided that there was no case to answer. Miller had not broken the law. His incompetence was a matter for the FBI. Miller's bosses in Los Angeles thought they should simply sack him for breaking regulations, write the whole thing off to experience and be thankful they were rid of him. But they were overruled in Washington by the FBI Director William H. Webster. No one was that inept. Miller was preparing to betray his country. He had spotted the surveillance and invented the story of the maverick operation simply to save his skin. Miller was brought back in and interrogated for five days without a lawyer present, signing away his rights under the illusion that they were simply preparing to sack him. Crucially, he signed a statement saying he had handed over the document to Ogorodnikova, who then passed it to the KGB. Miller was sacked and shown out of the building, only to be woken in the early hours of the next morning at his home in Bonsall, some 130km (80 miles) south of Los Angeles and arrested.

At the same time, Svetlana Ogorodnikova was being arrested at her home in West Hollywood along with her husband Nikolai, even though there was no substantial evidence of any kind to implicate him in any wrong-doing. Mrs Ogorodnikova's links with the KGB and the FBI were so tangled as to be difficult to unravel either way, although she always insisted that she thought she was working for the FBI. But despite protesting her innocence at her 1985 trial, she was eventually bullied under threat of incarceration for life into accepting a plea bargain under which she would be sentenced to eighteen years' imprisonment. In

return for the plea bargain, the prosecution insisted that her husband, Nikolai, accepted an eight-year prison term.

Miller's first trial in June 1985 ended in a hung jury. The
second resulted in his conviction and two consecutive terms of
life imprisonment plus fifty years. That verdict was thrown out
on appeal and a third trial began in August 1990, six years after
Miller's arrest. The defence opted for no jury and, after hearing
the evidence, Judge Robert Takasugi accepted that Miller had
been on a quest to redeem himself through a maverick operation to penetrate the KGB and leave the FBI in 'a blaze of glory'.
But Ogorodnikova's admission that she had been working for
the KGB, Miller's failure to let his bosses know what was going
on and the decision to hand over the secret document to the
KGB left the judge with little choice. Takasugi sentenced him
to twenty years' imprisonment with a recommendation for early
parole after he had served a third of his sentence. Miller's first
wife Paula had divorced him after his original conviction. He was
freed in 1994, moved to Utah and remarried.

Svetlana Ogorodnikova was released in 1996. Threatened with
deportation, she fled to Mexico, with a convicted drug trafficker
she had married in prison. She soon returned to the United
States and was allowed to stay after once again becoming an FBI
informant, this time to help foil an attempted contract killing.

Nikolai Ogorodnikov was released in 1990. He obtained a job
as a bus driver at Los Angeles International Airport and shortly
afterwards was hailed a hero for tackling a gunman who tried to
hijack his bus. Ogorodnikov pinned the attacker down until the
police arrived.

Despite repeated attempts to deport him, he had nowhere to
go and remained in the United States. The KGB never attempted
to take Svetlana Ogorodnikova or her husband back to Russia,
as it undoubtedly would have done had they been valued agents.

★★★

Aldrich (Rick) Ames is lauded as the '$2 million spy' but – while
his initial motivation was certainly financial – in many ways

his behaviour mirrored that of Richard Miller. Ames was not regarded by his superiors as a great intelligence officer; indeed, he was routinely inept and unprofessional, although he was never treated by his CIA colleagues in quite the same dismissive manner that Miller was within the FBI. There was also an element of fantasy to the way in which he initially contacted the KGB, and an air of false redemption in his obvious pride in his perceived status as the KGB's greatest ever spy within the CIA.

Ames was born in River Falls, Wisconsin, in 1941. His father, Carleton, was an early recruit to the CIA in the late 1940s but had a poor record as a front-line operations officer and spent much of his service confined to a desk at the CIA headquarters in Langley. He retired in 1967, the same year his son joined the Agency. Rick Ames underwent the normal psychological screening for a potential operations officer and came out badly, but the Vietnam War meant the CIA needed to recruit operations officers fast, and so he was accepted. His first overseas tour in Ankara did not go well; his bosses in Turkey suggested that, like his father before him, he should serve out his career as a desk officer. He returned to headquarters, where he became a Russian specialist supporting CIA operations against Soviet officials in Washington and New York. In 1981, he was sent to Mexico to specialise in recruiting Soviet Bloc agents, but his performance was as mediocre as it had been on his tour in Ankara. Ames's wife had stayed in New York and, with his marriage falling apart, he had an affair with a Colombian diplomat and CIA asset, Maria del Rosario Casas Depuy, in breach of the CIA's ban on relationships with agents.

Despite his bad reports, when Ames returned to Langley in September 1983, he was put in charge of counter-intelligence on all CIA operations involving Soviet agents or assets. This only served to reinforce his own opinion that his superiors were wrong to see him as a poor operations officer. In his own mind, he was in fact one of the Agency's leading authorities on the KGB. His new role was to look at every CIA case involving Soviet officials to check that they were genuine and watch for any security threats surrounding each case. As a result, he had access to every

operation the Agency was running against the Soviet target anywhere in the world.

A few months after Ames returned to America, he was joined
by his mistress, Rosario Casas Depuy, and her mother, both of
whom spent a lot of his money, so much in fact that he was soon
in serious debt. He admitted that the debt and the need to satisfy
his mistress's need for money for shopping was what motivated
him to contact the KGB, devising what he saw as 'a very rational,
clever plan' that would get him a quick $50,000 to pay off his
debts without betraying anything dangerous. If it was a ruse, it
was not a clever one. It was delusional, a stupid, arrogant trick that
any experienced case officer working the Soviet target should
have known would not end well.

As cover for what he later told the chairman of the Senate
Intelligence Committee was his 'very clever plan', Ames took
advantage of the common practice of Langley-based operations
officers assisting in the CIA's attempts to recruit agents inside
the Soviet Embassy and set up a series of meetings with a Soviet
diplomat specialising in arms control, ostensibly to see if he was
someone who might be recruited as a source. But Ames was not
interested in recruiting the arms control specialist as an agent; he
simply wanted to use the man as a cut-out between himself and
the KGB.

Ames's cover was that of a lowly State Department researcher
'Rick Wells'. The Soviet arms control specialist found their
conversations uninteresting and stood Ames up for a lunch
appointment at Washington's Mayflower Hotel on 16 April 1985.
Ames had intended to give him an envelope addressed to the
KGB *Rezident* at that meeting, so when the specialist failed to
turn up, he went to the Soviet embassy and asked to see him,
handing over the envelope.

It contained details of several potential recruits who in fact
the CIA had decided were 'dangles', attempts by the KGB or the
GRU (Soviet military intelligence) to draw the CIA into false
agent relationships that would allow deception operations to take
place. In Ames's version of events, he was not telling the Russians
anything they did not already know. But according to Viktor

Cherkashin, the KGB deputy *Rezident* who recruited Ames as an agent, the information in the envelope also gave details of two FBI agents inside the Soviet embassy, Sergei Motorin and Valery Martynov, who might otherwise have been in a position to report Ames to the US authorities. In return, Ames demanded $50,000, sufficient money to resolve the financial problems caused by Rosario and her mother.

The KGB had no choice but to test the waters. The arms control expert was instructed to invite Ames to the Soviet embassy on 15 May 1985, ostensibly to meet up before going out for lunch. When Ames arrived at the embassy, Cherkashin took him into a private room and exchanged a series of written notes with him, in order to avoid any bugging by the US authorities. In fact, Ames was, of course, aware that the US was not monitoring the meeting and subsequently talked freely.

How freely is far from clear from the accounts of Ames, in his subsequent FBI debriefing, or that of Cherkashin, but the reality of the KGB's standard reaction and what subsequently occurred leaves little doubt. The KGB would pay Ames the $50,000 he had asked for but was never going to do so on the basis of the original information. They already had that. There must be something else Ames was keeping up his sleeve, and Cherkashin duly demanded it. Ames told him about a British agent inside the KGB.

Two days later, Oleg Gordievsky, a long-term SIS agent-in-place inside the KGB, and arguably one of the best assets Western intelligence ever had inside the Soviet system, was recalled to Moscow from his post as deputy *Rezident* in London. He was suspended, drugged and interrogated, but not arrested, suggesting that Ames had not given Cherkashin enough to identify Gordievsky definitively as the SIS agent-in-place, but had provided sufficient information for him to become the focus of Moscow Centre's suspicions.

Cherkashin flew to Moscow to discuss the case with KGB Chief Vladimir Kryuchkov and agree how to run it. On his return to Washington, he told the arms control specialist to book a lunch with Ames at Chadwicks, a popular bar restaurant in Alexandria. The lunch took place on 13 June 1984. Cherkashin turned up with the arms control specialist, who then went off for a walk, leaving Ames alone with his KGB handler.

At this early stage in the relationship with a new agent, a case officer needs to build up trust and Ames was reticent about giving his real name. He eventually provided it but expressed concern over the number of CIA agents inside the KGB who might find out about him and report his betrayal back to Langley. Cherkashin said they could not protect him if they did not know who these agents were. Ames hesitated briefly before taking out a notebook and writing down a list of names. 'He tore out the page and handed it to me,' Cherkashin said. 'I was shocked. It was a catalogue of virtually every CIA asset within the Soviet Union. Ames said nothing about whether the men he had listed should be arrested or removed. "Just make sure these people don't find out anything about me," he said.'

Over the next eighteen months, every major source the CIA and the FBI had inside the KGB or GRU disappeared. Nine of those whose names were handed over in Chadwick's by Ames, in what would become known as 'the big dump', were subsequently arrested, tried and executed for treason. The killings were spaced out over a drawn-out period to make it more difficult to identify a single reason as to how each of the agents had been blown. Ames also gave Cherkashin enough information to confirm Gordievsky's role as the SIS agent-in-place inside the KGB. Fortunately, Gordievsky spotted the increased surveillance, activated his emergency exfiltration procedure and was smuggled out of Russia by SIS.

When Vitali Yurchenko defected to the US in August 1985, Ames was one of the CIA team that debriefed him. A few days later, Leonid Polishchuk, one of the CIA agents inside the KGB, was arrested at a dead drop that had been arranged at the insistence of Ames. Later that month, Gennady Smetanin, a CIA agent inside the GRU, was arrested in Moscow and subsequently executed. In November 1985, Yurchenko re-defected to the Soviet Union. Valery Martynov, one of the two FBI agents inside the Soviet embassy who had been given up by Ames in his original pitch, escorted Yurchenko back to Moscow. Martynov did not return. He, too, was arrested and executed. That same month, Gennady Varennik, a CIA agent inside the KGB's Bonn *Rezidentura*, was told to attend a conference in East Berlin. When he arrived there, he was bundled into an aircraft and flown to Moscow to be shot. The KGB was jubilant about the recruitment of Ames and the intelligence he was supplying, so much so that they told him that they had set aside $2 million for him. It was an extraordinary sum of money but in terms of managing Ames, it was less about payment than about validating his own opinion of himself as a misunderstood master spy, demonstrating that, unlike the CIA, the Russians recognised how important he was.

It was already clear that the CIA and FBI had suffered a major disaster in the operations they were running against the Russians and the new year brought no respite. Sergei Motorin, the other FBI agent inside the Soviet embassy in Washington, was arrested in Moscow in mid January and executed. Then, Sergei Vorontsov, a Moscow-based KGB official who had supplied intelligence on Spy Dust, an invisible chemical agent used by the KGB to track Western intelligence officers, was also executed. Ames had been involved in assessing Vorontsov's case in some detail. In June 1986, Vladimir Vasiliev, a GRU colonel who had passed documents to the CIA while stationed in Budapest, was arrested in Moscow and was later executed. General Dimitri Polyakov, a senior GRU officer who had worked for the Americans for more than a quarter of a century, handing over a wealth of valuable intelligence on Soviet foreign policy and GRU operations, had retired and was the last to die. Polyakov, the most important of the CIA agents to be executed, was not arrested until 7 July 1986. He was executed in March 1988, shot like all the others with a single bullet to the back of the head.

Details of these killings, and the loss of a number of other agents lucky enough to be jailed rather than executed, were not announced by the Russians at the time, so it was a while before the CIA realised the extent of the disaster. It was not until October, after it heard about the executions of Motorin and Martynov, that the CIA's Soviet–East European Division set up a Special Task Force to investigate the losses. Although there were

initial concerns that the Russians might have accessed communications, the investigation quickly became a mole hunt, working
in tandem with a similar FBI inquiry team.

There were further losses still to come. Vladimir Piguzov, a
CIA agent-in-place inside the KGB who had been recruited in
Indonesia, was arrested in February 1987 and shot, while the
devastating news that Polyakov was dead did not emerge until
late 1988. The investigation was later criticised for taking so long
by politicians who clearly did not understand the scale of the
problem, not least given the number of potential suspects and
the amount of paper files that existed in what was a relatively
early period of computerisation. The defection and treachery of
Edward Lee Howard, a CIA officer who had betrayed another of
the Agency's agents who had been arrested and killed during this
period, and whose existence had been revealed by Yurchenko,
also complicated issues, as did the as-yet-unknown existence of
Robert Hanssen, a KGB mole inside the FBI. The inquiry was
also repeatedly diverted up false trails, many of them laid deliberately by the KGB to prevent both Ames and Hanssen from
being discovered.

After a while, as the CIA managed to establish and run a
number of new agents against the Russians, the mole hunt began
to lose support. The disasters of the mid 1980s were history. The
problem appeared to have gone, and senior management wanted
priority given to current successes. Ames was on an operational
tour in Rome during this period, accompanied by Rosario, to
whom he was now married. He proved no more successful at
recruiting new agents in Italy than he had been in Turkey and
Mexico. Nevertheless, his own view of his capabilities stood in
remarkable contrast to that of his superiors. He persuaded the
KGB to pay him $10,000 a month, more than double his CIA
salary, further validating his belief in himself as a master spy. But
the cash payments gave Ames a problem: disguising the origins
of the money. He could not simply deposit it in his Italian bank
account without raising suspicion, and so he opened a Swiss bank
account at Credit Suisse in Zurich and made occasional visits to
Switzerland to pay the money in. After his conviction, he told

the joint FBI/CIA team debriefing him, without any apparent sense of irony, that he had bought a second-hand Jaguar car in Rome and, as he drove over the Alps with Rosario by his side, he pictured himself as the new James Bond.

Ames returned to Langley in July 1989 and was put in charge of a section in the Soviet–East European Division that gave him access to information on all US agents run against the Soviet target in Europe. The extent of his usefulness to the KGB in this position is clear, but his appointment had been opposed by senior officers who did not consider him good enough for the job, and he was soon reassigned.

The first indication that Ames was a major suspect for the disasters of the mid 1980s came as a direct result of the new monthly payments. On his return from Rome, Ames had suddenly started spending much more, buying a brand new $43,000 Jaguar car for himself and a $540,000 house in an expensive area of North Arlington. He bought expensive paintings and audio equipment on which to listen to his jazz records. A CIA officer who had been friends with both Ames and Rosario in Mexico City was concerned over the sudden appearance of money, which Ames could not possibly have earned working for the CIA, and reported it to the Special Task Force. Added suspicion was roused by the fact that there was no mortgage on the house and it was unlikely that any CIA career officer could have afforded to pay $540,000 dollars in cash for a house. But Ames suggested to friends that Rosario's family was rich and checks by the CIA station in Bogota seemed to confirm this. Ames had also taken out a loan to pay for the Jaguar, which helped to move suspicion away from his sudden wealth.

In October 1990, his bosses in the Soviet–East European Division had him transferred to the Counter-Intelligence Center (CIC) because they did not feel he was pulling his weight, but this only served to give him access to details of virtually every agent-in-place that the CIA was running against the Soviet Union. By this time, he was meeting his KGB case officers in Bogota, which was easy to go to because he could claim to be visiting his wife's family, or in Vienna or Zurich, but even here he displayed an astonishing level of ineptitude, missing a meeting in Vienna because he had gone to Zurich by mistake and another in Bogota because he failed to turn up at the correct place.

Despite a clear lack of support from senior management, the members of the Special Task Force, who included Jeanne Vertefeuille and Sandy Grimes, who had worked on the Polyakov case, remained determined to find the traitor. They received the backing they needed in early 1991, when Vertefeuille, approaching retirement and feeling guilty that they had not found the person responsible for the deaths of so many agents, was given permission to go off and hunt him (or her) down on her own. The FBI heard about her mission and asked to take part, allocating Special Agent Jim Holt – who had been Martynov's case officer and was similarly obsessed with the case – and Jim Milburn, the Bureau's best Soviet analyst, to what became the Special Investigations Unit. A disillusioned and frustrated Sandy Grimes was about to resign, but Paul Redmond, who had been in charge of the original mole hunt and was now Deputy Chief of the CIC, knew that if she were offered a real opportunity to track down Polyakov's killer she would jump at the chance. She did. The team now had real backing to find the mole. They cut down the number of possible suspects to 160. Each member of the team was asked, in a relatively unscientific fashion, to look at the list and come up with the top five suspects in order of likelihood. Ames's name came up more often than anyone else's.

Nevertheless, in August 1991, despite having been kicked off dealing with Russia a year earlier, Ames managed to get himself back to carry out a special study of the KGB, a position that gave him access to Soviet agent records. It was not until December of that year that he was moved into the Counter-Narcotics Center and away from routine access to Russian case files, and not until August 1992 that Sandy Grimes finally found the evidence that would point the finger at Ames. On 17 May 1985, he had lunched with the Soviet arms control expert. The following day, he paid $9,000 into his bank account. On 5 July 1985, he again had lunch with the Russian and that afternoon deposited $5,000 in his bank. They had lunch again on 31 July 1985 and Ames paid in $8,500 the same day.

Grimes went direct to Redmond, who as Deputy Chief of the Counter-Intelligence Center was the investigation team's supervisor. 'It doesn't take a rocket scientist to tell what is going on here,' she said. 'Rick is a goddamn Russian spy.'

From that point on, the FBI took over, opening an investigation code-named Nightmover against Ames, which used the full force of the far more intrusive investigative techniques that were available to them (but not the CIA) inside the US, and collecting the evidence in a way that would ensure the case would stand up in court. Even as the FBI net closed in, Ames was trying to get himself out of the Counter-Narcotics Center, where his usefulness to the KGB was limited, and appointed to an upcoming vacancy as Deputy Chief of Station in Moscow.

Ames and his wife, Rosario, were arrested for espionage on 21 February 1994, provoking a storm of outrage and criticism over how long it had taken to track down the mole, some of it justified, much of it not. Two months later, Ames pleaded guilty and was sentenced to life without parole.

So why did he do it? For many people, the $2.5 million the KGB paid him would seem to be the obvious motivation – and certainly initially he needed money – but even his idea of the clever ruse to sting the Russians was based on a remarkable degree of arrogance and demonstrated a striking gap in knowledge for someone who saw himself as an expert on agent operations and on the KGB. Ames omitted to mention, when he was subsequently debriefed by a joint FBI/CIA team, that as part of that 'very clever plan' he had betrayed Motorin and Martynov, sending them to their deaths. It did not fit with the way he wanted to portray his initial pitch to the KGB – the clever trick that gave nothing away.

The conceit inherent in that plan is exposed by what Ames said after his arrest. 'I got myself in the position where I thought, and still think – call it arrogance, if you will – I know what's better,' he claimed. 'I know what's damaging and I know what's not damaging. And I know what the Soviet Union is really all about, and I know what's best for foreign policy and national security … and I'm going to act on that.'

There is an interview that Ames gave to the BBC in prison in which the self-satisfied smile on his face as he walks towards the camera betrays the extent of his own inflated feeling of importance. At one point, he explains how the British had never shared Gordievsky's identity with the CIA. 'We discovered this,' he said. 'In fact, I discovered it. I managed to put together some pieces that allowed us to identify who it was.'

The real motivation for Ames was ego and self-obsession. From the moment he embarked on his 'very rational, clever plan', he set out to prove all his CIA critics wrong. He had read his father's personnel file. He knew that his own perceived failings as an operations officer mirrored those of his father. (They also shared a recourse to alcohol under pressure.) It would have been a crippling blow for any operations officer to be told by his bosses on his first overseas tour that he was not up to the job and should serve out his time behind a desk at Langley. When it happened on his second tour in Mexico as well, the die was cast. None of this fitted with his view of himself as the top CIA expert on the KGB, a figure to rival James Bond. His best friend and colleague David Samson, one of the few people who knew him well, put his finger on Ames's view of himself. 'He saw he was never really going to be able to make a significant contribution to history in the mid-levels of the bureaucracy,' Samson said. 'But he had this access to priceless information to the Soviet Union and felt by passing this to the Soviet Union he could become more of a player on the world stage, perhaps alter history.'

Ames's treachery was originally driven by money, but ultimately it was all about him and what he saw himself as being. It was about his father. It was about the damning criticism of his superiors. In Ames's view, those who had denigrated his father and now denigrated him simply did not have the intellectual vision to appreciate his talent. He was the CIA's leading expert on the KGB. He had proved that in his work for the KGB, who unlike the CIA had gone out of their way to confirm to him that they saw him as a top spy.

★★★

The psychological aspects in the case of Robert Hanssen are more immediately obvious than those of Ames. Born in Chicago in 1944, he was emotionally abused by his father, a police lieutenant, and from a young age became obsessed with spies, particularly James Bond. He collected items associated with espionage, including a Walther PPK pistol of the kind carried by Bond and a Leica spy camera. After dental school, where he met his wife Bonnie, he went to business school, becoming an accountant, and then followed his father into the Chicago Police Department before joining the FBI and obtaining a job in counter-intelligence, tracking down Soviet spies.

Hanssen was a devout Catholic and family man. He converted to Catholicism when he met his wife. They went on to have six children and he became a senior member of Opus Dei, a leading Catholic lay institution. He was a very quiet, sober man who attended Mass every day. He was politically conservative and openly anti-communist.

In security terms, he was the very last person who would have been suspected of being a traitor. But behind that facade, there was another person, obsessed since a child with espionage and torn by temptation. He first became a Soviet agent in 1979, passing secrets to Soviet military intelligence, the GRU, in return for $21,000. The association with the Russians ended after eighteen months when Hanssen's wife discovered it and persuaded him to confess to a priest. Hanssen subsequently handed much of the GRU money over to the Little Sisters of the Poor, a Catholic charity caring for the elderly.

But still he could not resist the temptation to spy. He reached out to the KGB six months after Ames had done so, and again it was Cherkashin who initially ran the case. Like Ames, Hanssen immediately identified Motorin and Martynov as FBI agents inside the KGB's Washington *Rezidentura* in order to protect

himself, but some of his material was far more important at a strategic level than that of the CIA officer. He gave the KGB details
of the US government's preparations for a nuclear war, including the locations of all the key sites, the top-secret capabilities of
numerous different satellite systems targeting Russia, US nuclear
programmes, and the existence of a surveillance tunnel dug under
the Soviet embassy in Washington. Hanssen also betrayed the
identities of CIA and FBI agents-in-place inside the Soviet system
and what intelligence the Western agencies had on the Soviet
Union. Ultimately, Hanssen's information was far more damaging
to the United States than that which Ames passed to the Russians.

Unlike Ames, Hanssen never met his KGB handlers, and never
gave them his real name, preferring the alias Ramon Garcia, or
simply Ramon. He used a variety of means of communication
to pass thousands of pages of documents and numerous computer disks, including dead letter drops and packages posted to
the homes of Soviet diplomats whom he knew were not under
FBI surveillance. In return he received a total of $1.4 million in
cash and diamonds, including $800,000 held in a Moscow bank
account that he never touched. Hanssen did spend some of the
money he received from the KGB, but his only real expenditure
outside that of a normal FBI officer was on sending his children to private schools. Unlike Ames, there were no ostentatious
purchases of fast cars, expensive paintings or property. But there
were bizarre moments of risk-taking as the other Hanssen, the
man behind the pious Christian mask, surfaced in bouts of stunning recklessness.

Hanssen had three periods as a Soviet spy. The first was with
the GRU (from 1979 to spring 1981). The second period with
the KGB came to an end with the dissolution of the Soviet
Union in December 1991 and the possibility that a new more
co-operative relationship between the new Russian foreign
intelligence service, the *Sluzhba Vneshney Razvedki* (SVR), and
the CIA or some other Western intelligence service might result
in his role as a Soviet agent being discovered. Towards the end
of that second period, Hanssen was living a double life in which
he visited strip clubs and formed a relationship with a pretty,

young stripper, Priscilla Sue Galey, taking her on an official trip to Hong Kong, buying her a Mercedes car and expensive jewellery and providing her with an American Express card on which he paid the bills. In another bizarre departure from the persona of the devout Christian family man, and unknown to his wife, Hanssen set up a video surveillance system in his bedroom so that a close friend could watch them making love and he posted explicit descriptions of their love-making on an adult internet site.

Unable to live without the adrenalin rush that his self-professed 'addiction' to espionage provided, Hanssen tried in July 1993 to resume his career as a Russian spy, approaching a GRU officer in the garage of the Russian's Washington apartment building. He explained his past work for the KGB and tried to hand over an envelope containing a list of FBI agents-in-place inside the GRU. It was a ridiculously high-risk approach. The Russian understandably assumed it was an American attempt to compromise him, refused to accept the envelope, and reported it to his bosses, who lodged a protest with the State Department. An investigation was launched, but it focused on the CIA rather than the FBI and failed to find the culprit.

Hanssen resumed spying for the Russians in 1999 but the FBI was closing in. FBI surveillance teams spotted Hanssen driving slowly past a known signal site on a number of occasions and a search of his FBI office uncovered a flash memory card that contained a number of his letters to the SVR, leaving little doubt as to who the traitor was and, indeed, the psychological issues that lay behind the betrayal. The FBI was finally forced to accept that the traitor was one of its own. On 18 February 2001, Hanssen was arrested for espionage. He agreed to plead guilty and undergo debriefings by the FBI and CIA in return for a prison sentence rather than execution and was sentenced to fifteen consecutive life sentences. Like Ames, he will die in prison.

A Justice Department investigation found that Hanssen's motives were a complex mix of 'his obsession with espionage, his lack of self-esteem and desire for recognition, [and] his belief that he could commit espionage without being detected.' His actions were clearly those of a reckless risk-taker and fantasist and were perhaps best articulated in one of Hanssen's final letters to the KGB. Seeking to answer the question as to why he had continued to work for the Russians for so long, despite the risks, he said:

> I have come about as close as I ever want to come to sacrificing myself to help you. One might propose that I am either insanely brave or quite insane. I'd answer neither. I'd say, insanely loyal. Take your pick. There is insanity in all the answers. I have, however, come as close to the edge as I can without being truly insane.

Chapter 6

REVENGE

Revenge is one of the most powerful and enduring motives for a traitor. Nothing carries someone across the line between simply thinking that maybe they might pass secrets to the enemy and actual betrayal more reliably than the intense and deep-felt anger created by something unconscionable that they believe – for whatever reason – should never have happened. It is an unrelenting motivation, because each batch of secrets passed to the other side, each individual act of revenge, reminds the avenger of the original crime, 'keeps his own wounds green', and reinforces the determination to carry on.

One of the most valuable agents run by the British secret service prior to and during the First World War – indeed right up until shortly before the Second World War – was a German marine engineer who had the run of the German North Sea and Baltic dockyards, and as a result could report in detail on the German Navy's preparations for war. Karl Kruger was a former German naval officer who had resigned after being court-martialled and demoted for hitting a relative of the Kaiser. His SIS file says that this made him 'very embittered against his country' and in November 1914 he approached the British legation in The Hague offering to spy on the Germans. Kruger openly admitted to Richard Tinsley, the British station chief in Rotterdam, that he was intent on wreaking revenge on the Imperial German Navy. After making his initial approach, Kruger seems briefly to have had second thoughts, before being persuaded by Tinsley to go through with the deal. He was designated R16, or TR16, the sixteenth agent run by Tinsley from Rotterdam, and later as H16, the H standing for Holland.

Henry Landau, who worked alongside Tinsley, remembered Kruger being known within the SIS Rotterdam office as 'the Dane', possibly a deliberate security measure, since he was in fact German and lived in what is now the Bad Godesberg district of the former German capital, Bonn.

Landau recalled:

> Slight of build, fair, with blue eyes, he looked the reserved well-bred Scandinavian of cultured and professional interests. He certainly did not look the arch-spy he was. When I came to know him better, however, I realised why he was so successful. He was a marine engineer of exceptional quality. He was a man without nerve, always cool and collected. Nothing escaped his austerely competent eye and he was possessed of an astounding memory for the minutest detail of marine construction. He covered every shipbuilding yard and every Zeppelin shed in Germany. The key to his success was that he made the Germans believe that he was working for them against us. He was allowed to travel freely to Kiel, Wilhelmshaven, Hamburg, Bremen, Emden, Lübeck, Flensburg and other shipbuilding centres. His popularity with German clients and their trust in his apparently candid nature were unbounded. When in due time he applied for a pass to proceed through Germany to Holland it was readily granted.

Once every few weeks, on a regular basis, Kruger went to Rotterdam, initially to meet Tinsley, or from late 1915, Captain Charles Power, the head of Tinsley's naval section. The encounters took place in one of several safe houses the British had dotted around the city, and Kruger wrote out his reports from memory alone.

Landau added:

> He never carried any incriminating materials whatsoever – notes, lists, letters, even special papers or inks. On his arrival in the house, the Dane immediately got down to writing his report, which he did in German, and this occupied sometimes

three to four hours. With his extraordinary memory, he was able to sit down and write out page after page of reports, giving an exact description of the ships which were under construction or repair, and supplying us with the invaluable naval information on which the Admiralty relied absolutely. As soon as his reports were completed, they were rushed to our office on the Boompjes for translating, coding and cabling to London. From him we got full engineering details of the submarines which the Germans were turning out as fast as they could in order to put over their unrestricted submarine warfare campaign.

Kruger's surviving reports begin in April 1915, with two on German submarine construction that, despite some errors, match the facts as they are now known, including what would have been very interesting, and was certainly accurate, evidence that some U-boats were being built with only one skin, making them much more vulnerable to being rammed by Royal Navy warships. Subsequent reports dealt with all types of vessels, although the U-boats remained a key area of interest for the Admiralty, and therefore Kruger.

He covered all the main ports at Emden, Wilhelmshaven, Bremerhaven, Hamburg and Kiel, as well as some of the smaller ports such as Cuxhaven and Rostock, and made frequent trips to the eastern ports at Danzig and Stettin. Kruger had cultivated long-term intelligence sources in the dockyards, while other information he derived from officials and sailors he met on his visits there, men who were taken in by his air of being a patriotic German. Tinsley and Power seem to have provided him with lists of specific information that was required from his sources; a January 1916 briefing directed him particularly to enquire about any troop-carrying ships that might be moored in north German ports and to explore rumours that troops were being mustered in Emden and Wilhelmshaven, both preoccupations that arose from fears of a German invasion of Britain. At first Tinsley and Power did not entirely trust their agent, considering him only 50 per cent reliable, but his reports do in general tally with known facts and his controllers came to rate him more highly, especially when the information he provided could be double-checked against decoded German naval messages.

Tinsley's network of agents grew, until by early 1916 there were more than thirty of them reporting to him from inside Germany. Kruger, though, was always the most important of these, and the intelligence he passed on included the death-toll aboard the *Seydlitz*, a German battle-cruiser that suffered an on-board explosion during the Battle of Dogger Bank. Kruger's reported figure of 128 dead was not far from the final death toll, which we now know to have been 160.

Among Kruger's best pieces of reporting was his revelation of a new German remote-control boat, the *Fernlenkboot*, or FLB. He came across it while on a routine visit to the ports of Stettin and Danzig, and he witnessed trials of the wire-guided boat, which was to be loaded with explosive charges and employed to ram Royal Navy ships. The Germans hoped to use them disrupt the British bombardment of the ports of Zeebrugge and Ostend. Kruger provided his British masters with extensive details about the FLBs, including their appearance and operating speed. In October 1917, a year and a half later, Kruger's report was proven to be accurate, when a German remote-control boat rammed a Royal Navy warship and exploded (although, fortunately, it did not sink it).

In the aftermath of the Battle of Jutland (31 May to 1 June 1916), an urgent message went out to all SIS's agents in Germany, instructing them to find out whatever they could about the scale of German losses in the battle. This was particularly urgent, as British losses had been heavy in the largest naval engagement of the war between the Royal Navy's Grand Fleet with the German High Seas Fleet and the outcome had been portrayed by the Germans as a signal defeat for the British. The Kaiser even claimed that his navy had 'torn down the nimbus of invincibility of British sea power'.

The British had been led to expect a victory on the scale of Trafalgar, and one that would deliver a devastating blow to the Germans of the kind that had eluded the allies in the trench-ridden stalemate of the Western Front. It came as a terrible shock that the British had in fact suffered worse than the German foe – with more than 6,000 killed, as opposed to the 2,500 German dead, and fourteen of the Royal Navy's vessels sunk, compared to only eleven on the German side (though they initially claimed it had been just seven). Amid this atmosphere of growing gloom, Mansfield Cumming, the Chief of SIS, added his own personal message to the pleas to agents to find out more: 'Reliable information urgently required regarding German losses in North Sea action yesterday.'

Seventeen days of agonising waiting passed before the first reply came, from D15, an agent based in Denmark. He had been to Wilhelmshaven and discovered that the German losses were in fact 2,473 dead and 490 wounded (which is not far from the final German reported toll of 2,551 dead and 507 wounded). D15 also correctly named the most badly damaged German ships, the *Seydlitz*, *Defflinger*, *Markgraf* and *König*. The rest of D15's report, however, contained little accurate information. He named seven ships he claimed had been damaged, but five of them had not been hit during the battle (and two of them could not have been, as they did not even take part in it).

Kruger was still gathering information for his own report when Whitehall received D15's intelligence. In Rotterdam at the end of June, he stayed in one of the safe houses Tinsley had established and wrote two reports on the losses suffered by the German High Seas Fleet at Jutland. In one of these (dated 27 June) he recounted his tour of six principal naval dockyards (from Emden in the west, to Danzig in the east). He had been able to talk with naval officers and dockyard officials, all of whom believed that he was a patriotic German citizen, a belief that loosened their tongues considerably. His information on the damage levels to the ships that were in docks for repair was very accurate. He was able to identify the positioning of the torpedo nets on some German vessels as a factor in the loss of the battlecruiser *Lützow*, one of the two largest and most powerful German warships, the other being its sister ship, the *Derfflinger*.

'I went to Sande, near Wilhelmshaven, as this latter place is closed to all traffic,' Kruger continued. 'Here I met men of the *Lützow* and learned that part of her torpedo nets had got entangled in the propellers, which was the cause of reducing speed, and eventually of her loss.' The damage to the *Lützow* was so bad, and the amount of water she was taking in so great, that a German torpedo boat had to be called on to sink her. The *Derfflinger* also suffered with the same problem and had to limp back to port, trying not to let her loosened torpedo nets foul her propellers; as a result of these problems all anti-torpedo nets were subsequently removed from the German warships.

Admiral William 'Blinker' Hall, the Director of Naval Intelligence was so impressed with the report that he wrote '100%' at the top of it. Yet the second of Kruger's reports, sent the day after, must have been received even more favourably in the Admiralty.

It did not appear, at first sight, to contain promising news for the British, as it recounted that the *Hindenburg*, one of the ships the Royal Navy claimed to have sunk, had not even taken part in the battle. 'Contrary to the rumours that have been about, that the *Hindenburg* was lost in the action off Jutland, I can definitely report that this ship is not commissioned yet, but is being finished as quickly as possible,' Kruger said. But he continued with much better news. 'Having spoken to some naval officers about the action in the North Sea, they said that the German Fleet had only been saved from annihilation by the failing light and the mist. The impression in the Fleet is that this experiment will not be repeated.'

Kruger's report helped the Admiralty with its argument that, although the British had suffered heavy losses, relatively speaking and, perhaps more importantly, in psychological terms the German losses had been more significant. The British Grand Fleet was still much larger than the High Seas Fleet, a disparity that helped ensure it would never again attempt to take on its British counterpart. This left the Royal Navy unhindered to enforce the economic blockade against Germany, a strategy that strangled German efforts to sustain its war machine and ultimately helped ensure its defeat.

As 1918 wore on, and the German economy began to buckle, Kruger's reports became full of the labour problems in the naval dockyards and the generally worsening conditions across the country. These included an upsurge in socialist activity, which manifested itself in unrest (including waves of strikes), and an increase in food shortages.

'I was in Cologne during the air raid the day before Whitsunday,' Kruger wrote in May 1918. 'The effect of the raid was frightful. The number of those killed (forty-five) given in the papers is generally contested in Cologne, for the authorities have not included in that number the casualties caused by anti-aircraft gunfire and falling houses.' The real number of dead was more than 100, Kruger said, and following a further British raid on the city, in August 1918, he reported that 'the destruction was great and the streets were closed for several days'. Meanwhile, labour unrest was spreading. 'In Westfalia, the miners are on strike. About forty pits are idle,' Kruger said. In Oberhausen, on 2 August, I saw considerable damage to houses, done by the miners. The newspapers are silent.'

By October 1918, a few weeks before the end of the war, Kruger was reporting widespread mutinies, with German troops refusing to leave for the Western Front:

Already on my return from Rotterdam at the end of September, things were pretty unsettled in the Rhine district. At the victualling stations in Rheydt, Dusseldorf, Mehlem etc. the troop transports refused to proceed to the front. This was in particular Bavarian and other south German troops, who commenced to mutiny already in Bingerbrück. Several companies of infantry with machine guns from the neighbouring garrisons were posted at the victualling stations in order to arrive on the troops by force, but without success. The troops were then sent back as prisoners. Such occurrences take place every day as I heard. Before everything else the principal reason is the bad and insufficient feeding of the troops and, since the new offensive, the hopelessness of the German fighting. Large bodies of soldiers indulge in plundering in their own country.

Three-quarters of all the thefts are perpetrated by soldiers. The
railway trains all carry military patrols to arrest the deserters
who stream along continuously.

Kruger did not cease reporting to the British even after the
November 1918 armistice brought a halt to the fight. He
described how the return of German troops from the front
was accompanied by widespread disorder, the blame for
which government officials squarely pinned on the growth of
worker's and soldiers' councils that had been set up by left-
wing groups in a bid to replicate the Bolsheviks' success in
the Russian Revolution. 'I read his reports from time to time
and marvelled at them,' said Landau. 'He was paid huge sums,
far in excess of any of our other agents. In my opinion, he was
undoubtedly by far the most valuable agent the allies ever had
working in Germany.'

Kruger's most important reporting during the 1920s and '30s
was on the German Navy's covert submarine construction programme, which used a company set up in the Netherlands to
circumvent the ban under the Versailles Peace Treaty on Germany
possessing any submarines or developing new ones. Under this
arrangement several new U-boat prototypes were designed and
built in Spain and Finland. By November 1934, Kruger was
reporting that the Germans had begun a domestic U-boat construction programme, but the Admiralty dismissed his reports on
the grounds of 'improbability'. There was a palpable feeling of
shock in the Admiralty when the first new German U-boat was
commissioned seven months later.

Within months, Kruger had handed over the secret German
plans for the construction of a large U-boat fleet. Thousands of
workers were being trained to mount round-the-clock mass production at six German naval shipyards, he said. The programme
would use prefabricated parts manufactured secretly in factories
across Germany. The aim was to produce seven U-boats a month,
creating enough submarines to blockade Europe and prevent
supplies of food and fuel getting through from America. It was
vital intelligence ahead of the Second World War.

But in April 1938, Kruger was arrested while trying to collect intelligence on a secret German air base. This time, he managed to talk his way out of detention, but he was now under suspicion and when he next crossed the border into the Netherlands to file his reports, he was subjected, unusually, to a thorough search. All meetings with SIS were suspended for at least two months, and at the first meeting thereafter he was shadowed throughout by a Dutch agent working for the SIS station in The Hague in order to ensure he was not being followed by German spies.

Unfortunately, the Dutch agent had been turned by the Germans and was reporting to them. On his return to Germany, Kruger was arrested for a second and final time. Shortly after the outbreak of the Second World War, the Nazi authorities announced that he had been executed by axe after being found guilty of 'working against Germany in favour of foreign powers'.

***

Revenge was also the motivation for another German, a man who was probably the most important traitor recruited by SIS in the 1930s. Johann de Graaf, whose SIS code name was Jonny, was one of the many who turned to communism as a result of the carnage of the First World War. Born in 1894 in Nordenham, a small town across the Weser from the German port of Bremerhaven, Jonny ran away to sea at the age of 14. During the First World War, he joined the Imperial German Navy and in 1917 was one of the leaders of a communist-inspired mutiny on board the battleship *Westfalen*. Jonny was court-martialled and sentenced to death, but was released and joined the communist party, working his way up through the ranks of the Hamburg organisation where Richard Sorge, later famous as the leader of a successful Russian spy network in Japan, was training young party activists. Jonny followed Sorge to Moscow and, like him, was recruited into an elite unit of Soviet military intelligence attached to the Comintern, a Soviet-controlled body that aimed to spread communism around the world.

Members of the unit operated undercover in non-communist countries, where they set up intelligence networks and acted as political commissars, ensuring local party activists followed the Moscow line and teaching them how to subvert democracy and foment revolution.

On some missions, the agents were paired with a member of the opposite sex on the grounds that a married couple travelling abroad was less likely to arouse suspicion than one person on their own. Although in theory the couples only existed for cover and work purposes, their relationships frequently developed into something more serious, and this had been the case with Jonny and one of his 'wives'. When he heard from Moscow that she had been purged, he was furious and decided to defect to the West. Jonny approached the US embassy in Berlin, but the Americans were not interested. So, in early February 1933, he went to the British seeking asylum and offering intelligence on the Communist Party of Great Britain.

One of Jonny's first missions for the Comintern had been to London, where the party had failed to capitalise on the rising unemployment in Britain and the anger it provoked, including hunger marches. As a result of this failure, it was under pressure from the Comintern leadership to reform. Jonny had recruited new young activists and had helped to foment the 1931 Invergordon Mutiny, a traumatic moment in the Royal Navy's history, when sailors went on strike over a 10 per cent cut in pay. Jonny could provide MI5, the British Security Service, with invaluable intelligence on the operations of the communist party and on Soviet infiltration of the armed forces.

The SIS head of station in Berlin, Frank Foley – now better known for his work saving Jews from the Holocaust – immediately recognised an opportunity to obtain far more than a simple dossier of intelligence on the British communist party. In theory, Foley was supposed to send a detailed signal to SIS 'Head Office' in London and ask for instructions. But that could take time, and Jonny was only in Berlin for a while between missions. The Comintern might send him anywhere at any moment, and then the opportunity would be lost. Foley took the documents Jonny had brought with him as proof of his credentials and arranged to meet him the following evening in a quiet backstreet restaurant. That second meeting over a meal and a drink was simply an opportunity to delve a little further, to get Jonny to feel comfortable talking to him and to assess his potential. Once a relationship of trust had been created, a series of debriefings took place, during which Jonny described his work training pro-Moscow activists not just in Britain, but in France, the Netherlands, Romania, Belgium and Austria.

It was Foley who gave Jonny his code name and managed to persuade him that he was better off pretending to continue working for Moscow. That way he could get his revenge for the Soviet treatment of his wife and as an 'agent-in-place' could thwart their attempts at subversion in the West.

Next day, Foley sent a coded signal to London. 'I am in touch with Johann, who is a member of the executive of the Communist International and secretary general of illegal Red Front Fighters Union here,' Foley said. 'He can give me complete information about communist propaganda amongst British Armed Forces and continue to keep me informed of most communist work in England arranged from here. Consider this most important contact I have yet made and convinced his genuineness. May I continue negotiations?'

The message caused a flurry of activity at SIS headquarters. Urgent meetings were set up between 'C', now Admiral Hugh 'Quex' Sinclair, and Colonel Valentine Vivian, the head of Section V, the SIS department that handled counter-espionage. 'Head Office sent Vivian to Berlin immediately to find out what was going on,' a former SIS officer said. 'Jonny had visited the UK in 1931 and 1932 and there was a lot of excitement about it all because of this.'

Vivian agreed to Foley's plan, and so Jonny remained in place, carrying out each mission he was given by the Comintern. He let the British know what was going on at every step of the way, for which he received 500 Reichsmarks a month. Shortly afterwards, he was sent back to London, travelling on a false passport as Ludwig Dinkelmeyer, a wine merchant. His itinerary included a weekend stay at a country house, where Vivian subjected Jonny to an extensive debriefing. His information was considered by MI5 to be 'of the highest importance ... a flood of fresh light' on Soviet-inspired subversion activity by British communists in the armed forces. Jonny also identified several police officers based at Scotland Yard who were working for the Russians, giving MI5 the ammunition it needed to take over counter-espionage and counter-subversion from the Metropolitan Police Special Branch.

Jonny's next mission was to Shanghai, which was dominated by the international settlements controlled by the British, French, American and Japanese. It was China's most industrialised city and was famous for a scandalous nightlife that featured prominently White Russian women who, having fled the Bolsheviks, had settled in the French quarter of the city, turning Frenchtown, as it was known locally, into the city's red-light district.

Shanghai was also the focus for the Chinese communist party's efforts to take over the whole country. The Comintern had a very strong presence and many of its most famous members spent time there in the early 1930s, including Sorge, the American communist Agnes Smedley, and Arthur Ewert, a leading member of the German Communist Party and political adviser to the Chinese communist leadership.

To support the communist rebels, Soviet military intelligence officers such as Sorge and Jonny were despatched to Shanghai, where they provided training in political subversion and military tactics. Among Jonny's pupils was Zhu De, a senior communist general, to whom he gave instruction on guerrilla tactics, explosives and sabotage. As a senior Soviet adviser, Jonny's full access to details of Comintern operations in China allowed him to pass invaluable intelligence to Harry Steptoe, the local SIS station chief, about ambitious plans for a communist takeover. He also broke into Ewert's desk, removing a list of all the local communist party activists that he handed to Steptoe, who in turn passed the names on to the local police. This coup led to a series of arrests that ripped the communist party in Shanghai apart.

Both Ewert and Jonny were recalled to Moscow, but the loss of the list of activists from his desk – together with a large stash of Comintern money, which Jonny had kept for himself – led to

Ewert getting the blame for the debacle while Foley and Jonny were lauded in London.

Over the next few years, Jonny was sent to Austria, Romania, France, Czechoslovakia, the Netherlands, Belgium and back to Britain, training the various communist parties in those countries to set up structures aimed at bringing down the state. All the while, he was providing SIS with complete details of the communists' plans that could not only be incorporated into its own reports on their activities but could also be traded with the security services in the countries Jonny had visited for other intelligence the British needed.

The information that Jonny provided on the British, European and Chinese communist parties was priceless, but perhaps his most spectacular success came during an attempted communist coup in Brazil in 1935. The leadership of the Soviet Union had decided in the early 1930s that the experience gained in China could be transferred to Latin America. The establishment of a Soviet-style regime there would provide the stepping stone for a communist takeover of the United States of America. Brazil was chosen because the Comintern controlled a Brazilian leader around whom the discontented masses would rally. Luís Carlos Prestes, the so-called Knight of Hope, had become a national hero in Brazil in the mid 1920s after an attempted revolution known as 'the Lieutenants' Uprising'. When this failed, he led a ragged band of little more than 1,000 rebels on a 25,000km (15,000-mile) retreat through the country's impoverished heartland, collecting new supporters in every village they visited.

After the revolt's collapse, Prestes left Brazil and travelled in secret to the Soviet Union, where he was groomed to lead a new communist-backed revolution in Brazil. In November 1934, Jonny was called to the *Westbureau*, the Comintern's base in Copenhagen, to be briefed on his role in the coup and to collect his travel documents. He sent Foley a telegram calling an urgent meeting in the Danish capital.

This was by now a routine procedure every time Jonny received a new mission. Foley would always take the same train from Berlin to Copenhagen. It was a simple matter for Johnny to arrange to be at the station the same time each day and wait for Foley to turn up. Agent and controller spotted each other at once and Foley followed Jonny as he made his way to his hotel. There Jonny paused briefly and as his controller passed him, murmured his room number. Foley did not break stride, giving no indication of the information that had passed between them but, Foley walked on by as if nothing had been said between them and, after a safe interval, then doubled back and went up to Jonny's room.

Jonny's role in the plans for the Brazil coup presented an extraordinary opportunity to undermine Soviet ambitions in South America. After debriefing Jonny, Foley went to the British embassy to send an urgent coded telegram to Vivian asking him to set up a meeting in Paris. Foley could not run Jonny while he was in Brazil. He had too much on his hands in Berlin tracking communists and reporting on the activities of the Nazis. Vivian would take over from here.

A team was despatched by the Comintern to Rio de Janeiro towards the end of 1934. Jonny arrived there first, under the alias Franz Gruber, accompanied by his latest 'wife', Lena (who assumed the name Erna Gruber). Next came Arthur Ewert, whom the Comintern had selected as head of its South American Bureau, an appointment that upset Jonny as it gave Ewert the lead position in fomenting the revolution. The Comintern's team also included Rudolfo Ghioldi, the leader of the Argentine Communist Party. Jonny's role was as Political Commissar, with a brief from Moscow to ensure there were no deviations from the plan, and an additional brief as the revolution's the military adviser and explosives expert. Lena was chosen as the conspirators' secretary and as a driver for Prestes. The group's focus was to help build an opposition alliance with Prestes at its head, while carefully concealing the fact that it was basically a communist front.

The *Aliança Nacional Libertadora* included socialists, liberals and communists among its ranks, who worked for the planned return of the 'Knight of Hope' to Brazil. In fact, Prestes was already back in the country, having been smuggled back to Rio de Janeiro, and was holed up in a safe house on the Rua Barao da Torre.

Vivian turned up unexpectedly in Brazil in early 1935. When he rang the doorbell at Jonny and Lena's Rio de Janeiro house, 'a negro servant opened the door, screamed and shut it in my face'. He tried again, but this time there was no response at all, so he entered via an open window he found at the side of the house. 'As I scrambled in and fell down the other side, an enormous arm protruded from a curtain levelling a 500 automatic Colt at me.' The gun was Jonny's, who was understandably wary of surprise visitors.

The Comintern's plan was that *Aliança* agents in the Brazilian armed forces were to use their position to take over the north of the country, operating under the mantle of a popular revolt. With the north under their control, the revolutionaries would move on the capital. The *Aliança,* under the leadership of Prestes, would remain a convenient cover until the Comintern team had secured all the levers of power. Non-communists were to be removed from positions of authority until finally a Soviet-style regime, still with Prestes at its head, would be installed. 'Next would come the Sovietisation and complete appropriation of the property of the landowners and bourgeoisie, then the distribution of land among the population,' Jonny told Vivian. 'Once the northern provinces had been made Soviet, there would be a breathing space to allow communist influence to spread over the remainder of Brazil and the other states of south America. The process of Sovietisation would continue until it covered the whole of Brazil.'

As the military expert on the team, Jonny was well placed to ensure that the carefully planned revolution failed. 'It was my job to organise the Army for revolution and train party members accordingly,' he later said. 'Through careful planning, I worked it so that half the army was in favour and half opposed.'

Jonny's propaganda work was so successful that the revolution broke out early in mid November 1935, ahead of the Comintern-sanctioned start date. The revolutionaries soon overran garrisons in the key northern cities of Natal and Recife, a premature success that pushed Prestes and Ewert into advancing the outbreak of the revolution in Rio de Janeiro. An infantry barracks in Orca, a fashionable suburb at the base of the Sugar

Loaf Mountain, was taken over by revolutionary troops, but
Jonny's parallel work, in making sure that the majority of officers in the capital were opposed to the revolution, meant that the
uprising was doomed to failure. The local population collected
on the mountain to watch as troops loyal to Vargas laid out artillery on the Copacabana beach before bombarding the troops in
the barracks into submission. At the end of it all, more than 100
people were dead, and several thousands more had been arrested
by the authorities.

Jonny and Ewert were taken into custody, along with Ghioldi,
but the local SIS representative secured Jonny's release, and along
with Lena and other members of the group he fled abroad. Prestes
went on the run shortly before police raided the house on the
Rua Barao da Torre. Jonny was supposed to plant a booby trap in
the safe to prevent the Brazilian authorities getting hold of the
team's documents if the coup went wrong. He had been tasked
with planting a bomb that would instantly kill anyone who tried
to break into it without using the correct combination, while the
explosion would also destroy the secret documents. But although
he had filled the safe with an impressive combination of TNT
and dynamite, he made sure it would not detonate. Jonny's ploy
meant that when the police arrived, they found documents, letter,
maps and notes intact, a trove that allowed them to identify hundreds of people who had been involved in the abortive coup. This
confirmed information they already had about the names of most
of the *Aliança* contacts. Lena had been assiduously working, not
only with Prestes, but with many of the other Comintern agents
and their Brazilian collaborators. As a result, she was aware of the
names and addresses of the whole range of communist activists
and sympathisers in the political organisations and the Brazilian
armed forces.

Following the collapse of the Brazilian revolution, an inves-
tigation was set up in Moscow under Stella Blagoeva, a senior
Comintern official. Jonny was blamed and accused of being in
the pay of the anti-Bolshevik White Russians. The evidence that
Jonny had deliberately thwarted the coup seemed strong. Like
Ewert, he had been involved in both the Chinese and Brazilian

arrests but, unlike Ewert, he had managed to escape arrest in Brazil and was now living with Lena in Buenos Aires. There was also something suspicious about her, since the Comintern had no record of her. It was Jonny who had brought her into the plan. Jonny and Lena were ordered back to Moscow immediately.

Jonny arrived in Moscow in 5 March 1937, but Lena was not accompanying him. He claimed that she had taken her own life in Buenos Aires. He had returned to Europe on board a British ship, in contravention of basic security protocols, and then travelled on to Moscow via Berlin. Jonny explained this away by claiming that he had gone to the German capital to break the news of Lena's death to her mother. It was a barely plausible excuse, but he could scarcely tell Blagoeva that he had gone to Berlin to be debriefed by Frank Foley, the SIS head of station, and that Lena was a British agent.

While in Moscow Jonny stayed in Room 670 of the Nova Moskovskaya hotel, a location often used by Russian intelligence to debrief officers after foreign trips. He wrote two reports. One on the operations in Brazil, the arrests, and the reasons behind them, and a second that blamed Ewert for the previous debacle in China. He tried to persuade Blagoeva and other Comintern leaders to send him back to South America with substantial funds, which he could use to secure the release of Ewert and Ghioldi. He would then bring them back to Moscow so they could be asked to explain why the coup failed.

Jonny also claimed to be in contact with an Argentine scientist, supposedly a member of the Argentine Communist Party, who had invented a type of 'electric cannon' (which produced no smoke or sound) and that he could put Soviet military experts in touch with him. If the Comintern sent him back to Buenos Aires, he would be able to provide Moscow with the cannon's blueprints, as well as further his work 'where it is urgently needed' in training would-be communist insurgents inside the Argentine armed forces. Blagoeva was highly sceptical of Jonny's claims and called in the NKVD, the Soviet secret police, to carry out an investigation. They placed Jonny under continuous surveillance. Blagoeva's suspicions appeared to be confirmed when a hotel cleaner discovered a revolver concealed in Jonny's room, and another member of the hotel staff noted that the German was receiving nocturnal visits from a woman. Anyone who had come into contact with Jonny was taken into custody and questioned about their association, but in the end he talked himself out of trouble, successfully assuring the NKVD and his bosses inside the Comintern that he was innocent. He was sent back into the field, continuing in his role as a British 'agent-in-place' inside Soviet military intelligence. The danger for Jonny had been very real; it was the very height of the Stalinist purges and even many innocent people, let along bona fide traitors, were being executed. His escape was nothing short of miraculous and would not have been possible without his immense resourcefulness and mesmerising powers of persuasion.

The Comintern ordered Jonny back to Brazil in May 1938 to continue with his work of developing a network of underground Communist activists. Back in South America, he established an agent network that he used to report on pro-Nazi officials and the arrival of German ships in the Brazilian ports for both Moscow and SIS. Jonny stayed in place inside Soviet military intelligence until the outbreak of the Second World War, when the British sent him to Canada to assist the Royal Canadian Mounted Police to track German spies. He also played a minor role in the Double Cross System, looking after Werner von Janowski, an *Abwehr* spy who landed by submarine on the Quebec coast and was used against his German paymasters.

At the end of the war, Jonny was sent back to Germany to assist in the hunt for leading Nazis, but he soon became disenchanted and resigned. He was resettled in Canada, where he ran a caravan site and resurfaced during the 1950s, embarrassing the authorities by revealing his past and embarking on a string of lectures and newspaper interviews in which he warned of the dangers of Soviet subversion of Western society. He died in 1980.

★★★

None of the agents recruited by SIS during the 1920s and 1930s was more determined to gain revenge than the White Russians – the collective term for those who fought the Bolsheviks during the civil war that followed the Russian Revolution – to punish the Soviet in the inter-war years. Dealing with White Russian émigrés was a difficult task for the SIS officers working against the Soviet target, not least because their communities were so heavily penetrated by the Russian intelligence services. Sidney Reilly was an early victim. But those such as the Ukrainian patriot Boris Bazhanov, who were recruited during the civil war, tended to be more reliable.

Harold Gibson, one of the prime candidates for the SIS officer who recruited Bazhanov, was bilingual in English and Russian having been brought up in Moscow, where his father owned a chemicals factory. Gibson was based in Petrograd in the wake of the Bolshevik Revolution and spent most of 1919 working his way across the Ukraine and southern Russia collecting intelligence and spotting potential agents. One of those he found was to become a legend within the service and invaluable in juggling the many difficult issues involved in running agents inside the Soviet Union.

Some SIS agents were so good they almost assumed the status of intelligence officers in their own right and Viktor Vasilyevich Bogomoletz was one of them. He was an ethnic Russian, born in Kiev on 8 May 1885, who after studying law had served as an intelligence officer in the Tsar's Imperial Russian Army. Bogomoletz's primary motives were his determination to get back at the Bolsheviks, money – since espionage was his livelihood – and a remarkable loyalty to the British.

Gibson recruited Bogomoletz as his assistant and took him with him when he was sent to Constantinople (now Istanbul) to set up a station using the then Turkish capital as a base to spy on Russia and the Balkans. Bogomoletz acted as Gibson's main agent runner, travelling extensively across the region and setting up networks and maintaining contacts with the agents recruited by Gibson in 1919. The Russian's successes included establishing a spy ring inside the Sevastopol base of the Black Sea Fleet and others on Red Army bases in the Ukraine and Siberia. The intelligence obtained was deemed by one senior SIS office to 'have proved accurate time after time'.

But it was as a pioneer of an extraordinarily imaginative use of SIS 'liaison relationships' with other countries' intelligence services that Bogomoletz produced some of his best results. He formed close working arrangements with the Bulgarian, Romanian, Polish and Czechoslovak intelligence services. His most interesting ties were with Mihail Moruzov, a Romanian military intelligence officer, during the early 1920s. Moruzov was trying to persuade his government to set up an intelligence service to perform a similar function to SIS or the Russian OGPU. Gibson moved to Bucharest at the beginning of 1923, operating under 'unofficial cover' as the correspondent of the British right-wing newspaper the *Morning Post*, with Bogomoletz as his 'fixer'.

A year after they arrived in Bucharest, Moruzov established the new Romanian secret service, the Serviciul Special de Informaţii. The relationship between Bogomoletz and the Romanians was so close that he was able to operate under cover as if he were himself working for their new secret agency, running the networks inside Russia as Romanian rather than British assets. The Romanians facilitated border-crossing operations over the Dniester river into the Ukraine and provided substantial resources to back up Bogomoletz's operations against the Soviet Union.

This arrangement worked very well for the Romanian service, which needed early successes to get on its feet, but held even greater advantages for Gibson. By sharing the British intelligence networks with the Romanians, Bogomoletz also obtained access to the intelligence the Romanians were receiving themselves. More importantly, it provided an ingenious form of 'cut-out' for Gibson, protecting his cover as a journalist when things went wrong. The intelligence collected by Bogomoletz's sub-agents included the identity of Artur Niman, the head of the Russian OGPU intelligence service in Bucharest, who operated a substantial network of spies across Romania. Niman's identity was shared with the Romanian secret police, who arrested him twice and searched his home but were unable to find any evidence. So, Bogomoletz had one of his agents, 'a beautiful, clever woman', seduce Niman to uncover all his secrets.

The use of the Romanians confused the Russians, who saw Bogomoletz as a freelance intelligence officer willing to work with anyone, and it ensured the networks could not be traced back to the British. Bogomoletz played on this image to offer himself to the Russians and the Germans as a double agent. At various times, both the OGPU and the *Abwehr* believed that Bogomoletz was working for them, passing them intelligence on the Romanians and the British, when in fact the information on the British – although probably not that on the Romanians – was meaningless or inaccurate and the real purpose was to collect intelligence on the Russians and the Germans themselves.

Gibson was posted to the Latvian capital Riga in 1931 where the ambassador was Sir Hughe Knatchbull-Hugessen – the same man who as ambassador to Turkey would later allow the *Abwehr* to copy his files – and his attitude to SIS was simple. It was 'a cancer it was desirable to remove from the diplomatic body'. There was no way he was prepared to allow Gibson or anyone employed by him to run agents into the Soviet Union from Latvia. Bogomoletz had no difficulty getting around this problem. He not only kept up his close links with the Romanians, he set up a similar liaison arrangement with the Poles – a precursor to a hugely productive wartime relationship between SIS and Polish intelligence. Rather than compromise the networks in Russia by operating from Latvia, Bogomoletz used Polish territory to carry out operations against the Soviet Union while sharing the intelligence with the Poles. One of the agents run in this way was an old Russian schoolfriend of Gibson in Moscow. 'Gibbie's Spy', as he was known, had risen to a senior position in the Soviet Communist Party but had become disillusioned with Stalin's regime and was providing high-grade intelligence from inside the Kremlin. His position was too precarious to share his intelligence with the Poles but, unfortunately, he was betrayed by one of the Cambridge spies, Anthony Blunt, when he joined MI5 in 1940.

The relationship with the Romanians was briefly threatened in 1935 by growing problems with Russian penetration of the White Russian networks. Bogomoletz had made frequent visits to Paris and Berlin to recruit émigrés as agents, often with good results, but in 1935, the Romanians arrested two brothers, Mikhail and Alexander Flemmer, who had been among his recruits, but were in fact working for the Russian secret service. Even Bogomoletz himself came under suspicion, but Moruzov absolved him of any guilt and although the relationship between SIS itself and the Romanians was seriously damaged by the incident, that between Bogomoletz and the Romanians survived.

During the late 1930s, Gibson and Bogomoletz were in Prague, where the Russian continued his valuable relationship with the *Abwehr*. Yet again, there were highly productive links with the local intelligence service, the Czechoslovak military intelligence department, under Colonel Frantisek Moravec. This gave the British access to the reports of Paul Thümmel, an *Abwehr* officer, and highly decorated Nazi Party member, who had become disillusioned with Hitler's drive to war and from early 1937 provided Moravec with detailed intelligence on Wehrmacht capabilities. Thümmel warned in advance of the German invasion of Czechoslovakia in March 1939. On the eve of the invasion, Gibson bribed a Dutch KLM pilot to fly Moravec and ten of his leading intelligence officers to London. At the same time, he had the Czechoslovak intelligence files moved into the British embassy to protect them from the Germans, sending them to the United Kingdom in batches in the diplomatic bag.

At the beginning of 1941, Gibson was posted to Istanbul as station chief, where he and Bogomoletz found themselves reunited with the ridiculous Knatchbull-Hugessen. When Frank Foley was sent out to Turkey in early 1942 to have a look at possible improvements to operations run by Gibson across the Balkans, he described the ambassador's attitude to secret service work as 'a serious handicap' and urged Stewart Menzies, the wartime SIS Chief, to persuade the Foreign Office to intervene. Sadly, they did not. Gibson himself was as derisive about Knatchbull-Hugessen as the latter was about the 'cancer' of secret service and rightly determined to spy against the Germans not just in Turkey, but across the Balkans, saying: 'I consider we are here to

do a job of work not as part of a house party.' It was not an attitude shared by his ambassador, who hindered that work in more
ways than one.

While Foley's ostensible mission was to write up a report on
the operations from Turkey, he had another important task in
mind. He had just been put in charge of the Double Cross agents
run by SIS. MI5 controlled all the double agents based in the
United Kingdom, but SIS ran those abroad. Many of the double
agents operating overseas were based in Lisbon, which was now
the espionage capital of Europe, and Foley needed someone to be
his eyes and ears there. He had worked with Bogomoletz against
both the Russians and the Germans during this time in Berlin
and he knew Gibson well, having used Prague for secret meetings
with Jonny de Graaf. He needed a good agent in Lisbon. Viktor
Bogomoletz fitted the bill, and Menzies had given him permission to send the Russian to the Portuguese capital.

Shortly after Foley's visit to Istanbul, Bogomoletz arrived in
Lisbon, where, like Fidrmuc, he based himself in the fashionable
resort of Estoril. Bogomoletz took an expensive suite in the Hotel
Palacio and spent much of his time watching the various Axis
and Allied spies who gathered in the English bar or the Casino
Estoril. Bogomoletz was frequently seen in the company of the
self-styled Marquesa Carmen de Najara, a mysterious Mata Hari-
like figure who also lived in the Hotel Palacio and much of whose
days were spent at the gambling tables in the Casino Estoril. The
Marquesa was no beauty, and already in her early thirties, but she
possessed a sexual magnetism, an allure only increased by her love
of alcohol, drugs and the good life in general. Rumours about her
background swirled around her, encouraged by both Bogomoletz
and the Marquesa herself.

'Before the war she was involved in several scandals in Biarritz
and Cannes in which money and men were concerned,' the
Abwehr station in Lisbon told their bosses in Berlin. 'She is in close
contact with Bogomoletz, a Romanian with an English passport
who is considered to be Russia's Chief Agent. She is said to have
received money from Bogomoletz. She has gambled heavily here
and lost a great deal of money.'

Abwehr headquarters in Berlin was more interested in Bogomoletz than the femme fatale he was drinking with. It was pleased to hear that he had resurfaced. The Lisbon station was told that he was an important agent who had provided them with exceptional intelligence on both the Russians and the Romanians in the past and they were to recruit him immediately. Bogomoletz declined the generous German offer, although he engineered and accepted a separate one to provide the PVDE, the local secret police, with information on the spies who congregated in the English Bar and the Casino Estoril. This had the useful side-effect of allowing him to control what the Portuguese knew about any SIS agents and operations while at the same time allowing him to carry out surveillance without any interference from the local authorities. Bogomoletz also kept in close contact with the Romanians, using them as cover for his presence in Lisbon and forming a close friendship with the Romanian ambassador Victor Cădere.

One of the Double Cross agents Foley wanted Bogomoletz to look after was Johann Koessler. He was an Austrian and like Bogomoletz had studied law, but his mother was a Russian Jew. As a result, he had been listed as Jewish, and forced to sign his property over to a Nazi. Koessler moved his business to Brussels and cultivated the local *Abwehr* officers, persuading them to send him to Lisbon and use his business to run a network of agents who would report to the Brussels station.

Koessler's plan resembled Garbo's method of operating. He mixed up a cocktail of intelligence, true, false, exaggerated and some wholly imaginary, all in a bid to reinforce the belief among senior German officers (of which he was aware from his contacts in Brussels) that Germany would ultimately lose the war. There was no element of patriotism involved. His sole motive was revenge on the Germans for their treatment of the Jews and in particular his own family.

Foley told Bogomoletz to get in contact with Koessler and run him, initially as a straightforward agent providing intelligence from his German military contacts in Brussels. The Austrian and his new Russian friend were soon being seen together on a regular basis, sitting in the English Bar or the Hotel Palacio arguing over the latest news from the Eastern Front. Foley flew to Lisbon in December 1942 to recruit Koessler as a Double Cross agent, telling him that if he worked for the British, he was 'in a position to double the power of the instrument of revenge he had forged'. Justifying his faith in Koessler to his MI5 colleagues, and no doubt with the experience of the case of Jonny de Graaf in mind, Foley told them that with regard to agents 'revenge is the best motive'.

Bogomoletz also used his contacts in the Balkans to run an escape line for agents out of Yugoslavia through Switzerland to Portugal in tandem with an MI9 officer based in the British embassy, but eventually, probably as a result of the machinations of the *Abwehr* station in Lisbon, the PVDE secret police realised that he was playing them for fools and expelled him from Portugal. The British then provided him with a visa for Egypt.

Bogomoletz later claimed that while in Cairo he had heard of the 'extraordinary success' of his cousin, the noted Soviet physician Alexander Bogomoletz, who under orders from Stalin had developed a serum made from rabbit's blood that supposedly prolonged life. When he heard in 1946 that Alexander had died, he 'decided to develop certain aspects' of his cousin's work, setting up a private practice in Paris advising the rich on how to stay young and publishing an international bestseller on *The Secret of Keeping Young* that, according to the blurb on its jacket, 'caused the widest controversy in medical circles'.

★★★

One of the most important agents-in-place ever run by the CIA or SIS was an ambitious GRU officer whose career was brought to a dead halt when it emerged that his father had been on the wrong side in the Russian civil war. More than any of the spies whose roles are discussed here, Oleg Penkovsky really did prove the adage that 'revenge is the best motive'.

Penkovsky was born, in April 1919, in Vladikavkaz on the northern edge of the Caucasus Mountains in south-western

Russia. His father, Vladimir, an officer in the Tsar's Imperial Russian Army, was killed fighting on the side of the White Russians just a few months after holding his new-born son in his arms. At the end of the civil war, with the Bolsheviks firmly in charge, Penkovsky's mother – determined to ensure the safety of both herself and her son – invented a story of how her husband had died of typhoid. When her son was old enough, she told him the truth. From a young age, Penkovsky lived with a cover story, in the jargon of the spy 'a legend', designed to hide the truth.

Penkovsky joined the Komsomol, the Communist Party youth organisation, and served with the Red Army during the Second World War as a political commissar, an official assigned to a military unit to ensure Communist Party control. He married a general's daughter, Vera Gapanovich. It was to be a feature of Penkovsky's military career that he went out of his way to cultivate generals. Ultimately, this was the characteristic that would make him such a valuable agent.

In late 1943, while serving in the Ukraine, Penkovsky was assigned to the staff of General Sergei Varentsov, who was in charge of all artillery forces in the region. Six months later, they were both wounded and brought back to Moscow. Varentsov spent four months in hospital and during this time Penkovsky looked after his wife and daughter, ensuring they had sufficient food. The general's daughter from a previous marriage died while he was in hospital and Penkovsky sorted out the burial arrangements. 'I sold my last watch and went down to Lvov to bury the girl, purchasing a black dress and her coffin.' Penkovsky said. 'After I returned to the front with the Marshal and he knew what I had done, he said, "You are like a son to me."' In a move that was to be absolutely critical to Penkovsky's value as a spy, Varentsov became the young officer's lifelong friend and mentor.

After the war, Penkovsky was selected for a post in the GRU (Soviet military intelligence) and spent four years from 1949 to 1953 studying 'strategic intelligence' at the Military–Diplomatic Academy in Moscow before being assigned to work at GRU headquarters, initially on the Egyptian desk and then, in the mid 1950s, as an assistant military attaché at the Soviet embassy in

Ankara. His time in Turkey – where he had a difficult relationship with his boss and another colleague – appears to have been a
seminal moment in his decision to betray his country.

'They both were dead set against me and made my life so
miserable that I wrote a letter to headquarters requesting a transfer – anywhere,' he told his SIS and CIA debriefers at their first
meeting. 'By nature, I am a vengeful person but at least on the
basis of fairness. Even then when I saw how unjustly I was being
treated I had already decided to come over to you.'

Penkovsky spent the latter part of his tour in Ankara flirting
with Turkish counter-intelligence and 'dangling' himself in front of
Americans at diplomatic receptions, but any approach was ignored.
A career officer with a good record and an apparently bright future
was an unlikely traitor. Penkovsky was clearly a plant, designed to
draw the Americans into an elaborate GRU deception.

On his return to Moscow, Penkovsky was sent on a nine-month
course in missile technology. The Soviet Union desperately
needed to improve its ability in this field if it were to keep up
with the West, and the GRU was tasked to collect intelligence
on sophisticated Western technology. Already looking to betray
his country to the West, Penkovsky spent his evenings 'studying'
classified documents and lectures in the library, copying them out
painstakingly by hand, ready to pass to the CIA when the opportunity presented itself.

At the end of the course, he was appointed as the GRU intelligence officer on the State Committee for the Co-ordination of
Scientific Research, which set up visits abroad by delegations of
Soviet scientists and electronics experts. It was an ideal platform
for the GRU to obtain intelligence on Western technology.

The final straw that pushed Penkovsky across the line came in
May 1960, when a KGB vetting exposed the fact that his father
had been an officer in the White Army. He was called in front of
a senior GRU officer and accused of deliberately concealing the
true nature of his father's death.

An SIS note in the transcript of Penkovsky's initial debriefing,
said: 'This is the most salient theme in subject's recent life and has
contributed significantly to his decision to approach the West. It

involves his life-long legend that his father had died of typhus.' Penkovsky was furious that the allegation that his father was 'an enemy of the people' had been placed on his GRU record, effectively blocking all chances of further promotion. 'For them I am politically unreliable,' he told the SIS and CIA officers debriefing him. 'They watch me closely.'

Three months later, while returning from a holiday in the Crimea, Penkovsky saw a group of American language students on the train. A few days later, back in Moscow, he spotted two of the group in Red Square and followed them down to the Bolshoi Moskvoretskiy Bridge, where he gave them an envelope containing a letter offering his services as a spy and asked them to hand it to the US embassy. They passed it on, but the CIA officer in the embassy failed to get in touch with Penkovsky.

Fortunately, SIS had become aware of the GRU officer's attempts to contact the West and found another way of getting in touch with him, using one of those patriotic businessmen the service liked to employ as agents. Dickie Franks, an SIS officer who would later become the chief of the service, picked out Greville Wynne, a business consultant who helped British companies sell their products across Eastern Europe.

He took him to the Ivy, a select London restaurant, and suggested he did his bit for Queen and country by linking up with Penkovsky's scientific research committee. A few months later, Wynne was part of a delegation hosted by the committee.

The Russian tried to pass an envelope to an American member of the delegation, without success. He turned instead to Wynne, suggesting he organise a Soviet delegation to London to meet British electronics companies. Wynne agreed, and in the spring of 1961 flew back to Moscow to finalise the details of the delegation's itinerary. Shortly before the Englishman was due to return home, Penkovsky handed him a large envelope containing the missile intelligence he had copied out. Wynne realised the dangers and refused to take it, but Penkovsky was not prepared to be denied yet again. 'I gave him the letter and one document,' Penkovsky said. 'Wynne did not want to do it at first. He was very much against it. He was afraid. Oh, how he was afraid. How

I begged him and persuaded him. Wynne was my last chance.' Eventually, shortly before he got on the flight for London, Wynne relented, accepting a smaller envelope and, once he was back in London, handing it over to SIS.

When the delegation arrived in London, Wynne was told to arrange for Penkovsky to meet two SIS officers and two CIA officers in a room at the Mount Royal Hotel, close to Marble Arch. The first meeting took place on 20 April 1961. Information poured out of the Russian, but the most important intelligence he had to offer concerned Soviet long-range missiles. His mentor Varentsov was now Marshal Varentsov, in charge of all Soviet military missile systems and one of a small select group of officers who were privy to the problems the Russians were experiencing with missile technology, and in particular with the electronic guidance systems. Penkovsky was a frequent visitor to Varentsov's home, and at the weekend to his dacha, and since the GRU man's intelligence responsibilities focused on missile technology, they had frequently discussed the issue.

The alleged missile gap between America and Soviet Union at the time, with US inter-continental ballistic missile (ICBM) capability supposedly way behind the Russians, made Soviet missile systems a key target for Western intelligence. Nikita Khrushchev, the Soviet leader, had made belligerent statements, talking up the number of Soviet ICBMs, which seemed to back up claims made by the 1957 Gaither Report into US offensive and defensive nuclear capabilities by a US Air Force that was determined to stay on top in the Cold War, and even by the CIA's own much lower estimates.

Penkovsky was adamant that the missile-gap argument was nonsense. He revealed at the first meeting that the Soviet Union had no inter-continental ballistic missiles (ICBMs) at all. The programme to build the R16 missile, the first Soviet ICBM, had stalled spectacularly the previous October when the fuel in a missile ignited ahead of a test launch, killing scores of people, including the head of the Soviet missile programme Chief Marshal of Artillery Mitrofan Nedelin and the missile guidance engineer. The Russians, Penkovsky explained, were pouring money into their missile programmes, scrambling to catch up with the Americans.

'There is a difficult situation in the country right now,' Penkovsky said at that first meeting. 'Everything is subordinated to the armaments race. Everything is being directed to equipping our forces with rockets. Billions of roubles are being cut from other programmes to develop rocket technology. The greatest deficiency is in the field of electronics. Our main launch test site is at Kapustin Yar and the impact area is Kazakhstan. There were very many cases where rockets had struck railways or a settlement because they had deviated from their assigned course. The electronics development is far behind.'

Asked what Varentsov had said about Khrushchev's recent claims that the Russians had 'all kinds of ICBMs' ready to fire, Penkovsky quoted his mentor as saying that it was simply a bluff to make the West believe in a threat that did not in fact exist. 'He has so often told me: "You know, Oleg, with respect to ICBMs up to now we don't have a damn thing. Everything is only on paper and there is nothing in actual existence. For short ranges, we can fulfil the missions but beyond that what? There is nothing."'

There were a series of meetings during that first visit to the UK in April and May 1961. The SIS and CIA officers followed the delegation around as it travelled from London, to Birmingham and Leeds, and back to London, Penkovsky was trained to use an SIS Minox spy camera and given a series of intelligence targets: details of GRU operations and agents operating in the west, particularly the 'illegals', agents operating under unofficial cover and living in the community; had the Russians broken the British and American codes, and if so which ones? And missiles: continuous updates of the Soviet strategic missile systems; how many did they have? Which ones worked? Which ones didn't? How accurate were they? Where were the bases? What were their targets? How many atomic warheads did the Russians have? Where were they stored?

Penkovsky had an interesting approach to betrayal. He insisted on being seen as a soldier who had switched sides and now owed his allegiance to Queen Elizabeth II and to President John F.

Kennedy. 'I was thinking of becoming a soldier in a new army,' he said, 'to adopt a new people, to struggle for a new ideal, and in some measure, to avenge my father and millions of other people who have perished in a terrible way as well as for my close relatives.'

At one point in one of the London debriefings, Dick White, the SIS Chief, or 'C', arrived to meet Penkovsky, bringing with him a message from Lord Mountbatten, the British Chief of Defence Staff, but more importantly perhaps, the Queen's cousin. Mountbatten regretted not coming himself, 'I am filled with admiration for the great stand you have made and we are mindful of the risks that you are running,' his message said. 'I have also had reported to me the information which you have passed on to us. I can only tell you that it would be of the highest value and importance to the free world.'

Penkovsky's response was extraordinary: 'I would also like to add and to express the great desire which I have carried in my soul,' he said, 'to swear my fealty to my Queen Elizabeth II and to the President of the United States Mr Kennedy whom I am serving as their soldier.'

Despite the quality and detail of the information Penkovsky had provided, there was some resistance in the CIA to the idea that he was genuine. The British, in contrast, were absolutely convinced and determined to push ahead no matter what. Penkovsky had provided them with too much valuable intelligence, much of it highly damaging to the Russians. Maurice Oldfield, another future 'C', who was the SIS head of station in Washington, and John Maury, head of the CIA's Soviet division, had to fight hard to ensure the joint operation went ahead. At one point, after a fractious discussion of the case with Angleton, the CIA chief of counter-intelligence staff, Maury felt compelled to put his thoughts on record. During the meeting, he had shown James Angleton one of Penkovsky's comments and asked him how he thought revealing this particular piece of intelligence could have helped the Russians.

'After reading the source comment, he confessed he could see no way in which it would be to the Soviet interest to give us this line,' Maury said. 'However, Mr Angleton then took off on the notion that Penkovsky was an anarchist or a crank and for some obscure reason was trying to get us in war with the Russians. I frankly do not know what he was talking about in this regard and doubt very much that he did.'

Oldfield and Maury ensured the Americans stayed on board. There were more debriefings in Paris in the late summer of 1961. Back in Moscow, Penkovsky was run by the British. They devised a system of collecting his intelligence based on the long-standing SIS tradition of occasionally giving the wives of officers serving abroad a role in agent-handling operations, particularly in countries such as the Soviet Union where the SIS officers themselves were likely to be under surveillance.

Janet Chisholm, a former SIS secretary married to Ruari Chisholm, the SIS Head of Station in Moscow, would meet Penkovsky on a Sunday afternoon stroll in a park with her young children, one of whom was young enough to be pushed in a pram. Penkovsky would put the Minox cassettes and any messages into a box of sweets 'for the children' and drop them in the pram as he passed.

Penkovsky was an incorrigible collector of top-secret documents who seemed to have no fear of being caught. During the eighteen months that he was run by SIS and the CIA, Source Ironbark, as he was known to the British (Hero to the Americans), handed over 110 cassette films, including photographs of 8,000 pages of documents. The Penkovsky 'take', coming at a critical period of the Cold War that included the creation of the Berlin Wall and the Cuban Missile Crisis, was extraordinarily valuable, none of it more so than that on the missiles that Khrushchev planned to base in Cuba.

In the summer of 1962, Varentsov was put in charge of all Soviet surface-to-surface missiles, from those used by army divisions on the front line to the development of the ICBMs, and Penkovsky had access to his office. One of the documents he photographed was a manual entitled 'Methods of Protecting and Defending Strategic Rocket Sites'. A comparison of images taken by an American U-2 spy plane overflying Cuba and the details in the Penkovsky manual confirmed that the Soviet Union was planning to site R12 medium-range missiles at a new military base under construction at San Cristobal, 80km (50 miles) west of the capital Havana.

This was a direct threat to the United States and it broke Khrushchev's pledge to Kennedy that Soviet military aid for Castro would be purely defensive. It was this information that sparked the Cuban Missile Crisis in October 1962, leading to a US blockade aimed at preventing the missiles arriving and a stand-off between Kennedy and Khrushchev that arguably brought the world closer to a nuclear holocaust than it has ever been.

But the most important intelligence Penkovsky had to offer was what ensured that the crisis came to a peaceful end. His inside knowledge, courtesy of Varentsov, had revealed beyond a shadow of a doubt that the missile gap was massively in America's advantage. 'With Cuba, for example, I simply can't understand why Khrushchev should not be sharply rebuked,' Penkovsky had said at the first meeting, the day after the Kremlin first offered military aid to Cuba. 'Kennedy should be firm. Khrushchev is not going to fire any rockets. He is not ready for war.' The documents and intelligence that Penkovsky subsequently provided confirmed that he was right and allowed Kennedy to demand that Khrushchev should back down, safe in the knowledge that the Soviet leader did not have the necessary missiles to fight a war with America.

On 22 October 1962, just hours before Kennedy demanded the removal of Soviet missiles from Cuba, Penkovsky was arrested by the KGB, who had been watching him for some time. He confessed almost immediately. From then on Khrushchev knew that Kennedy was aware that all the talk of Soviet missiles and their capabilities was just a bluff. A week later, the Soviet ships carrying the missile warheads turned around and the world was hauled back from oblivion.

At the end of the crisis, Dick White called his staff together at Century House (the headquarters of MI6). He said:

I have been asked by the CIA to let you know of the abso-lutely crucial value of the Penkovsky intelligence we have been passing to them. I am given to understand that this intelligence was largely instrumental in deciding that the United States should not make a pre-emptive nuclear strike against the Soviet Union, as a substantial body of important opinion in the States has been in favour of doing. In making known this appreciation of our contribution, I would stress to all of you that, if proof were needed, this operation has demonstrated beyond all doubt the prime importance of the human intelligence source, handled with professional skill and expertise.

Greville Wynne, the British businessman and MI6 courier who had been Penkovsky's go-between, was arrested in Hungary ten days later. He and Penkovsky were put on trial in May 1963. Penkovsky was sentenced to death and was shot shortly afterwards. Wynne was sentenced to eight years' imprisonment but exchanged a year later for Gordon Lonsdale, a Soviet spy arrested in Britain. Varentsov was retired and reduced in rank to major-general for his inadvertent role in the affair.

★★★

Where Penkovsky's desire for revenge was cold and determined, Edward Lee Howard was one of the most petulant and vindictive espionage agents ever to betray his country. Howard was born in New Mexico in October 1951 and, after graduating from the University of Texas, carried out volunteer work with the Peace Corps in South America, where he met his wife, Mary. He returned to the United States and took an MA in business studies at the American University in Washington before working for a while for a private company.

Howard joined the CIA in 1980, admitting during the recruitment process to having used marijuana and cocaine while with the Peace Corps and was warned that if he ever took drugs again he would be dismissed. Howard was selected for operations work, training at the Farm, the legendary CIA operations training camp near Williamsburg, Virginia. He was a potential high-flier who excelled in counter-surveillance skills and he was assigned to the Soviet–East European Division, where he worked first on East Germany before being moved to a section dealing with agents operating in the Soviet Union. By 1983, he was so well regarded that he was given a plum posting to the CIA station in Moscow. In preparation for the job, Howard was briefed on the main agents and operations being run in the city. Then, a routine polygraph examination indicated that not only had he lied about the extent of his use of drugs but that he had a history of petty theft. Howard was sacked. His reaction raised immediate warning signals. Much the worse for alcohol, Howard rang the Moscow embassy on a telephone line that he knew was monitored by the KGB to inform the head of station that he would not be coming over to join him.

Attempts were made at counselling Howard, who moved back to New Mexico to work for the state government, but he remained furious at his treatment and took refuge in drink. In the summer of 1984, still extremely angry and struggling financially, Howard contacted the Soviet embassy and offered to provide them with details of CIA agents in Moscow.

Howard and his wife travelled to Vienna in September 1984, where he was debriefed at length by senior KGB officers about what he knew. Although he had only been in the agency for a short while, his work on CIA agents in the Soviet Union and the briefing he had received ahead of the abandoned posting to Moscow meant he had extremely valuable intelligence to impart. During two separate debriefings, one in September and a second in early 1985, Howard destroyed several of the operations that were being run from the CIA station in Moscow and sent one long-serving agent to his death.

He revealed the secrets of a long-term CIA technical intercept programme that had produced important intelligence on the Soviet nuclear weapons programme. In the late 1970s, a US spy satellite had spotted a series of new and identical manhole covers leading from the centre of Moscow to a nuclear weapons centre just outside the city. A new telephone line had been installed solely serving the research centre. The CIA placed an intercept device around the telephone line and taped all the conversations, but shortly after Howard's first debriefing the tapes went blank. The secret intercept programme was blown.

The luckiest agent Howard betrayed was Boris Yuzhin, a KGB officer who had operated under cover in San Francisco for the official Soviet news agency TASS. He was recruited by the FBI in 1979 and copied KGB documents in the Soviet Consulate-General using a miniature camera. Yuzhin was careless and left the camera in the consulate-general. When it was found, the KGB opened an investigation into who might have been using it. Yuzhin was one of the suspects but remained undetected when he returned to Moscow in 1982. Information provided by Howard during his first debriefing in Vienna led to Yuzhin's arrest. Fortunately for him, the FBI had refused to allow the CIA to run him as an agent in Moscow, so KGB surveillance and searches of his home turned up nothing incriminating. He was jailed but released in a 1991 amnesty ordered by President Boris Yeltsin.

Adolf Tolkachev was less lucky. He had been recruited by the CIA's Moscow station in 1979 after his half a dozen approaches over the previous two years had been rebuffed for fear he was part of a KGB deception operation. Tolkachev was in fact an extremely valuable agent. He was an armed forces technical expert with access to all the latest Soviet military technology. His motives were money and anger at the regime, his wife's family having suffered badly during various purges. For six years, Tolkachev provided hundreds of rolls of film on a variety of military technology and equipment, including Soviet stealth technology and new tactical nuclear missiles, before their introduction into service. The Moscow station's last meeting with him was in January 1985. On 13 June that year, Paul Stombaugh, a CIA officer, was arrested by the KGB on his way to a planned meeting with Tolkachev. He was held for four hours in the KGB headquarters at the Lubyanka before being released. Tolkachev had been arrested four days earlier and was subsequently executed.

The loss of the agents and the secret intercept programme remained a mystery until August 1985, when Vitaly Yurchenko defected. He revealed the existence of a CIA officer who had contacted the Soviet embassy in Washington the previous year. Yurchenko did not know his name. He only knew that he was code-named Robert, that he had offered to work for the KGB after being rejected for a posting to the CIA station in Moscow, and that he had been debriefed in Vienna in the autumn of 1984.

Howard was the only person who fitted the bill and the FBI put a surveillance operation in place. His phone was tapped, but he soon realised that he was being watched. Both he and his wife behaved completely normally and had no contact at all with the KGB. After several weeks of surveillance the FBI decided that they had no choice but to confront him with the evidence that he was a Soviet spy.

Howard agreed to be questioned but revealed nothing. Then on 20 September 1985, he approached the FBI and agreed to talk if there was a lawyer present. A date was set for the following week. That night, Howard and his wife went out for dinner. She drove and as she slowed the car to turn right, he jumped out, leaving a dummy in the passenger seat to fool the surveillance team. When Mary Howard arrived home, she made a telephone call to an answer machine, playing a recording of her husband leaving a message. Edward Howard flew first to New York and then to Finland, where he walked into the Soviet embassy. The KGB looked after Howard, giving him an allowance, an apartment in Moscow and a *dacha* in the expensive resort area of Zhukovka. He occasionally met his wife and son, either in Russia or in places abroad but he drank heavily and, in July 2002, he fell down the steps of his *dacha* and broke his neck.

Chapter 7

THE RIGHT THING TO DO

The popular reputation of espionage and 'secret agents' in particular is bound up with the idea that spies are unscrupulous, ruthless people prepared to do anything to get what they want. It is undoubtedly true, as some of the case studies in this book show, that often people will betray their country or their cause, or even send people to their deaths, for very selfish reasons. But while these tend to be the most famous cases and the ones that truly shock, the reasons agents do what they do are as varied as the motives for which people choose to do anything. Sometimes spies are simply people doing the best they can in a bad situation and very often – far from being selfish – they are putting their own lives at risk to provide intelligence because they believe they should. That might of course be for patriotic reasons, but very often it is for reasons of belief, ideology or simply a moral duty, a decision that this is the right thing to do.

John Merrett was born in London in 1879 and was the son of a chartered accountant. He was apprenticed as an engineer and in 1909 moved to St Petersburg (or, as it later became known, Petrograd). He set up a successful engineering company, Merrett and Jones, and became a leading member of the city's relatively large British expatriate community with a smart house on the Moika, the riverside district that was home to members of the Russian aristocracy. Merrett knew everyone who was anyone and, after the October Revolution, he was used by the British secret service as a conduit to General Mikhail Alekseyev, the former Imperial Russian Army commander-in-chief, providing him with large sums of British government money to fund the Civil War against the Bolsheviks.

When the 'Red Terror' broke out in September 1918, in the wake of 'the Lockhart Plot', most of the British intelligence officers based in Petrograd were arrested or forced to flee, leaving several British secret service officers who went underground to continue operating. These included not just Sidney Reilly and George Hill, but also Jim Gillespie, an officer in the Royal Naval Volunteer Reserve who had been using the Petrograd embassy as a base from which to set up agent networks across Russia. Gillespie's role now was simple, to try to protect the British agent networks, to keep them together and ensure they remained in place until a new system could be created to run them.

The restrictions on what Gillespie could do were severe. He was a known British spy and the Bolshevik secret police, the *Cheka*, or Extraordinary Commission, were looking for him. He badly needed someone who was not marked out as a British spy to help him, to be his leg man. Merrett was that man. He had no training and no idea of how to run an agent network, but he was going to have to learn fast. It would be too dangerous for Gillespie to hang around for long. He needed to make sure his agents knew they were now working to Merrett, so that he could get out before the *Cheka* found him (an eventuality that had to be avoided at all costs since, no matter how strong he was, if he was interrogated it was likely to lead them eventually to some, if not all, of the British agents).

Gillespie gave Merrett 200,000 roubles to fund the networks before getting out to Finland to take over the British secret service base in Tornio that provided the 'letter box' for the couriers smuggling intelligence across the border. Merrett's role was to babysit the networks, collecting the intelligence, paying the agents and couriers and sending the reports down the line to Gillespie, who would pass them back to London via the British embassy in Stockholm. It seemed a natural thing for a patriotic Englishman to do, but Merrett soon found himself doing far more than just running the intelligence networks. The British expatriate community were in serious trouble with many already incarcerated in Petrograd's Peter and Paul Fortress and those who were still free under threat of arrest at any time. Merrett knew where his duty lay, in doing the right thing, not just by continuing the intelligence networks, but by using the money Gillespie had given him (and also his own funds) to help those in trouble. Despite the great risk he was already running, he bribed *Cheka* guards to get food and clothing to the Britons held in the Peter and Paul Fortress, and became what one of those he helped described as a latter-day Scarlet Pimpernel.

'Apart from the members of the Embassy, British subjects in general were being imprisoned, and as I was fortunate enough to avoid arrest, I was determined to do all in my power to alleviate the sufferings of the less fortunate,' Merrett said. He used 10,000 roubles of his own money to buy bedding, clothes and food for the Allied prisoners and, with the aid of the American Red Cross, set up a kitchen to ensure they were properly fed. But that was not all he did. As well as passing the agents' intelligence reports along the courier lines to Finland, he began using those routes to get Britons out before they too were arrested, hiding people in apartments until one of his guides was able to take them across the border.

'I know how ungrudgingly Mr Merrett gave his help both to his countrymen and frequently to others who were in trouble supplying them in many cases with funds and food,' one of those he saved recalled. 'During the period from August to December 1918, when the Bolsheviks were imprisoning and killing persons, often merely on suspicion of counter-revolutionary sympathies, and were particularly hostile to Great Britain, many of these persons were escaping not only from prison but from the country through the aid of Mr Merrett.'

But Merrett was betrayed to the *Cheka*. His house was ransacked and his wife, Lydia, was arrested and held a hostage in an attempt to force him to give himself up. Despite his concerns for her safety, Merrett went underground and continued his work getting both intelligence reports and refugees down the lines to Finland. 'The work entailed considerable danger to myself and involved my actual arrest on one occasion by the Red Guards,' he said. 'Fortunately, I succeeded in escaping on my way to prison, and was thereafter only able to avoid re-arrest by adopting disguises and sleeping in ever changing and out-of-the-way quarters.' On another occasion, he only avoided arrest by sliding down a drainpipe into the backyard of a neighbouring house as the Red Guards burst down the front door.

Despite the constant pressure from the *Cheka*, Merrett continued to work to get people out of prison and across the border. 'Mr Merrett used every endeavour to discover, not without great risk to himself, new routes by which British subjects might safely leave Russia,' said W.H. Murray-Campbell, one of the directors of the Anglo–Russian Bank. 'He organised very successfully guides and conveyances and made all arrangements by which food could be obtained by those who were escaping the vigilance of the Bolsheviks.'

One of those Merrett helped escape recalled that before the revolution he was one of the best dressed men in the city. 'What was my surprise on entering Mr Merrett's house to see my host transferred into a bearded, shabbily dressed Russian in top boots.' Another called Merrett a 'Scarlet Pimpernel' and asked how it felt to know he might be arrested at any moment. 'He laughingly replied that while the Bolsheviks were busy arresting him on the Moika, he was to be found in the country and when they were after him in the country, he was to be found somewhere else.'

Eventually, a British secret service officer arrived to replace Merrett and take control of the British networks. Paul Dukes, one of the most famous names of the early days of SIS, was operating under cover as a member of the *Cheka*. It was several days before Merrett trusted the new arrival enough to meet him. Dukes was surprised by his appearance, describing him as 'a huge fellow, whose stubble-covered face brimmed over with smiles beaming good nature and jollity. This giant was dressed in a rough and ragged brown suit and in his hand he squeezed a dirty hat.'

Dukes spent two weeks taking over the networks, then bribed a *Cheka* official to get Lydia Merrett out of jail and sent both her and her husband down the courier lines to Finland. In a letter to the Foreign Office backing Merrett's subsequent request for a refund of the £3,000 of his own money he spent helping his fellow Britons escape, Dukes said:

> I met Mr Merrett for the first time in November 1918 in Petrograd. I found him continuing the work of Mr Gillespie, who was in Government employ and who had been compelled to quit the country. At the same time, he was engaged in enabling allied subjects, particularly British, who were in difficulties and whom the Bolsheviks refused passes, to find means of crossing the frontier unobserved.
>
> I had the opportunity during a couple of weeks of observing Mr Merrett's work in this sphere. During this period, he enabled nearly a dozen people to escape, providing them in some cases with money and paying the smugglers and others through whose agency the transmission over the frontier was effected. Mr Merrett was certainly acting under circumstances of grave personal danger; when I arrived in Petrograd, I found him in hiding, changing his abode every night, in various disguises, and hotly chased by the agents of the Extraordinary Commission.
>
> I formed the judgement during those days that Mr Merrett was actuated partly, perhaps, by a love of adventure but mainly by a sense of duty towards the British colony in Petrograd. There was at that time absolutely nobody left who was attending to the material wants or discovering means of communicating abroad. Mr Merrett, I believe, felt that he could not leave Petrograd until someone arrived, or some arrangements were made for the continuation of the various activities for which he temporarily voluntarily assumed the responsibility.

In short, he spied out of a sense of duty.

***

A sense of duty is one manifestation of 'doing the right thing'; idealism is another. Communism attracted more than its fair share of idealists, in particular those who wanted to change the world and were therefore prepared to become agents for the Soviet and East European intelligence services. Markus Wolf, the East German spy chief, said it was a phenomenon that often affected educated, young people from good backgrounds.

'This feeling of belonging to a special community, an elite and secretive club fighting for a noble ideal, was, I often observed, of particular importance to Westerners from upper middle-class backgrounds with strong and complex personalities,' Wolf said. 'Perhaps this goes some way toward answering the question I am incessantly asked about why such people flocked to work for us. What we offered them was the chance of mixing idealism with personal commitment, something that is missing in many modern societies.'

This was particularly true in the period between the wars when the members of the Cambridge Spy Ring were recruited. The belief in communism shared by many young intellectuals at the time appears to be incomprehensible today, given what we now know about Stalinism, but during the late 1920s and early '30s the effects of the depression and the rise of Hitler and Mussolini led many to see the 'brave new world' represented by Stalin's Russia as the only answer to social and political injustice.

'The Wall Street Crash seemed to herald the end of capitalism,' said Robert Cecil, who like both Kim Philby and John Cairncross studied at Trinity College, Cambridge, in the 1930s before going on to work in SIS. 'In Germany and Italy fascism was in power. The USA remained aloof and in Britain and France the democratic trumpet gave a very uncertain and wavering sound. To this hard core of young intellectuals, the schematic and revolutionary message of Marxism seemed to hold all the answers; it was a cause to which they could devote their idealism, a cause that would assuage their despair.'

One of the young European intellectuals who saw a better future for the world in communism was Edith Tudor-Hart. She was born Edith Suschitzky in Vienna in August 1908 to a family of well-to-do Jewish Social Democrats. Her father and his brother ran a bookshop and independent publishing house specialising in progressive causes, particularly feminist issues such as equal rights for women, access to birth control and the right of a woman to decide on whether to have an abortion. Edith, known to her closest friends as Edie, came to Britain in 1925 to work as a kindergarten nurse and met a young medical student, Alexander Tudor-Hart, with whom she fell in love. He was a communist and it was he who converted her to communism.

Edith returned home to Vienna intermittently and studied photography at the legendary Bauhaus art school in the German town of Dessau, but she was deeply in love with Tudor-Hart and returned to the United Kingdom to live with him. Her close friends now included leading British communists such as Rosa Shar, a courier for Soviet intelligence, and Maurice Dobb, one of Kim Philby's tutors at Cambridge. Edith was recruited in 1929 by Arnold Deutsch, a Soviet intelligence officer working under-cover in both Austria and the United Kingdom. She was also in contact with the representative of the Soviet news agency TASS, which was used extensively by the Soviet intelligence services as cover for operations abroad, and she carried out courier and other minor operations in Paris and London.

Although her activities on behalf of Soviet intelligence were not known to the British authorities at this stage, the involve-ment of a foreigner in the activities of the Communist Party led inevitably to interest by Special Branch and, after taking part in a communist-led demonstration for workers' rights in Trafalgar Square in October 1930, during which she was seen talking to leading members of the Communist Party, Edith was ordered to be deported to Austria. Despite 'spirited resistance', she was sent back to Vienna in January 1931, much to the fury of Maurice Dobb, who described such behaviour by the authorities as 'mon-strous ... especially when it happens to one of the nicest and most charming people one knows'.

Back in Vienna, Edith joined the Austrian Communist Party and worked as a professional photographer for the Vienna bureau of the Soviet news agency TASS, which was run at the time by Sigmund Ebel, a Soviet intelligence officer oper-ating under journalistic cover. She carried out a number of missions in Austria and Italy under the direction of a Soviet intelligence colonel, possibly Ebel himself. Edith's main work appears to have been as a go-between or courier, and her contacts included Deutsch and the Hungarian communists Arpad Haasz and Theodor Maly, all of whom were Soviet intelligence officers or agents.

The Austrian government was run at the time by the right-wing Christian Social Party, while the city government in Vienna was controlled by the left-wing Social Democrats, and there were frequent clashes on the streets between supporters of the right and left. In the summer of 1933, after coming down from Cambridge, Philby told Maurice Dobb that he wanted to travel in Europe and do something for the cause. Philby later claimed that his tutor put him in touch with the Paris-based World Committee for the Relief of Victims of German Fascism and they told him to go to Vienna to help the Communist underground. It seems more likely, given Dobb's closeness to Edith and the violent clashes that were then going on between supporters of the left and right in Austria's main cities, that it was Dobb who sent Philby to Vienna with Edith's contact details. Certainly, Philby knew Edith in Vienna and it was there that she took one of the most enduring images of the young Philby, in which he is seen smoking a pipe. That photograph was to come back to haunt them both. Edith is also almost certainly the person who introduced Philby to her close friend Lizy Friedman, a young communist activist working for the Comintern who lived with Philby in Vienna.

Philby worked as a courier for the communists and helped those members of the left who were on the Austrian government's wanted list to flee the country. 'I greatly admired Kim Philby,' wrote one of those helping the refugees:

> Here was a young Englishman, determined to risk much to help the underground freedom movement in a small country which must have been of very limited interest to him. But doubts began to dawn on me when Philby appeared as a communist go-between and when he declared that he could provide all the money we needed for our work. The money Philby offered could only have come from the Russians.

Edith's involvement with the communists and suspicions of her role with Soviet intelligence led to her arrest and for several weeks she was held in prison before being released for lack of evidence. She was ordered by Soviet intelligence to cease all operations from that point. Her letters to Alexander Tudor-Hart from Vienna were described by MI5, which was monitoring their correspondence closely, as 'passionate to the point of being unbalanced' and, in August 1933, he travelled to Vienna to marry her, thereby providing her with the protection of British citizenship and the ability to return to the United Kingdom. When the clashes on the streets broke out into full-scale 'civil war' in February 1934, Philby married Lizy and brought her back to Britain, where she moved in with the Tudor-Harts.

Philby later admitted that it was Edith and Lizy between them who engineered his recruitment by the NKVD. Edith took him to Regents Park and led him to a bench where Arnold Deutsch was sitting waiting for him. 'Here we are,' she said, and left them to it. Philby's own reaction to this meeting casts interesting light on why so many young people in the 1920s and '30s decided for ideological reasons to back the obscenity of Stalinism as a solution to the world's problems; it may even have relevance in explaining how some in the modern world have decided to back Islamist extremism. The inspiration of being someone who can make a change and at the same time adhere to something, an ideal, with the ability to change the world, will always be a powerful incentive for potential agents:

> I was being offered a very interesting future, a very interesting life. I had a life goal and I was being offered the means to reach that goal. I could give the communists and anti-fascists information that they could not get from anyone else. It was an amazing conversation, and he was a marvellous man. Simply marvellous. I felt that immediately, and it never left me.

Deutsch told Philby to go back to Cambridge and come up with other potential recruits with the ability to infiltrate the British establishment. He compiled a list of seven names, at the top of which was Donald Maclean, one of the other members of the 'Ring of Five', the Cambridge Spy Ring. Guy Burgess, Philby's friend, another member of the network, was the last on his list. It was Burgess who would recommend Anthony Blunt, the fourth member, and Blunt who would recommend John Cairncross, the final member of the Cambridge Five. Blunt described Edith as 'the grandmother' of the Cambridge Spy Ring, but she also tried to recruit a similar spy ring in Oxford.

'Through Edith we obtained *Söhnchen* [Philby],' one report from the NKVD *Rezidentura* in London said. 'In the attached report, you will find details of a second *Söhnchen* who, in all probability, offers even greater possibilities than the first. Edith is of the opinion that Wynn is more promising than *Söhnchen*. From the report, you will see that he has very definite possibilities. We must make haste with these people before they start being active.'

Wynn was Arthur Wynn, a highly committed communist who was a contemporary of Philby's at Trinity and by now was carrying out academic research at Oxford. He was recruited by Deutsch on Edith's recommendation, given the code name 'Scott' and provided the names of twenty-five potential agents in Oxford, including at least one who was successfully recruited. Wynn subsequently travelled widely in Germany and Austria, and MI5 believed him to be working with the Comintern, but the Oxford spy ring did not come close to fulfilling Edith's expectations. Wynn's idealistic view of Soviet communism did not survive Stalin's initial alliance with Hitler. During the Second World War, Wynn worked on research on radar and navigational aids for the RAF and subsequently became a civil servant working to improve safety in the mines. After retiring from the civil service in 1971, he became a prominent social researcher and commentator whose work was highly respected across the political spectrum.

Despite Edith's enthusiastic efforts on behalf of Soviet intelligence, her marriage to Alexander was not a happy one. A few months after their son Tommy was born, his father went off to fight in the Spanish Civil War. Edith lived alone with her son, making a comfortable living as a photographer specialising in children. Her work did not just consist of portraits of young children taken for private clients, it included many extremely moving photographs depicting the deprivation caused by the economic crises, which had worsened the already bad conditions in the slum areas of London and South Wales where her husband worked as a doctor and had increased levels of poverty throughout Britain. Edith's photography brought home the impact of that poverty on young children in a very effective way. 'In the hands of the person who uses it with feeling and imagination, the camera becomes very much more than the means of earning a living,' she said. 'It becomes a vital factor in recording and influencing the life of the people and in promoting human understanding.' In a report in September 1936 on an exhibition entitled: 'Photography serves Mankind,' *The Times* highlighted 'Miss Edith Tudor-Hart's engaging studies of children'. Meanwhile, her work on behalf of Soviet intelligence continued, but it was placed in danger in 1938 when a camera used by a Soviet spy ring operating in the Woolwich Arsenal was traced back to her. She denied involvement and avoided arrest.

By the time Alexander Tudor-Hart returned to Britain their marriage was all but over. They separated but remained friends and eventually divorced. Edith was treasurer of the Austrian Communist Party, which was in exile in the United Kingdom, and acted as liaison with the Communist Party of Great Britain. During 1940, when there was no Soviet intelligence officer in the UK to handle the members of the Cambridge Spy Ring, she passed intelligence from Blunt and Burgess to Bob Stewart, a British communist party member working for the Russians, who then sent it to the Paris *Rezidentura*, using Lizy Philby as a courier.

For much of the war, Edith was in an intimate relationship with another member of the Austrian Communist Party. Engelbert Broda, a nuclear scientist at the Cavendish Laboratory in Cambridge, was supplying the Russians with continuous updates on the laboratory's work on Tube Alloys, the British code name for the Anglo–American atomic weapons programme, known in the United States as the Manhattan Project. Broda, code-named Eric, was one of the three main Soviet sources in Britain on the

atomic weapons programme, along with John Cairncross and
Melita Norwood, a secretary in the British Non-Ferrous Metals
Research Association, which carried out research on the proper-
ties of various metals used in the Tube Alloys programme.

After the war, Edith had little involvement with communist
activities, but when Guy Burgess and Donald Maclean fled to
Moscow in May 1951, Philby came under immediate suspicion
because he was a good friend of Burgess and one of the few
people who knew that Maclean was about to be arrested. The
MI5 investigation began to uncover the details of Philby's communist past and Edith Tudor-Hart's involvement. She was clearly
aware of the problem, and by September of 1951 was already
talking about destroying the negatives of photographs she had
taken of Kim and Lizy Philby in Vienna.

In late 1951, Edith was put under intensive surveillance, with
eight MI5 'watchers' working in tandem twenty-four hours a day,
a telephone tap put on her home and all her mail intercepted and
read. She probably spotted the surveillance because, when two
MI5 officers arrived at her door in early January 1952 to interview her, claiming to be from the War Office, she was already
in a highly depressed state of mind and had taken to her bed.
The two MI5 officers claimed to be interested in Lizy Philby's
new husband but asked about Lizy as well. Edith denied knowing
her in Vienna, claiming they had only met when she moved to
London, and when they showed her a photograph of Kim Philby,
she insisted she had never seen him before.

Clearly panicked by the visit of the MI5 officers and certainly
now realising that she was under surveillance, Edith destroyed
the negatives of her photographs of Philby and Lizy in Vienna
and activated an emergency procedure, sending a telegram with
a birthday greeting from 'Syb and Tommy' to a cafe in West
Wickham in Kent. In an apparent response, she received an invitation to Bob Stewart's 75th birthday party at the Polish Club
in Portland Place. But she had stopped doing anything for the
party, and Stewart's view was that she was completely mad and
no longer any use to them. MI5 continued its surveillance of
her after the interview and her complaints to friends that she

was being followed everywhere, although true, led them to be
concerned over her mental state. She eventually had a genuine
breakdown and was admitted to a psychiatric hospital suffering
from a 'persecution complex'.

After recovering from her illness, Edith worked initially at the
Heal's furniture shop in Tottenham Court Road before attempting to resume her career as a photographer. But she met with little
success, and by the mid 1960s was running an antique shop in
Brighton, at which point MI5 decided she no longer needed to be
kept under surveillance since she had 'settled down to a responsible
bourgeois life'. Edith's ground-breaking role in espionage history
went unrecognised until after her death from cancer in 1973.

***

The overwhelming nature of the British class system during
the 1930s was another important element in persuading idealistic young Britons, such as the members of the Cambridge Spy
Ring, that communism offered a better way. Ironically, only one
of those five Soviet agents had not come from the wealthy, upper
middle-classes with their ready access to private schooling and
Oxbridge education.

John Cairncross was born in 1913 in the small Lanarkshire
town of Lesmahagow, where his father was the local ironmonger
and his mother a former schoolteacher. The family were regular church-goers and were not poor; they had a maid, although
with eight children they practised thrift, and, most importantly
for their children's future, their parents encouraged learning. John
Cairncross was educated at Hamilton Academy and Glasgow
University, where he studied French, German and Economics.
After around eighteen months studying French literature in Paris,
a period during which he also travelled to Berlin and Vienna,
experiencing the same conflicts between left and right that
inspired Edith Tudor-Hart and Kim Philby, he won a scholarship
to Trinity College, Cambridge.

Arriving in Cambridge in September 1934, Cairncross took
rooms in New Court, where those sharing his staircase included

the communists Jack Klugman, who became a good friend, and 'a Research Fellow in Modern Languages named Anthony Blunt, to whom I took an immediate dislike'.

It was Blunt who recommended Cairncross to the NKVD as a potential recruit after the young Scot, having come top of both the Foreign Office and Home Office entrance examinations, had left Cambridge and joined the Diplomatic Service. Blunt invited him back to Cambridge with the main intention of introducing him to Guy Burgess, who befriended Cairncross and arranged to meet up in London when his potential as a Soviet agent was assessed by Burgess during a long evening of conversation.

'Cairncross is 23 years old, he comes from a lower middle-class family and is of humbler origin than I,' Burgess told Theodor Maly, who was now the NKVD *Rezident* in London, in a report that said as much about Burgess as it did about Cairncross. 'He speaks with a strong Scottish accent and one cannot call him a gentleman. He is a lower middle-class intellectual. His Presbyterian background instilled ambition in him and it was his dream to get into the Foreign Office at any price. After five years of academic work, he came spiritually to Marxism.'

Cairncross was convinced that communism was the right way forward but he could not act on that conviction without losing the Foreign Office career he had fought so hard to attain. This made him an ideal recruit, Burgess said. He could be offered the opportunity to retain his career and ambitions, while working for the cause underground as a Soviet agent. Burgess, though, felt it was too dangerous for either him or Blunt to approach Cairncross, since he might react badly and report them. Jack Klugman, a friend of all three men, agreed to make the initial approach instead, and offered an unspecified opportunity to work for the cause while retaining his career, and Cairncross happily agreed to do so.

'We shall call him "Moliere",' Maly told Moscow. 'He gave Klugman his agreement to work, but knows, of course, only half of what we want from him. So far, his only contact is Klugman. We shall take him over from him by the end of May.' Klugman introduced Cairncross to Arnold Deutsch, just as Tudor-Hart

had done with Philby, and Deutsch then recruited him as an
NKVD agent, explaining to him that they wanted him to act as
a spy inside the Foreign Office. Although Klugman served in the
Special Operations Executive in Cairo during the war, where he
dealt with the resistance in Yugoslavia and was a proponent of
the British decision to back the communist leader Tito, a former
KGB officer familiar with the case insisted that the recruitment
of Cairncross was the only work that Klugman did for Soviet
intelligence and that his arguments in favour of Tito were his
own and had nothing to do with the NKVD.

Cairncross always denied being a Soviet sympathiser, claiming that he had merely 'flirted' with communism at Cambridge
and was drawn into working for the Russians against his will. He
feared being sacked if he reported the NKVD approach to his
bosses in the Foreign Office, he said, and had to console himself with the thought that the Soviet Union was providing more
effective opposition to Hitler than Britain. But the next telegram
from Deutsch to Moscow appears to contradict those claims. 'We
made direct contact,' it said. 'He was very glad that he could make
contact with us and not feel himself cut off from the party. He is
very well-educated, serious and a convinced communist. He at
once expressed his readiness to work for us and his attitude to our
work is extremely serious.'

For a while Cairncross – who was working in the same office
at the Foreign Office as Donald Maclean – was 'held in reserve' by
the London *Rezidentura*. But in August and September of 1938,
while attached to a special unit set up inside the Foreign Office
to deal with the Munich crisis, Cairncross passed the NKVD
documents that showed that there was an influential lobby within
Whitehall, backed by the British ambassadors in Berlin and Paris,
for some form of accommodation with Hitler. This came at the
crucial moment when Stalin was deciding whether he should
back Hitler or the Western powers, although how much impact
Cairncross's information had is impossible to assess.

Shortly afterwards, Cairncross was transferred to the Treasury,
where he worked as assistant to the head of the section dealing
with the Post Office and several other Government departments.

Cairncross later claimed that he only passed the Russians small amounts of relatively minor information during the period before the war. 'I did not have access to secret data in the Treasury,' he said, 'unless the construction of new Post Offices could be regarded as confidential.' In fact, the Post Office was heavily involved in the construction of a network of intercept sites around the country and in connecting them to Britain's secret wartime code-breaking centre at Bletchley Park, which the NKVD code-named *Kurort*, the German for spa, and Cairncross duly handed over to the Russians details of this along with documents listing all of the staff of MI5 and the locations of every one of its offices.

In August 1939, many of those who had seen Stalin as a bulwark against fascism were dismayed to learn that he had done a deal with Hitler. Under the so-called Molotov–Ribbentrop Pact, Germany and the Soviet Union carved up Eastern Europe between them. By now, Maly and Deutsch had been recalled to Moscow and control of the Cambridge Spy Ring had been taken over by Anatoly Gorsky, code-named Henry.

Cairncross claimed that at his next meeting with Gorsky they had a long discussion on the implications of the alliance with Nazi Germany and he extracted an agreement under which he would not have to pass any information to the Russians. There would be a 'closed season' while Stalin and Hitler were allies. 'My contact with Henry during the Molotov–Ribbentrop Pact was nominal and our infrequent meetings were merely a formality,' Cairncross claimed. 'I passed no documents to him, nor did he expect anything.' The files of the former KGB, opened briefly in the mid 1990s, show this to have been a nonsense. His dedication to the cause was such that he continued to pass over numerous secret documents, including two War Office directories listing every member of the intelligence services.

In February 1940, the NKVD closed its London *Rezidentura*, but before Gorsky left for Moscow, Cairncross told him about a post that was opening up as private secretary to Lord Hankey who, as a minister without portfolio in the Churchill government, was in charge of investigating a wide range of top-secret projects. Gorsky told him to apply for the post and, when he returned to London in December 1940, was delighted to hear that Cairncross, now code-named Liszt after one of his favourite composers, had followed his advice.

'We drew Liszt's attention to the desirability of his getting the job,' Gorsky told Moscow Centre. 'Liszt pointed out that Boss [the NKVD code name for Hankey] was an enthusiastic vegetarian and looked with great approval on modern young men who were also vegetarians. Liszt also discovered that Boss frequently visited the Vega vegetarian restaurant near Leicester Square.

'We instructed Liszt to become a devoted vegetarian and to frequent the restaurant at the same time as Boss. This simple scheme led to Boss finally noticing "this modest young man who apparently was a fanatical vegetarian". The acquaintanceship was established and Liszt succeeded in creating a favourable impression on Boss.'

Cairncross's new job would be the most productive period of his time working for the NKVD. He was in charge of the registry of all the department's documents and so had access to anything he wanted to see. He was handing over so many reports by the Chiefs of the Imperial General Staff and SIS on the progress of the war that Gorsky complained that only the most urgent could be sent by encoded telegram, with most dispatched to Moscow in the diplomatic bag. In 1941 alone, Cairncross handed a staggering 3,449 documents and reports to the Russians. One batch, sent by diplomatic bag in May 1941, shortly before the German invasion of the Soviet Union, contained sixty films of various documents supplied by Cairncross, including the reports of two investigations into MI5 and SIS counter-intelligence operations, with detailed profiles of the leading members of both organisations; numerous SIS reports; a report on radio measures against night bombers; and another on British bacteriological warfare capabilities.

The extent of the secret information Cairncross was now able to provide, which also included an investigation by Hankey into every one of the British intelligence services, made the Centre suspicious and – amid an investigation in Moscow into the credibility of the entire Cambridge Spy Ring – led to Cairncross having to explain why he had such extraordinarily valuable access.

The truth was that, as Hankey's private secretary, he shared exactly the same access as his boss and in addition saw many more documents that the minister had no need to read. 'Of course, I return the great majority and retain only a few really interesting ones and those which affect subjects he is interested in,' Cairncross said. Foreign Office reports and telegrams, secret SIS reports, the weekly operations reports of the Chiefs of Staff, the daily War Office record of operations and intelligence, the daily reports on the damage caused by German bombing and large numbers of other secret documents all passed across his desk, he said, adding that he was enclosing some more samples so that his detractors in Moscow could judge their value for themselves.

By far the most important information that came into Cairncross's possession while he was working for Hankey concerned the British Tube Alloys atomic weapons programme. At this stage of the war, the British programme was ahead of its American counterpart, the Manhattan Project. Hankey was chairman of a committee known as the Scientific Advisory Committee, which reviewed two reports summarising British research into the potential of the atomic bomb. These reports, 'Use of Uranium for a Bomb' and 'Use of Uranium as a Source of Power', were passed to the Americans, a transfer of information that helped to kick-start the US atomic weapons programme. But thanks to Cairncross, who was the committee's joint secretary, they were handed to the Russians, and formed the basis for their atomic weapons programme as well.

Hankey not only chaired the Scientific Advisory Committee but was also a member of the Tube Alloys Consultative Committee, which subsequently oversaw the British atomic weapons programme. His boss's position gave Cairncross extensive access to invaluable information that could help the Russians.

Cairncross's first report on Tube Alloys provided the minutes of a meeting of a cabinet sub-committee on 16 September 1941, which was told that: 'It is quite feasible to develop a uranium

bomb, especially if Imperial Chemical Industries (ICI) under-
takes to do this in the shortest possible time.' He also reported
that the armed forces chiefs of staff had decided four days later to
start 'the construction of a plant in Britain for the manufacture
of a uranium bomb'. A week later, Cairncross handed Gorsky the
two reports that had been passed to the Americans.

Pavel Fitin, the NKVD's head of foreign intelligence, cited
Igor Kurchatov, now regarded as 'the father of the Soviet atomic
bomb', as saying that the material provided by Cairncross
formed the basis for the Soviet atomic weapons programme. The
Russians gave atomic weapons research the rather apt code name
Enormoz. Fitin wrote:

> Extremely valuable information on the scientific developments
> of Enormoz reaches us from the London *Rezidentura*. The first
> material on Enormoz was received at the end of 1941 from
> John Cairncross. This material contained valuable and highly
> secret documentation, both on the essence of the Enormoz
> problem and on the measures taken by the British govern-
> ment to organise and develop the work on atomic energy. This
> material formed the point of departure for building the basis
> of, and organising the work on, the problem of atomic energy
> in our country.

Cairncross always insisted that he was not paid for his work for
the NKVD and only took the occasional payment when he
needed to settle an expensive bill, but it was during his time with
Hankey that he managed to acquire an apartment in the expensive Dolphin Square complex in London's Pimlico district, close
to Whitehall, having until this time lived in what Deutsch had
described as 'a cheap furnished room in a working-class district
of London'.

At the beginning of 1942, Cairncross was informed that he
was about to be called up, putting his work for the NKVD at
risk, but his ability to cultivate senior officials saved the day. He
befriended Colonel Freddie Nicholls, who as head of MI8, the
military intelligence section that dealt with code breaking, was

looking for good linguists to work at Bletchley Park. Gorsky told Moscow Centre:

> In the course of his professional duties, Liszt became acquainted with Nicholls and by rendering small services established friendly relations with him. During lunch at the Travellers' Club, Liszt complained to Nicholls that he was about to be called up by the Army, where he would be unable to use his knowledge of foreign languages. Nicholls started to persuade him to come and work in *Kurort*. After he received his call-up papers, Liszt told Nicholls about this, remained in his unit for one day and was then put at the disposal of the War Office which conditionally demobilised him and seconded him to *Kurort*.

Cairncross worked in Hut 3, which produced intelligence reports based on the deciphered German army and air force Enigma messages. He smuggled them out of Bletchley Park stuffed down the legs of his trousers and passed them to Gorsky, who even provided him with the cash to buy a second-hand car so that it was easier to transport them to London.

The most important material Cairncross gave the Russians during this period – what he referred to as his only worthwhile contribution to the Soviet cause – was a series of decrypted messages from the German commanders in 1943 laying out the complete plans for Operation Citadel, the Battle of Kursk, and a separate German report giving the full technical details of the new Tiger tank, which Hitler believed would turn the tide in Germany's favour.

The information was crucial to the Russian victory in what was to be the decisive battle on the Eastern Front and arguably one of the most decisive battles in the war against Germany.

There is no reason to doubt that the material Cairncross provided to the Russians had a significant influence on the war effort. A brief biography of Fitin published by the SVR highlights the Bletchley Park intelligence on the German preparations for the Battle of Kursk as one of Fitin's main achievements. Yet

Cairncross was wrong to assume the British were not passing this intelligence to Moscow. They were, but in a sanitised form that did not reveal the source for fear that Bletchley Park's ability to break the German high-grade ciphers, not just the Enigma ciphers but also the Tunny teleprinter ciphers, might leak to the Germans with catastrophic results. It would only have taken a few relatively simple changes to the German cipher systems to prevent their being broken, robbing the Allies of a vital source of intelligence. Cairncross put that source at grave risk. Nevertheless, it is undoubtedly the case that Stalin distrusted the information he received from the British, so Cairncross played an important role in passing the raw intelligence to Moscow, thereby persuading the Soviet leader that the British were telling him the truth.

The difficult hours at Bletchley Park led Cairncross to ask for a transfer to SIS. It is not clear why the NKVD backed his move to Section V of SIS, given that Kim Philby was already based there and passing the Russians everything he could lay his hands on. However, Cairncross was in a far better position to provide unique intelligence once he was moved to Section I of SIS, which dealt with political intelligence. The reports he produced there included the section's correspondence with Cecil Barclay, the SIS Head of Station in Moscow.

Although Cairncross's motive for working for Moscow continued to be what Gorsky described as 'our ideology', he was also paid for the intelligence and in November 1944 the NKVD provided him with a £250 bonus to celebrate the anniversary of the Bolshevik revolution. 'I am delighted that our friends should have thought our services worthy of recognition and am proud to have contributed something to the victories which have almost cleared the Soviet soil of the invaders,' Cairncross wrote in a thank you letter. 'The premium presented to me is of the most generous nature, and I shall try to express my gratitude for it by redoubled efforts in the future.'

Cairncross left SIS in June 1945, returning to the Treasury, but not before giving the Russians details of British agents in Finland, Sweden, Denmark, Spain, Portugal and South America, and plans to monitor Russian radio relay traffic. Cairncross always claimed that the files that crossed his desk in the Treasury 'were of a purely routine, non-secret nature' and that the information he passed the Russians was 'innocuous', but in fact one former Treasury colleague recalled that during the summer and autumn of 1945 Cairncross was responsible for authorising funding for research into atomic, biological and chemical weapons, guided weapons, submarines, torpedoes and radar. 'He therefore had access to some of the most sensitive of all British defence secrets,' the former colleague said. 'He knew what expenditure was planned before it happened and could legitimately ask for as much detail about plans as thought necessary for the Treasury to give its approval.'

The defection of Igor Gouzenko, a cipher clerk in the Soviet embassy in the Canadian capital Ottawa, led to the Russians suspending links with Cairncross. For three years, he was inactive as a spy. But in mid 1948 he was reactivated by Yuri Modin, the KGB's new London *Rezident*, after Burgess reported that Cairncross was working in the Treasury department dealing with top-secret defence estimates and details of Britain's contribution to the fledgling NATO alliance. Some of the documents he supplied during this period ran to more than 100 pages, one former KGB officer said.

Now code-named Karel, Cairncross handed over 'a large quantity of important documents' regarding Britain's defences, Modin said. 'Documents of the highest secrecy pass through his hands.' Asked in early 1949 to find out whether the British were still able to break Soviet ciphers, Cairncross invited Henry Dryden, a former colleague at Bletchley Park who was still working for GCHQ, to lunch at the Travellers Club. 'In the middle of the meal, he disconcertingly asked: "Are we still reading Russian ciphers?",' Dryden said. 'I had no first-hand knowledge of any current work on Russian and the only off-putting response I could think of, on the spur of the moment, was to shake my head and mutter "one-time".' This was a reference to the theoretically unbreakable one-time pad cipher system the Russians were using.

After the disappearance of Burgess and Maclean in May 1951, MI5 searched Burgess's flat and, among a collection of classified documents, found one with an accompanying note written by

Cairncross that referred to the discussions between Stalin and Benes over the 1939 invasion of Czechoslovakia. He was followed to a meeting with Modin, but the Russian spotted the MI5 watchers and aborted the meeting. 'As soon as I got back to the embassy, I dispatched a report to Moscow, expressing my personal view that the British secret service would continue to hound Cairncross in the foreseeable future,' Modin later wrote. 'The answer came back promptly. I was to cease working with him altogether.'

Cairncross was interrogated by MI5, but maintained that, although he did have communist sympathies, his relationship with Burgess was entirely innocent and he had no connection with espionage. He admitted innocently passing a secret document to Burgess and, damned as a security risk, he resigned from the Civil Service. But in the absence of any convincing evidence against him, a prosecution was impossible.

He left Britain, initially working as a journalist in Italy and Thailand before briefly becoming an academic at Western Reserve University, Cleveland, Ohio. When Philby defected to Moscow in 1963, MI5 reopened its mole-hunt and Cairncross was again questioned. This time he made a partial confession, identifying eight KGB officers and even agreeing to get back in contact with the KGB as a potential double agent, but to the FBI's intense irritation, the Immigration and Naturalisation Service insisted that he be expelled from the USA because of his communist past. His identity as the so-called Fifth Man in the Cambridge Spy Ring was only publicly confirmed in 1990, by the Soviet defector Oleg Gordievsky. By this time, Cairncross was living in the south of France. He wrote his memoirs and moved back to Britain in 1995, shortly before his death. In all that time, he did not apparently waver from his strong ideological conviction that spying for the Russians had been the right thing to do.

★★★

The Cuban intelligence service, the *Dirección Generalde Inteligencia* (DGI), specifically targeted agents whose moral opposition to US policy in Central America, particularly during the Reagan era, made them susceptible to recruitment. This enabled it to attract a number of high-profile agents, including one of the most damaging traitors ever to serve inside the US intelligence services. Ana Belén Montes, a Hispanic American angered by Reagan's policy in Central America, was a Cuban agent-in-place inside the Defense Intelligence Agency (DIA) for sixteen years.

Ana Montes was born in February 1957 on a US military base in Nurnberg, Germany, where her father, Alberto, was an army psychiatrist. Her parents were from Puerto Rico and she was the eldest of four children. When her father left the army, the family settled in Towson, just outside Baltimore, where Alberto Montes set up a successful private practice. He was a very strict man and his children were frequently punished with a leather belt. When Ana was 19, her mother divorced him. A secret CIA psychological assessment of Ana Montes subsequently concluded that her father's abusive behaviour 'made her intolerant of power differentials, led her to identify with the less powerful, and solidified her desire to retaliate against authoritarian figures'.

Montes studied international relations at the University of Virginia. Part of her course was spent in Spain and while there, under the influence of a left-wing boyfriend, she took an active part in anti-American demonstrations. 'After every protest, Ana used to explain to me the "atrocities" that the US government used to do to other countries,' one fellow student recalled. 'She was already so torn.'

After graduation, Montes went to Puerto Rico, hoping to make a life there, but could not find a job that matched her ambitions. In 1979, she took a post in Washington DC at the Department of Justice, initially as a clerk typist before becoming a para-legal working on appeals for the release of government information, a post for which she was granted security clearance to read top-secret documents.

At the same time, she took a part-time master's degree at the School of Advanced International Studies at Johns Hopkins University. There, she made no secret of her opposition to the Reagan administration's policies in Central America and particularly its support of the Contra rebels who were fighting the Sandinista government in Nicaragua, a view that was widely held by her tutors and fellow students. 'It was in this atmosphere that she developed a sense of moral outrage at the US participation in the hostilities in Nicaragua,' according to the Pentagon investigation into her career as a Cuban spy. 'She saw the United States as waging a war against that country, killing innocent people, and attempting to overthrow a legitimate government.'

The DGI had talent spotters, or 'access agents', at all the leading US universities, looking for politically motivated students with the ability to go on to take prominent positions in government. Montes was the ideal candidate. Not only did she already work in a responsible role in government, she already had clearance to see top-secret material.

It did not take long for her to be spotted by a DGI access agent, who made a 'soft pitch', not raising the possibility that she might become a Cuban spy, but simply asking if she would be willing to meet some friends who wanted some news reports about Nicaragua translated from Spanish into English. When she agreed, the access agent introduced her to a DGI intelligence officer based at the Cuban Mission to the UN in New York. The Cubans worked closely with their Russian and East German counterparts and used a similar approach. The DGI officer asked her whether she might be willing to provide them with any information that passed across her desk that would help the Sandinista government defeat the Contras. The recruitment focused solely on the issue that had fuelled her anger with US policy, the military backing for a right-wing group that was trying to overthrow a legitimate government purely because it was left-wing. They 'tried to appeal to my conviction that what I was doing was right', Montes said, and she didn't hesitate. According to the CIA psychological assessment, 'her handlers assessed her vulnerabilities and exploited her psychological needs, ideology, and personality ... to recruit her and keep her motivated to work for Havana'.

Montes flew to Cuba in March 1985, covering her tracks by flying first to Madrid, and then to Prague using a false Cuban passport, before flying on to Havana, where she was briefed by senior officers on her mission and taught tradecraft and security, including secret communications and counter-surveillance techniques. On her return to Washington, she began applying for other government posts that had better access to information that would be useful to the Cubans and in September 1985 she obtained a post as a junior intelligence analyst in the DIA department working on Latin America. Her first job was working on El Salvador and Guatemala, both Central American countries where proxy wars were going on between right-wing governments backed by the Reagan administration and left-wing guerrillas supported by the Cubans.

She now had access to top-secret material on the US special operations forces and CIA personnel on the ground in both countries and on what the Americans knew about the left-wing guerrillas and their Cuban advisers. Although it was not her specific responsibility, she would also have had access to material on the conflict between the Sandinista government and the Contras, including details of US special operations involvement and agents inside the rebel forces and their Cuban support forces. In early 1987, she also spent five weeks in El Salvador and a week in Guatemala being briefed on US support operations for the governments of Jose Napoleon Duarte and Vinicio Cerezo. Michelle van Cleave, who as National Counterintelligence Executive oversaw the damage assessment report on the Montes case, told Congress that it was 'likely that the information she passed [to Cuba] contributed to the death and injury of America and pro-American forces in Latin America'.

Initially, Montes held meetings with her Cuban handler at restaurants in New York, and was accompanied to the first two meetings by her initial contact, but she soon became concerned that her frequent train journeys to New York would raise suspicions among colleagues and asked the Cubans to make her handler an illegal, a DGI officer operating under cover who was not associated with the Cuban government and could meet her in Washington. They would meet in the US capital once every two to three weeks, usually at the weekend, normally in restaurants. If either she or her handler needed a meeting that was not on the agreed schedule, they would page each other using a public telephone. There were various pager codes requesting or cancelling meetings or signifying that an urgent report needed to be collected. Montes did not use payphones too obviously close to her home; she walked a short distance away to the Smithsonian National Zoo to use one there or travelled further north to phone booths outside a department store in Chevy Chase and the Friendship Heights metro station. She never went direct to the payphone; she always approached it carefully via a circuitous route to ensure she was not under surveillance. The pager numbers and codes were all kept on water-soluble paper that could just be dropped down the toilet and disappear without flushing.

When she was not using them, Montes kept all the codes and instructions given to her by her handlers in a safety deposit box at her bank. Montes was extremely careful to avoid doing anything that might lead security officers or colleagues to become suspicious of her. She never removed documents from her office in the DIA's headquarters at Washington's Bolling Air Force Base. She memorised the information in the reports and wrote it down or typed it into her computer once she got home. For the most part, she only sought access to files that she could justify seeing for the work she was doing, and deliberately refrained from expressing her personal views on US policy in Central America. She also tried to ensure that no matter how much she tailored her reports to help the Cubans, it could always be justified by the available intelligence. She refused to take any money from the Cubans, other than for expenses, and lived very frugally. She had a modest apartment and drove a small, economical Toyota car. She limited any socialising with colleagues to ensure that no one showed any interest in her personal life. 'She was very private,' a former colleague said. 'She never attended parties. When we had office parties, she might show up for only a little while.' She was given the nickname, '*La Otra*', the Spanish word for outsider. In many ways, she was the perfect spy.

Every few years, Montes would travel to Cuba – using the same circuitous route via Europe and several different false passports – to brief senior DGI officers and be briefed herself on what material really interested the Cubans. It was not just information on the US and Central America that they wanted to see. They were also interested in top-secret US intelligence programmes on which she had been briefed that had a much wider role. These would be of interest to the Cubans' main intelligence partners, the Russians, thereby ensuring they continued to receive high-grade intelligence in return from the KGB and its post-Soviet successors.

Montes was regarded by her bosses as 'a stellar employee'. She produced detailed reports on the situations in El Salvador and Guatemala that were highly praised by the members of the administration, by senior military officers and by other parts of the intelligence community. Then, in 1990, she was put in charge of the Nicaragua desk. It was her dream job. But ironically, the Sandinista leader Daniel Ortega lost the presidential elections in February of that year and was replaced by the National Opposition Union candidate Violeta Chamorro, thereby removing the US interference in Nicaragua that had fuelled her anger and facilitated her recruitment. When Chamorro visited Washington in 1991, Montes was chosen to brief her on the threats to her government. Despite the changes to the political situation in Nicaragua, Montes continued to provide the Cubans with intelligence on the Chamorro government, while at the same time seeking to move to a role on the Cuba desk where she would be of far more use to her DGI controllers. She later claimed that her 'moral realignment' from spying for Cuba to counter US interference in Nicaragua to helping the Cubans directly was a result of her fear that, with the reduction of Russian assistance that followed the collapse of the Soviet Bloc, the US might find a pretext with which to invade Cuba.

Montes was appointed as a senior analyst on Cuba in February 1993 and, thanks to her understanding of the country and its political system, acquired over seven years of working for the DGI and several clandestine visits to Havana, was soon seen as the leading analyst, briefing the National Security Council and the Joint Chiefs of Staff on the threat from Cuba and its future political direction following the break-up of Warsaw Pact. She made several official visits to Cuba during this period on behalf of the US intelligence community, including one funded by the CIA-run Center for the Study of Intelligence, quite apart from her clandestine visits to Havana to meet with senior Cuban intelligence officers.

During the nine years she worked on the Cuban problem, Montes passed virtually everything she could to Havana. By the mid 1990s, the DGI and its agents abroad used relatively sophisticated computer encryption systems. Montes simply wrote her reports in plain text on to her laptop computer and it was automatically encrypted. She then copied the encrypted reports on to floppy disks, which she passed to her handler. The DGI passed messages to her in five-figure enciphered messages read out by a woman on a specified short-wave frequency. The messages to each agent were carefully timed, with each individual message introduced with the words '*Attencion! Attencion!*' Montes simply had to listen at the scheduled time, type the numbers into a computer programme installed on her laptop and the DGI messages appeared on the screen in plain text.

She compromised US agents in Cuba and every intelligence collection programme targeted against the Cubans, including the most sophisticated electronic and signals intelligence systems, some of them covertly planted in Cuba by US intelligence and special forces operatives. Any data captured by the systems was therefore automatically suspect. She also told the Cubans everything that the Americans knew about their most secret bases and reported the imminent arrivals of at least four different US intelligence officers who visited the island, compromising any activity they carried out. (The Cubans did not arrest the US intelligence officers or give them any indication that they knew who they were.) Montes was now regarded as one of the DIA's top intelligence analysts but she repeatedly refused promotion in order to remain on the Cuban desk and in a prime position to serve her Cuban masters. There was only one minor hiccough in 1996 when a colleague reported his concerns over what he regarded as 'aggressive' attempts by Montes to see material to which she did not need to have access. The complaint was investigated but

Montes was too well regarded within the DIA and she was ruled innocent of any wrongdoing.

Michelle van Cleave said that, aside from the intelligence she provided to Cuba, and despite Montes's efforts to back up her judgements with intelligence, the damage assessment investigation found that she operated as 'an agent of influence' on behalf of Cuba and that what she said in her analysis or in discussions with other intelligence officers and policymakers was 'coloured by her loyalties to Cuba'. Although the significance at the time was not recognised, this element of her work on behalf of Cuba burst into the public domain in early 1998, when a DIA report written largely by Montes, although she was never named, was attacked in Congress for 'blatantly minimising' the threat from Cuba and had to be toughened up by Pentagon chiefs.

The report, written in November 1997, concluded that the disintegration of the Soviet Bloc in 1989 triggered a profound deterioration of the Cuban Revolutionary Armed Forces and that Castro's regime posed a 'negligible' military threat to the US. 'At present, Cuba does not pose a significant military threat to the US or to other countries in the region,' the report said, adding that it had 'little motivation to engage in military activity beyond defence of its territory and political system'. Ironically, the report did say quite honestly that Cuba's 'intelligence and counterintelligence systems directed at the United States appear to have suffered little degradation'.

Unknown to Montes, the FBI was already looking for a Cuban agent inside the US government. In May 1996, Miguel Mir, a Cuban intelligence officer based at the UN Mission, defected to the United States. A year earlier, in early 1995, he had driven Luis Carrera, a senior DGI case officer, to Washington for a meeting with an agent. During the journey, Carrera bragged that he was running 'a very important person who works at the highest levels of the American government'. Mir told the US officials who debriefed him and an investigation was put in place to try to find the mole.

The inquiry team had what seemed at the time to be limited assistance from a CIA agent. DGI officer Jose Cohen Valdes decided in 1994 to defect to the United States. In an attempt to boost his value to the CIA, he persuaded several colleagues to defect with him. One of them was Rolando Sarraff Trujillo, who worked in the section that created the encryption systems agents such as Montes used to communicate with their handlers. The information Cohen Valdes was providing was now so valuable that the CIA persuaded him to stay in Cuba as an 'agent-in-place'. As an incentive, he was paid a large sum of money, which he spent carelessly, and both he and Sarraff Trujillo were put under surveillance. Cohen Valdes realised that he was under suspicion and was swiftly extracted, along with one of the other would-be defectors. Sarraff Trujillo was not so lucky. He was arrested and jailed, and only released in a 2014 spy swap. But the intelligence he had provided on communications encryption techniques allowed US officials to read some of the messages between Luis Carrera and his agent, providing small details that might help identify the mole, including the fact that at the end of 1996, the agent bought a reconditioned Toshiba Satellite laptop. Nevertheless, the information the FBI had was not enough to narrow down the suspects and the mole-hunt ran into the sand.

In September 2000, frustrated by the lack of progress, and with no idea which department of government the traitor worked for, one of the inquiry team tipped off the DIA security staff in the hope that they might be able to provide more information. The DIA launched its own investigation and Ana Montes soon came up as a possible match for the agent, in large part as a result of the 1996 complaint over her 'aggressive' attempts to obtain intelligence she had no reason to see. Montes became the focus of the investigation and eventually, after initially dismissing the DIA suspicions, the FBI put her under surveillance. Montes was about to be handed a top promotion to the National Intelligence Council, which was based at Langley and advised the head of the CIA on all intelligence operations. The promotion was quietly shelved.

FBI officers tracked Montes going to public payphones by circuitous routes in a way that strongly suggested classic counter-surveillance techniques. They searched her bank records and discovered that in November 1996 she opened a credit account at the Alexandria branch of the CompuSave office supplies company to buy a 'refurb' Toshiba Satellite laptop. The FBI sent in a 'black bag' team to surreptitiously search her apartment and copy the laptop's hard drive. Although Montes had deleted her communications with Havana, the files were still recoverable from the hard drive, including precise instructions on how to encrypt her reports.

The FBI wanted to watch her and track all her contacts in the hope of finding more Cuban agents, but in the wake of 9/11, with Montes now holding a senior role in the DIA, there were concerns that US operations against al-Qaeda and the Taliban in Afghanistan might be compromised. She was arrested on 21 September 2001 and agreed a deal under which she pleaded guilty to one charge of conspiracy to commit espionage and briefed the damage assessment team on what she had passed to the Cubans. In return she received a twenty-five-year prison term rather than a death sentence.

Michelle van Cleave said the investigation into how much damage Montes had done took three years to complete. 'Few people realise the extent of the damage her sixteen years of meticulous espionage caused this country, including putting lives at risk,' van Cleave said. 'Montes was one of the most damaging spies in US history.'

The separate Pentagon investigation found that her 'traitorous decision to betray her country was based on a combination of factors including an ingrained hostility toward US policy on Latin America; and a misguided sense of morality.'

In a statement ahead of sentencing, Montes told the court that she had betrayed her country because she believed it was the right thing to do:

> I obeyed my conscience rather than the law. I believe our government's policy towards Cuba is cruel and unfair and I felt morally obligated to help the island defend itself from our efforts to impose our values and our political system on it. My way of responding to our Cuba policy may have been morally wrong. Perhaps Cuba's right to exist free of political and

economic coercion did not justify giving the island classified information to help it defend itself. I can only say that I did what I thought right to counter a grave injustice.

★★★

In the twenty-first century, ideologically motivated espionage has come in new forms. The appeal of Islamist extremism to young people who have become radicalised on internet websites or in mosques across Europe is the modern-day equivalent of the idealistic belief in a communist utopia that persuaded people such as Edith Tudor-Hart and John Cairncross that Stalin's Russia offered the answer to the failures of capitalist society. The age groups of those involved are broadly similar, most of them being in their mid twenties. Supporting groups that include Islamic State appears to its recruits to offer the same combination of a protest against the establishment and the prospect of a better, more peaceful world.

The belief that Islamic State's brutality might offer a route to peace is clearly as nonsensical as the idea that Stalin's Russia was utopia, but many recruits to Islamic State and groups like it have fallen for the argument peddled by extremist websites and radical imams that by travelling to Syria to help eliminate non-believers they could help cleanse the world. Once they got there, many of them realised their mistake and tried to return. Since Islamic State kills deserters and the authorities in their own country now saw them as terrorists, this was difficult, but some of them have nonetheless found a way out.

The increasing pressure on Islamic State in Syria and Iraq from a number of different players, led by the Americans, made the group desperate for new recruits, making it easier for intelligence agents to penetrate. A small number of extraordinarily brave Western agents have infiltrated Islamic State, either by allowing themselves to be recruited or because, having returned home disillusioned, they have been persuaded to go back as agents for the intelligence services of their own country. Just as they were originally persuaded that eliminating 'infidels' was the right thing to do, having seen the reality on the ground they have been convinced that helping to bring Islamic State down is the right thing to do.

Alex Younger, the 'Chief' of MI6 (or 'C'), revealed in late 2016 that the British secret service had agents working on the streets of Raqqa, the then capital of Islamic State (the group being also known by the derogatory acronym Daesh). 'I will not seek to hide the challenges that come with work against an organisation as murderously efficient as Daesh,' Younger said. 'Some of our agents operate in the most dangerous and hostile environments on earth. They know that the result of being identified as an MI6 agent could be their death. But they do what they do because they believe in protecting their country and religion from the evil that Daesh and other terrorist organisations represent.'

One of those MI6 agents played a vital role in the elimination of the Islamic State executioner known as Jihadi John, who became infamous as a result of a series of videos depicting the beheadings of Western hostages. Jihadi John's real name was Mohammed Emwazi. He was born in Kuwait, but when he was 6 his family moved to London, where the young Mohammed lived a comfortable middle-class life in an affluent area of northwest London. A diligent young man, he studied computing at Westminster College, where he was radicalised by fellow students.

After graduation, Emwazi attempted to go to Somalia to join the fundamentalist Islamic group al-Shabaab. He and a friend flew via Tanzania but were arrested and deported to the Netherlands, where Emwazi was interrogated by MI5. He was eventually released for lack of evidence but, at the end of 2012, he went to Syria, telling his parents he was going there as an aid worker. In fact, he was joining the Islamic State as one of an increasing number of Western Muslims attracted by the organisation's supposed idealism and success in fighting against the Iraqi and Syrian regimes.

The videos of innocent hostages being beheaded turned Emwazi into the public face of Islamic State, and both David Cameron and Barack Obama, who were the then British Prime Minister and the US President respectively, vowed to track him down. A joint US and British special operations forces team was singling out Islamic State leaders in order to take them out, either in 'snatch' raids or by using Hellfire missiles fired from drones, but people such as Emwazi were hard to find. He was a computer expert and too aware of the dangers involved in using a phone or the internet. He disappeared from the radar. Stories were put about that he had fled Syria and was now in Libya. He had not. It was disinformation to try to confuse the US and British intelligence services who were trying to track him down.

The British and the Americans needed an agent inside Islamic State who could lead them to Emwazi, a human source on the ground to get close to him and report his precise location. The best person would be someone who knew him, one of those who had been part of Islamic State but was now looking for a way out. MI6 began sifting through the files on foreign fighters who had returned to Europe and eventually selected one who knew Emwazi personally and – in return for being given a new life away from the brutality of Islamic State – was prepared to help track him down.

The agent went back to Syria and found Emwazi hiding out in Raqqa. On 12 November 2015, the agent reported the terrorist's location back to his MI6 handler. Emwazi was in a building sandwiched between the city's Islamic Courts and Clocktower Square, the spot where the group's executions took place. A US spy satellite homed in on the building and US Reaper drones began circling the skies above Raqqa like hawks, placing Emwazi's hideout under a 'persistent stare', and waiting for him to come out. Everyone in Raqqa would have known the drones were up there. They would have heard them even if they couldn't see them. Emwazi remained inside the building all day, hoping that once it was dark he could sneak away without being spotted.

It was just nine minutes to midnight when Emwazi hurried out of the building to a waiting car. He was trying to get out of the city, accompanied by a team of bodyguards. Even as he opened the car door, a Hellfire missile fired by an American Reaper drone several thousand metres above Raqqa was heading towards him at close to 1,600kmh (1,000mph). He would have barely realised something was wrong before he was dead. The missile destroyed the car, leaving little evidence that Jihadi John and his friends had ever existed. The Pentagon said he had been 'evaporated'. David Cameron said Emwazi had been intent on murdering many more people. The missile strike was 'an act of self-defence', the British Prime Minister said. 'It was the right thing to do.'

Chapter 8

UNCONSCIOUS AGENTS

Agent motivation is an extraordinarily complex issue. This book has sought to identify a number of different motivations, and to place agents into one of the different compartments: sex, money, patriotism, revenge, ego, and ideology. Often, though, there is actually no single compartment into which any one agent fits, no single reason for betrayal. Aldrich Ames is a prime example. On the face of it, the main reason 'The $2 million Spy' betrayed his country was money. This book has argued that his treachery had far more to do with ego, with Ames driven by the need to prove those who had decided that he, and his father, were not quite up to the job wrong. Ames needed to prove to himself that he was a brilliant spy, a real James Bond, and the Russians gave him the opportunity to do so.

The reality is that there are often multiple reasons as to why spies spy. Ames was both greedy and egotistical, so what was his principal motivation? Money or ego? Did Gabi Gast spy for love or was her inspiration, as Markus Wolf claimed, ideology – a moral belief in communism as the right way forward? Or did the first motivation merge into the second later in her career as a spy? Penkovsky claimed to have realised the failings of communism and that this was why he betrayed the Russians, but it is very clear that his prime motivation was revenge rather than ideology. He should be excused this. He was not alone in seeking to justify his real motives with a half-truth. Many agents do this, often simply in order to justify their betrayal to themselves. Very few Soviet intelligence officers ever crossed the lines and said they had come to the West because they would enjoy a much better lifestyle there. It was almost always a result of a realisation that Soviet-style communism was evil. How many of them were actually telling the truth is a moot point.

Motivation frequently changes over time; an agent who initially betrays his or her country for one reason will often end up spying for a completely different one, as the cases of at least two of the Cambridge Spies demonstrate all too well. They were recruited in the 1930s. The 1929 economic crash and the inequities caused by the British class system seemed to shine a light on Stalin's Soviet Union as the 'brave new world' of the future. Kim Philby, Donald Maclean, Guy Burgess, Anthony Blunt and John Cairncross all saw the rise of fascism as the disaster it turned out to be and believed that communism offered a better way forward. They were not alone in that belief, but for most people the illusion died in 1939 when Stalin threw his lot in with Hitler. What happened to 'the war on fascism' now? At that stage, most of those who had flirted with communism during the 1930s realised their mistake. But for the Cambridge Spies there was no turning back. The KGB had evidence of their betrayal and was ready and willing to release it if they did not do as they were told.

Maclean clearly struggled to cope with the contradictions, although he steadfastly continued to fight for the communist cause. Burgess was different; he desperately needed to be part of something, and constantly sought to persuade his KGB controllers that he was a valuable source of intelligence. Blunt's role as an MI5 officer was more discreet, protecting the other four, and sticking to the cause right or wrong. The most revealing responses came from Philby and Cairncross. Both men continued to spy for the KGB, providing everything they could, no matter how damaging. But in the end, it was no longer simply about their belief in communism; it was as much about their own vanity, their own arrogance, their belief that they knew better than anyone else what was the right thing to do. Cairncross later lied shamelessly about what he had done, trying to suggest that he had passed Moscow nothing that was damaging to the West. In truth, he not only gave the Russians the head-start they needed to produce an atomic bomb by passing them the details of the British atomic weapons programme, he also risked the Enigma secret, deciding for himself that this was the right thing to do, despite knowing that it was the Allies' trump card against the Germans.

Philby took charge of the MI6 Soviet section in the immediate aftermath of the Second World War and was aware of joint Anglo–American operations to send hundreds of émigrés into the Ukraine, the Baltic Republics, Poland and Albania to mount resistance operations against the Russians. Tipped off by their man in London, the KGB was waiting. Hundreds of men whose only crime was to believe their country should be free of the Soviet yoke were shot as a direct result of his treachery. In 1947, Philby was posted as MI6 head of station in Turkey, where he controlled similar operations into the southern Soviet republics of Georgia and Armenia. Yet again, none of those sent in ever came back, dispatched to their death by a man who was spying in the end not for a cause, but because he could.

***

Very few agents were ever more conscious of the damage they were doing, or the deaths they were causing, than Philby, but there is another kind of agent, one who is not even aware that he or she is being used as an agent. This is the 'unconscious agent', known to the Americans as an 'unwitting agent', someone who is being used by an intelligence service in order to obtain information they need or to achieve some other aim, and so influence a situation in a way that benefits the service's country or cause.

'Unconscious agents are an interesting category – especially from the point of view of agent motivation,' one former MI6 officer said. 'For an intelligence officer, the aim is to get someone to do what he wants and thus to "control" him. Control rather than consciousness is the key factor and an unconscious agent has several advantages. It is obviously easier, for example, in extremis, to deny that one has recruited him – thus facilitating deniability.'

The Russian intelligence services' campaign to influence the 2016 US Presidential Elections was probably the most infamous and certainly one of the most obvious use of 'unconscious agents' in recent times, with a large number of people associated with Donald Trump's campaign used in this way as part of an 'influence operation' designed to ensure Trump won the presidency, or perhaps more to the point, that Hillary Clinton did not win. Russian President Vladimir Putin was apparently concerned that, if elected, Clinton would adopt the same tough stance she had taken against his regime during her time as Barack Obama's Secretary of State.

The Russians have been adept at running what they call 'Active Measures' (*aktivnye meropriyatia*) to confuse, deceive, and influence the West since the time of the Czars. Operations by the Russian *Okhrana* to discredit émigré opponents in London form the backdrop for Joseph Conrad's 1907 novel *The Secret Agent*. When the Bolsheviks came to power, their own intelligence services continued the tradition, penetrating and manipulating Russian émigré organisations abroad. One such group, known as The Trust, was used in 1925 to entice Sydney Reilly, the so-called 'Ace of Spies', to Russia, where he was interrogated and then murdered.

Yet, despite this long history, the full complexity of such operations was not understood by the Western intelligence agencies until the 1980s when several KGB 'Active Measures' experts defected, at a time when the Soviets were pursuing continued efforts to build up the multiple conspiracy theories over the assassination of President John F. Kennedy while also mounting extensive operations to discredit the introduction of US cruise missiles into Europe.

'Active Measures' involve the use of a large number of different capabilities to exert influence over the political world of a target country and achieve aims favourable to Russia. They employ multiple techniques, usually in parallel and completely at random, to seek various ways of achieving the same aims – deception, disinformation, and confusion. This ensures that they influence the widest possible audience. The techniques include covert action (such as false-flag operations) to discredit opponents, and the exploitation of front organisations, either co-opted, often unconsciously, or created for the purpose. They involve substantial use of agents inside the target country – the large majority of them 'unconscious' agents – and include the release of disinformation, fake news, linked to, or interwoven with genuine, easily verifiable facts. The expansion of news and information sources via the internet and the widespread use of mobile telephones to access social networks has greatly increased their effectiveness.

The operation to disrupt the US presidential elections was initially confined to an influence operation by the Internet Research Agency (IRA) targeting US social media and in particular Facebook, Twitter, YouTube and Instagram. The IRA was ostensibly a privately funded Russian 'troll farm'. It was based in St Petersburg and was set up in 2013 by Yevgeny Prigozhin, a multi-millionaire Russian businessman who had made his money from mass-market restaurants. Prigozhin was so close to the Russian President he was known as 'Putin's Chef'. Whether he actually provided the funding for the IRA is unclear but there is no doubt at all that it was run like a classic Russian intelligence operation and, privately funded or not, it was to form a key part of the Russian intelligence operation to prevent Clinton winning the presidential election.

In June 2014, Aleksandra Krylova, a senior manager at the IRA, went on an 'intelligence-gathering mission' to the US with her colleague Anna Bogacheva, during which they visited Nevada, California, New Mexico, Colorado, Illinois, Michigan, Louisiana, Texas, and New York to gather ideas for social media webpages of fictitious organisations that would focus on issues ranging from right-wing opponents of immigration, through Black Lives Matter, to both Christian and Muslim religious concerns. They also obtained the use of computer infrastructure that would allow them to create Virtual Private Networks (VPNs) inside the US to disguise the fact that they were operating from Russia. They used intelligence terms throughout, discussing potential 'evacuation scenarios' should their mission be blown and producing a final 'intelligence report' on their return.

The IRA then employed teams of operators working around the clock to create social media accounts and group pages that addressed the various divisive US political and social issues identified by Krylova and Bogacheva on their tour of the US. Every one of these social media pages was designed to look like it was run by US activists. The IRA operators encouraged US fans of the pages to take an active part in their administration – as 'unconscious agents' – and used multiple US personas, some fake and some stolen, to post material that would help to inflame passions and increase the webpage audiences.

Even before Hillary Clinton announced her candidature for the Presidency in April 2015, the IRA's operators were required to intersperse their posts with criticism of her, to the point where they were admonished if their anti-Hillary posts did not reach the required level. After the IRA's operations were terminated in 2017, Facebook discovered that pages controlled by the IRA had reached at least 29 million people in the US and that the number of individual Americans actually reached might be as high as 126 million, two-fifths of the US population.

At the same time as the IRA was creating its web of social media pages to influence the views of US voters, the Russian Federal Security Service, the FSB, and the GRU, Russian military intelligence, were preparing the two other major strands of the 'Active Measures' operation in the full knowledge that its aim was to prevent Clinton becoming president.

In February 2016, Putin gave the go-ahead for a full-scale 'Active Measures' operation. Almost immediately, the IRA-controlled webpages stepped up their criticism of Clinton and began openly backing Trump while the GRU began operations to hack into the computers of Clinton's campaign committee and the Democratic National Committee (DNC), the Democratic Party's administrative body. The GRU 'Fancy Bear' cyber teams, led by Military Unit 21265, which specialises in hacking foreign government organisations, used human agents on the ground – largely among the Russian émigré community in America – to help them hack into the DNC and campaign committee computers.

When people think of hacking, they imagine a Hollywood image of a lone, obsessive geek sat behind a row of computers with strings of computer codes cascading down each of the screens. Russian cyber operations are far more sophisticated than that. Even a professional cyber-criminal will sometimes need human intelligence to make the initial breakthrough or progress through the target systems. The more information that is available to the hacker, the quicker he or she can take control of those systems and ensure that the attack goes undetected. This will frequently involve the use of human agents obtaining intelligence on the ground to assist the professional hackers to break into the target computer systems.

Christopher Steele, a former SIS Russian specialist turned private intelligence operative, began tracking the Russian efforts to interfere in the elections in mid 2016. Steele had run agents for SIS in Moscow and gone on to control operations against the Russians from London. He was a fully paid-up member of what the old SIS called 'the Master Race', the Russian specialists who had run the service during the Cold War. Steele left SIS in 2009 to set up Orbis Business Intelligence, a London-based company that gathered intelligence and provided advice for companies dealing with or operating in Russia. The US company Fusion GPS, which had been employed by the Democrats to investigate the truth about Russia and Trump, brought in Steele.

His sources told him that Russian diplomats based at the embassy in Washington and at consulates elsewhere in the US had organised funding for the Russian agents involved in the hacking operation who were largely Russians émigrés living in the US and included sources with access to the Democratic Party offices. The agents were a mix of human intelligence informants and 'offensive cyber-operators'. The money was handed out under cover of supposed Russian armed forces pension payments to ethnic Russian veterans living in the United States. The operation 'depended on key people in the US Russian émigré community for its success,' one source told Steele. 'Tens of thousands of dollars were involved.'

The GRU hackers used standard 'spear phishing' techniques to attack the internal emails of more than a dozen people working on the Clinton presidential bid, including campaign chairman John Podesta. The lists of emails, which were for use only on the campaign committee and DNC systems and not publicly available, were almost certainly stolen by Russian agents who infiltrated the campaign offices to give the hackers the starting point they needed. Like the IRA operations, the GRU used computer systems based in the US – in the case of the hackers in Arizona – to prevent their operations being traced back to Russia. Crucially, they obtained the log-in details of key system administrators who had unrestricted access to the DNC systems and by the beginning of June they had hacked into the computer systems of both the DNC and the campaign committee, stealing hundreds of thousands of documents and emails.

The DNC announced on 14 June 2016 that its computer systems had been hacked, with a number of documents believed to have been stolen. The next day the GRU began publishing excerpts from the stolen data – carefully salted with embarrassing fake information – through two fictitious online personas, a website called 'DCLeaks' and a mysterious self-styled Romanian hacker called 'Guccifer 2.0'. WikiLeaks swiftly contacted DCLeaks offering to give the stolen data 'a much higher impact'.

The GRU passed a collection of thousands of emails and documents hacked from the DNC's computers to WikiLeaks in July 2016. Some of the emails showed Democratic Party bosses working to ensure Clinton's nomination rather than that of her former rival, Bernie Sanders. The leak caused considerable embarrassment to the Clinton campaign and was a major boost to Trump, with some supporters of Sanders switching to the Republican nominee. US intelligence officials were not slow to point out that the signature of the hacking was that of the GRU.

Trump seized on the fact that the emails had been stolen by the Russians to suggest the hackers track down some 30,000 'missing' emails that Clinton had stored on her personal email server in breach of security restrictions while she was Secretary of State and had refused to hand back to the State Department on the grounds that they were of a personal nature. At a news conference in Miami, he first appeared to appeal to the GRU to produce the emails. 'Russia, if you're listening, I hope you're able to find the 30,000 emails that are missing,' he said. Within five hours, the GRU had begun attempting to hack into the computer systems in Clinton's personal office.

At the same time as the other two strands of the 'Active Measures' operation were taking place, Russian intelligence officers were working to cause further confusion in a widespread infiltration and influence operation aimed at manipulating the Trump campaign in Russia's favour.

With hindsight, the first real evidence of Russian infiltration came in a relatively low-key way in March 2016 with Trump's announcement, during a meeting with the editorial board of the *Washington Post*, of a number of new foreign policy advisors. They included Carter Page and George Papadopoulos, both relatively unknown oil industry advisors with limited foreign affairs experience and both, crucially, keen to forge closer relationships between Trump and Russia.

The appointment of Page was particularly instructive. He had worked for investment bankers Merrill Lynch in Moscow between 2003 and 2007 and shortly after his return to the US, in 2008, was in contact with Russian intelligence officers. Page had been interviewed by the FBI in 2013 over further contacts with two Russian intelligence officers. Both of the Russians were expelled and a Russian illegal, an agent operating without diplomatic immunity, pleaded guilty to a charge of conspiring to act as a foreign agent.

Page was the owner of Global Energy Capital, a consultancy specialising in Russian oil and gas that, conveniently for his new appointment, was based in offices next door to Trump Tower in Manhattan. Page was invited to Moscow in July 2016, where he gave a speech praising Putin's aggressive foreign policy and comparing it favourably to 'hypocritical' US foreign policies. He met Russian Deputy Prime Minister Arkady Dvorkovich and other officials, who according to his emails to the campaign team included 'senior members of the Presidential Administration'. Not only had Dvorkovich expressed strong support for Trump but 'based on feedback from a diverse array of other sources close to the Presidential Administration, it was readily apparent that this sentiment is widely held at all levels of government'.

Steele's informants claimed that one of those Page met was Igor Sechin, the chairman of the Rosneft oil company and a close ally of Putin. Like the Russian president, Sechin had been a Soviet intelligence officer. He was a GRU Africa specialist, stirring up trouble in Angola and Mozambique during the 1980s, and was de facto leader of the *Siloviki*, the retired Russian intelligence and armed forces officers who had used the skills honed in their previous jobs to go on to become oligarchs. When the US government imposed sanctions on Sechin in 2014, Page defended him as someone who had done more to improve ties between the United States and Russia 'than any individual in or out of government from either side of the Atlantic'.

Page would later describe the Steele reports of a meeting with Sechin as 'complete garbage', but the former MI6 officer's sources, who included a senior associate of Sechin, said the Rosneft chairman offered Page and other Trump associates a stake in his company in return for the lifting of sanctions (imposed after Russia's annexation of Crimea from Ukraine in 2014). Page was said to have responded by confirming that 'were Trump elected US president, then sanctions on Russia would be lifted'.

Page subsequently denied meeting 'any sanctioned individual' and complained of a 'witch-hunt' against him based on 'completely false media reports'. Asked about his contacts with Russian intelligence officers, Page said that none of the oil industry documents he handed the Russians was classified. 'I didn't want to be a spy,' he said. 'I'm not a spy.'

Unlike Page, George Papadopoulos had no links to the Russians before his appointment but shortly after it was announced, during a working trip to Rome, he was introduced to Joseph Mifsud, a London-based academic with extensive ties to Russia. Ten days later, Mifsud met Papadopoulos for lunch in London, introducing him to one of his 'former students', a young Russian woman Olga Polonskaya, whom he described as Putin's niece. Putin does not have a niece.

Both Mifsud and Polonskaya said they were very keen to help Papadopoulos set up a meeting between Trump and Putin. Aside from the alleged link to Putin, Polonskaya claimed to have connections to a number of other senior Russian government officials, including Aleksander Yakovenko, the Russian ambassador to the UK, who was allegedly a personal friend. The idea that Papadopoulos might be able use these contacts to set up the meeting between Trump and Putin, thereby proving his value to the campaign, was consistently dangled in front of Papadopoulos. He was also put in touch with a Russian Foreign Ministry Official, Ivan Timofeev, who repeatedly spoke about backing from senior Russian officials for the meeting 'when the time is right'.

Papadopoulos mentioned the meeting repeatedly in emails to senior members of the campaign team and raised it during a session with Trump in which the candidate showed a clear interest in the idea. Papadopoulos continued to discuss it with both Mifsud and Polonskaya, with the latter telling him in one email that: 'I have already alerted my personal links to our conversation and your request. We are all very excited by the possibility of a good relationship with Mr Trump. The Russian Federation would love to welcome him once his candidature would be officially announced.'

Following one of a number of visits to Russia that Mifsud made during this period, he arranged to meet Papadopoulos in the Andaz Hotel, near London's Liverpool Street station. Over breakfast in the hotel's '1901 Restaurant', an impressive Grade II-listed former ballroom with a beautiful stained-glass domed ceiling, Mifsud said that during his trip to Moscow he had discussed the possibility of the Trump–Putin meeting with a number of 'high-level Russian-government officials'. He spoke enthusiastically about the interest in Moscow in such a meeting before confiding in Papadopoulos that the 'high-level' officials he met had told him that the Russians had obtained emails which could damage Hillary Clinton's campaign. 'They have dirt on her,' Mifsud said. 'They have emails of Clinton. They have thousands of emails.' That meeting took place on 26 April 2016, just over six weeks after the GRU began hacking the DNC and Clinton campaign emails.

On 6 May 2016, ten days after that meeting with Mifsud, Papadopoulos suggested to the Australian High Commissioner to the UK, Alexander Downer, that 'the Trump campaign had received indications from the Russian government that it could assist the campaign through the anonymous release of information that would be damaging to Hillary Clinton'. Soon after WikiLeaks began releasing the hacked emails, Australian officials contacted the FBI to inform them of the conversation between Papadopoulos and Downer, leading the FBI to open a counter-intelligence investigation – aptly code-named 'Crossfire Hurricane' after the opening line of the Rolling Stones song 'Jumping Jack Flash' – into whether the Trump campaign had co-ordinated with the Russian interference in the election. Both Page and Papadopoulos were regarded as prime suspects along with Paul Manafort, Trump's campaign chairman and 'chief strategist'.

Manafort had joined the campaign team a week after Page and Papadopoulos were announced as advisers, strengthening the potential links with the Russians. Manafort had made millions advising former Ukrainian President Viktor Yanukovych, a Putin ally who was forced from power in 2014 and fled to Moscow. Manafort also worked for Oleg Deripaska, another of Putin's oligarch allies, on a scheme to 're-focus, both internally and externally, the policies of the Putin government'. He denied ever being 'involved with anything to do with the Russian government or the Putin administration'. But throughout his time with the campaign he had continued contacts with his long-standing associate Konstantin Kilimnik, a former member of the Russian military with close ties to Russian intelligence. Manafort provided Kilimnik with internal campaign polling data, which would have helped the IRA troll teams ensure they put out the right messages in areas of the US where the vote could go either way. Just two days after the FBI began the 'Crossfire Hurricane' investigation, Kilimnik met Manafort in New York to give him a peace plan for the Ukraine that the Russians wanted Trump to back and which Manafort subsequently admitted was a 'backdoor' way of Russia taking control of eastern Ukraine.

Two weeks later, Manafort was forced to resign from the campaign team. He subsequently dismissed as 'absurd' claims by unnamed US officials that the NSA had intercepted him talking on the telephone to Russian intelligence officers. 'I have never knowingly spoken to Russian intelligence officers,' he said. 'I have never been involved with anything to do with the Russian government or the Putin administration. It's not like these people wear badges that say: I'm a Russian intelligence officer.'

Following the election, Trump continued to dismiss the reports of ties between his campaign and the Russians as 'fake news'. He also denied having any business links with Russia. 'I can tell you, speaking for myself, I own nothing in Russia,' he said. 'I have no loans in Russia. I don't have any deals in Russia.' Not for want of trying. Not only had Trump sought repeatedly to do business in Russia, he had also had a number of business relations with prominent Russians based in the United States.

Perhaps the closest business connections between Trump and Russians had been in his relationship with the Russian-owned hotel group Bayrock. The firm's founder was Tevfik Arif, a former senior official in the Soviet Ministry of Commerce and Trade. When the Soviet Union broke up in 1991, Arif went into private business in the West, building hotels in Turkey and then moving to the United States. The role of Felix Sater, Bayrock's managing director, in the company was less clear, but he was always at Arif's side. Sater was born in Russia in 1966 but raised in Brooklyn. He became a stockbroker but was jailed after a fight in a New York cocktail bar in which he stabbed a man in a face with the broken stem of a margarita glass. Before working for Bayrock, he had been involved in a $40-million Mafia share scam, escaping prison by turning informant for the FBI.

Trump worked with Bayrock on two major projects: Trump SoHo, a forty-six-storey 'condominium-hotel' that featured in Trump's US television show *The Apprentice*, and the Trump International Hotel & Tower in Fort Lauderdale, Florida, a project dreamed up by Sater. Trump's son, Donald Jr, made no secret of where much of the money was coming from for his father's new investments. 'Russians make up a pretty disproportionate cross-section of a lot of our assets, say in Dubai, and certainly with our project in SoHo,' he said in 2008. 'We see a lot of money pouring in from Russia.'

At the beginning of January, two weeks before Trump assumed office, details of a joint CIA–FBI–NSA analysis of the hacking of the Democratic Party's computer systems were released. It concluded 'with high confidence that Russian President Vladimir Putin ordered an influence campaign in early 2016 aimed at the US presidential election, the consistent goals of which were to undermine public faith in the US democratic process, denigrate Secretary Clinton, and harm her electability and potential presidency'.

The US intelligence agencies confirmed that the leaked Clinton campaign emails released by WikiLeaks had been hacked by the GRU. Putin had a clear preference for Trump and 'aspired to help President-elect Trump's election chances when possible by discrediting Secretary Clinton'. The Obama administration reacted to the report by imposing sanctions on both the GRU and the FSB and by expelling thirty-five Russian diplomats who were in fact intelligence officers. There was some surprise when Russia chose not to respond with tit-for-tat expulsions of US diplomats.

The controversy over Trump's links with Russia continued after the inauguration when his National Security Adviser, former DIA Director Michael Flynn, was forced to resign. Flynn had misled Vice-President Mike Pence over his contacts with Sergei Kislyak, the Russian ambassador to the United States. Flynn had numerous known contacts with the Russians, including during a gala dinner in Moscow in December 2015 at which he sat next to Putin. He also had a number of telephone conversations with Kislyak both before and after the election. Pence insisted that none of those conversations were sanctions-related and that in no case had they taken place after sanctions were imposed. It then emerged that US intelligence had a recording of Flynn discussing a further round of sanctions with the Russian ambassador on the day they were imposed, the implication being that Putin had not responded to these new sanctions against the GRU and the FSB because he believed they would be reversed by Trump. The new

American president denied any knowledge of what Flynn was doing and attacked the US intelligence services for leaking secret information to the media.

The confirmation by FBI Director James Comey in March 2017 that the FBI was investigating Russian interference and 'any co-ordination between the campaign and Russia's efforts' increased the pressure on Trump, eventually leading him to sack Comey. This in turn resulted in the appointment of former FBI Director Robert Mueller as Special Counsel with a brief to investigate 'Russian interference in the election and any links or co-ordination between the Russian government and members of the Trump campaign'.

Mueller's inquiry team took nearly two years to complete its report. There was a good deal of consternation at the conclusions, in large part because of a misleading summary by US Attorney-General Bill Barr that led to headlines, and inevitably presidential tweets, proclaiming 'no collusion'. Mueller reacted by complaining to Barr that the attorney-general had failed to 'fully capture the context, nature and substance of our work and conclusions' and that as a result 'there is now public confusion about critical aspects of the results of our investigation'.

There was indeed public confusion but it was as much due to the nature of investigation Mueller chose to pursue. Mueller had been told to take the FBI's original 'Crossfire Hurricane' counter-intelligence investigation into his own inquiry, but from the start he adopted a more rigid approach. His inquiry looked solely for evidence of criminality that would stand up in court, limiting the material he could use. Intelligence from highly secret sources, including foreign liaison partners, was therefore excluded from use since it could not have been used in open court. The counter-intelligence investigation, which was always likely to be a far longer process, continued in parallel. FBI agents from the 'Crossfire Hurricane' probe sat alongside Mueller's team and relayed any intelligence relevant to their inquiries to their own bosses, but Mueller looked solely for criminal offences that could be proven in court. There would have to be co-ordination between the campaign and Russian government representatives that constituted a conspiracy, or evidence that would stand up in court that members of the campaign team were acting as Russian agents.

On numerous occasions, Mueller's team found evidence but not enough to sustain a conviction. 'A statement that the investigation did not establish particular facts does not mean there was no evidence of those facts,' he said. 'The investigation identified numerous links between individuals with ties to the Russian government and individuals associated with the Trump campaign.'

Page, Papadopoulos, Manafort and Flynn were all found to have lied about their Russian contacts and Mueller's investigators uncovered interactions between Russians and more than twenty members of the campaign team, including Trump's son, Donald Trump Jr, and his son-in-law, Jared Kushner. Mueller's investigation also led to the indictment of twenty-five Russians who were alleged to have taken part in the Russian hacking and social media influence operations.

The interactions between the Russians and the Trump campaign team included the meeting on 9 June 2016 in Trump Tower, New York, at which Donald Jr, Kushner and Manafort met Russian lawyer Natalia Veselnitskaya and her friend Rinat Akhmetshin. The meeting followed an email to Donald Jr in which he was offered documents that would 'incriminate' Hillary Clinton. The email said the offer of dirt on Hillary was being made as 'part of Russia and its government's support for Mr Trump'. Donald Jr's immediate response was: 'If it's what you say I love it.' But although Veselnitskaya claimed at the meeting that Clinton and other Democrats had received funds from illegal activities in Russia, she failed to produce any evidence.

As a result, the meeting with Veselnitskaya did not in fact lead to collusion but the intent was clearly there and reflected the general approach of the Trump campaign team, a situation perhaps best summed up by Mueller's conclusion with regard to the hacking of the Clinton campaign's emails: 'The investigation established that the Russian government perceived it would benefit from a Trump presidency and worked to secure that outcome, and that the campaign expected it would benefit electorally from information stolen and released through Russian efforts.'

Nevertheless, Mueller failed to find evidence of co-ordination or conspiracy between Russians and any member of the Trump campaign, including Page, Papadopoulos, Manafort and Flynn. As Mueller made clear, that does not mean that it did not exist. Even when individuals did agree to testify to his investigation – and Donald Trump Jr, for example, refused to do so – they sometimes lied, while a number of witnesses, including many of the Russians, did not live in the United States and were unavailable or unwilling to testify. Even some of those who did testify deleted communications relevant to the investigation or, like Manafort, used encrypted internet communications that the Mueller investigators were unable to access. The inquiry was unable to determine whether the campaign polling data that Manafort passed to Kilimnik was used by the Russians as part of their interference with the elections, or indeed identify any of the 'diverse array' of senior officials close to Putin whom Page said he met during his trip to Moscow. As a result, it concluded that it was unable to be certain the information it could not access would not shed additional light on its findings, or even cast them in a completely different light.

Given these difficulties and the very nature of Russian 'Active Measures', Mueller's admission that he and his team were unable to be certain of many of the facts they uncovered is scarcely surprising. The various threads of an 'Active Measures' web are overlaid with multiple 'denial and deception' operations designed to cover up what is going on or lead investigators away from the real aims. This process and the widespread use of 'unconscious agents' means that when it comes to unravelling such an operation, very little is quite what it seems. It was always going to be difficult to work out who was and who was not in touch with the Russians and whether there was sufficient evidence of 'conspiracy' between the two sides to sustain a conviction.

Although Steele's reports were far more credible than Trump and his supporters claimed, with much of his intelligence and certainly the central thrust of his reports confirmed by Mueller's findings, it is unlikely that the Russians did not know what he was doing, and probable that some of his material was fake or manipulated and provided by sources under FSB control. In addition, the complexity of 'Active Measures' is such that at least some of those on whom suspicion has fallen, possibly even all of them, will have been, like Trump himself, 'unconscious agents', manipulated from Moscow and moved around like pieces on a chess board.

The Trump Tower meeting, for example, drew three key members of the campaign team, including Trump's son and son-in-law, into a situation where they seemed keen to work with the Russians, something that appears to have been avoided only because the Russians failed to provide any evidence of their claims. George Papadopoulos, whose original claims that the Russians had 'dirt' on Clinton led to the FBI's original counter-intelligence investigation, looked for all the world like a classic 'unconscious agent'. Although even in his case it will have been difficult for Mueller to be absolutely certain.

Finally, there is the question of who the target was. Certainly, the main thrust of the Russian interference was to prevent the election of Hillary Clinton, but it achieved far more than that. One element of 'Active Measures' is a process known as Decomposition (*Razlozheniye*). It involves destroying the reputation and influence of a target individual, country, or organisation. In the case of a country, the aim is to induce internal strife, dissension, or tensions between its leader and various parts of its system of governance, which is of course precisely what the Russians achieved, helped in substantial part by Trump's own erratic personality.

One senior MI6 officer who operated against the Russians during the Cold War said Trump was an ideal 'unconscious agent', easily pushed into doing whatever the Russians wanted at any point. 'His vanities, narcissism, egocentricity, naivety, sensitivity to criticism, and his desire always for revenge and getting even, as well as his intellectual weaknesses and lack of knowledge of international politics are all factors to be exploited.'

The controversy around the Russian interference in the elections has dominated Trump's presidency and as his, and America's, reputation around the world has suffered so Putin's has risen exponentially among ordinary Russians, and just as importantly among the *Siloviki*. After years of seeing their country's influence decline, their president has restored it to what they see as its rightful place as a powerful player on the world stage. From Putin's perspective, the Russian intelligence operation to interfere with the 2016 US Presidential Election was a stunning success.

***

The GRU's signature use of a combination of agents on the ground and hackers to get into highly secure systems was one of the reasons why some experts suggested Edward Snowden, who stole large numbers of top-secret NSA documents on the extent of modern surveillance, might be a Russian agent rather than a whistle-blower. The truth is that, while there were a number of indicators that he was recruited before he downloaded the documents, there were many others that suggested he was precisely what he claimed to be, a whistle-blower angered by domestic surveillance of US citizens that went way beyond what many Americans deemed acceptable.

The suspicions surrounding Snowden's motivations stem from the fact that he openly admitted taking a post at the NSA's base in Hawaii in order to obtain as many documents as he could on the agency's cyber-hacking operations around the world. He subsequently told the *South China Morning Post* that the job, as a contract computer specialist supplied by technology consultancy Booz Allen Hamilton, 'granted me access to lists of machines all over the world the NSA hacked. That is why I accepted that position.' Snowden started work at the Hawaii Cryptologic Center at Wahiawa on 1 April 2013 and left seven weeks later. He then flew to Hong Kong, arriving on 20 May 2013.

'If he was a Russian agent and I was his Russian controller, Hong Kong is exactly the country I would have chosen as Snowden's first port of call,' one former MI6 officer said, explaining why so many inside the intelligence community regarded him as a Russian agent. 'There was never any likelihood that the Chinese would return him to the US and, of course, it diverts attention from Russia. There are also regular Aeroflot flights direct to Moscow.'

Once he had arrived in Hong Kong, Snowden handed some of the documents he had downloaded to the *Guardian* newspaper and gave his interview to the *South China Morning Post*. The United States had revoked his passport and although he had been offered asylum in Ecuador, the only way to get there without being arrested, given that he had no passport, was via Moscow. While his aircraft was en route from Hong Kong to Moscow, the Americans persuaded the Ecuadorean government not to take him and Snowden found himself stuck in Russia. He claimed, ludicrously, that the Chinese government would not have been able to get hold of the data he held on his computers and data drives while he was in Hong Kong. He also maintained that he had taken no documents with him to Moscow. (The latter claim is possible but, if true, he would have to explain why he clearly had access to them once he was there.) Once he was in Moscow, and having nowhere to go, he was entirely under control of the Putin government and the FSB, who would certainly have wanted to debrief him on the computer systems of both the NSA and the CIA. His subsequent frequent revelations of further NSA activities were clearly designed to cause disruption in the relations between the United States and its allies.

'Take the visit of Obama to Berlin,' one former MI6 officer said. 'A few days earlier Snowden "revealed" details of how the CIA was tapping into Merkel's phone. The outcome was a furore over the idea that the wicked, unscrupulous Americans were attacking their most faithful NATO ally. A little later it was revealed that the *Bundesnachrichtendienst* had done the same to the Americans, but this attracted little attention.'

Whatever the view taken by the American and British intelligence agencies, there is no denying that some of Snowden's revelations demonstrated that the 'War on Terror' launched by the West following the 9/11 al-Qaeda attacks on the United States had led to a worrying willingness to stretch the rules on what could and could not be done in terms of domestic surveillance in both the US and the UK. It caused widespread alarm in the

United States, where a Federal Court ruled the bulk collection by the government of Americans' phone records to be illegal and Congress passed the USA Freedom Act that put limits on the NSA's ability to collect and store bulk telephone data. In the United Kingdom, there was less public concern, largely because aggressive action by the government persuaded most media organisations not to follow the *Guardian*'s lead. Nevertheless, the UK's Investigatory Powers Tribunal ruled that GCHQ had acted unlawfully in its mass interception of private data, although ironically the agency had already altered the way it worked to make the operations legal some months before Snowden's disclosures. The controversy led to new legislation in the form of the Investigatory Powers Act, which left no doubt as to what would and would not be legal and placed important judicial barriers to unlawful breaches of the power to intercept domestic emails and phone calls, and to access computer systems remotely.

Snowden could, therefore, argue that what he did was for the good of the people and that those who believed you had nothing to fear if you had done nothing wrong were at best naive. The extent to which the understandable determination to prevent people dying in terrorist attacks led NSA and GCHQ to stretch the rules in a way that went beyond what most people would deem acceptable was perhaps best demonstrated by a GCHQ memo leaked by Snowden that gave staff the option of not monitoring video of people interacting on internet sex sites. It is difficult to see what might constitute a greater invasion of privacy.

The release of the documents initiated an important debate about the extent of domestic surveillance and led to legislation laying out what the intelligence services could and could not do. But the value of that debate was mitigated by the extent to which many of the documents Snowden released damaged operations that had nothing to do with domestic surveillance and compromised complex operations against terrorists and other countries, operations that were producing important intelligence and saving lives.

Like Cairncross providing the Russians with the information that helped them build their own atomic bomb, or releasing details of the Bletchley Park breaks into the Enigma cipher, Snowden and the media who published those revelations that had nothing to do with domestic surveillance took it upon themselves to decide what they should reveal, without a real understanding of what might or might not be damaging. For every article published around the world as a result of his disclosures that raised questions about the level of domestic surveillance, there were several more that clearly put their countries and the lives of innocent people at risk.

Whatever Snowden's motivation, and whether or not he was under Russian control before he arrived in Moscow, once he was there, he was an agent of the FSB. He might well have been an 'unconscious agent', but he was nevertheless extraordinarily valuable to the Russians as an agent of influence.

'Snowden was quite clearly an agent of the Russian intelligence services,' one former MI6 officer said. 'What is not certain is whether he was a "conscious" or an "unconscious" agent. In other words, was he fully aware that he was an agent? Given that he is presumably not total naive, I believe he must realise he was under the control of the Russians, but he may choose to delude himself that he was a genuine whistle-blower. Officers working in "active measures" are a pretty sophisticated group. They know how to get people to do their bidding by a variety of methods.'

***

The ambiguity surrounding Snowden's motivations, and whether he considered himself as being involved in espionage at all, underlines the problem that reasons why spies spy are often difficult to discern. That some of them do not even realise that they are being used as spies only makes the search for motivation more complex. But some agents do defy the norm. They spy for one single indisputable reason. Often it is money, which is of course an easy means of controlling an agent.

The carrot-and-stick approach allows the agent handler to starve agents of money until they produce the goods or pay them at varying rates depending on the quality of their material, so conditioning them to produce the best possible intelligence. There is one major flaw in the use of money. It is vulnerable to fraud, to agents producing material that is false in order to obtain more cash, but it has one significant advantage in that it is very easy to close the case down in a way that leaves the agent handler or controller far less uneasy over the end of the affair. Sex and love is a more difficult motivation, tying down as it does intelligence officers to a single case for long periods of time. For the East Germans, this was less problematic. For organisations such as the CIA and MI6, in contrast, it would have been virtually impossible to allocate one officer to a single agent for years on end. Ego has produced some spectacular cases of espionage, but in terms of agent control is probably the worst of all motivations. The most reliable agents are motivated by something they believe in passionately: patriotism; ideology; and revenge; the classic back stories of the spy novel. These will always be the best agent motivations, and the easiest to control, although money, particularly when it contributes to the welfare of children, can be a very useful incentive.

'The higher motives, such as ideological zeal for US objectives, patriotism, a parent's aspirations for his children, or religious devotion, are extremely reliable ones,' one former CIA officer said. 'In my own experience the best agent motivation has been his respect for the case officer and friendship with him, backed by an identity, even if not a total one, between his aims and the basic aims of the United States and its allies.'

Ultimately, the most important thing in the relationship between a case officer and his or her agent is the mutual respect between them, the 'relationship of trust'. The agents whose roles are described in this book were for the most part putting their lives at risk. They needed to know, often desperately, that their case officers believed in them and would go to the wall for their agent, for 'their Joe'. The intelligence officer handling them clearly had to take hard-headed decisions, and the agent knew that. They just had to accept it. The case officer was often their only link to the real world. They knew that he or she was their only real friend. But they also needed to know that he or she was willing to speak truth to power, prepared to explain to their bosses the value of what their agent could provide, to fight and rail against the bureaucratic resistance that all too often prevented the value of the intelligence provided by a particular agent from being recognised.

In one letter to his case officer, Ryszard Kukliński said that every time he went out to hand over intelligence to a CIA handler on the streets of Warsaw, he 'bid his family a discreet farewell'. Robert Hanssen complained to his SVR handler, shortly before he was arrested, about the lack of any response to his reports. 'I have come as close as I ever want to come to sacrificing myself to help you and I get silence,' Hanssen said. 'I hate silence ...' Both men needed to know they were valued.

From the perspective of the agent, Kukliński's case officer, David Forden, a CIA veteran, was the perfect case officer. 'The importance of your security, of your well-being and that of your family, is unmatched by any other consideration,' he told Kukliński, shortly before the emergency exfiltration that saw the Polish army officer and his family whisked to freedom. 'Sure, we will labour over every package from you, to examine and benefit from the documents you have selected and copied so expertly. They will have, as they already have had, tremendous value to my government. But, always, our first concern in opening each package is to find the personal note from you, to learn that you are OK.'

Whether or not any member of the US intelligence community other than Forden really cared whether Kukliński was OK, and however many voices at Langley or in Washington sought for their own reasons to dismiss his reports – as is too often the case – the Pole knew that someone believed in him and that knowledge will have kept him going through the very, very tough times he experienced before he and his family were safely brought to the West.

'Your personal letters and the entire pertinent correspondence are for me a special kind of reward for the tensions and anxieties which, after all, I included in my thoroughly thought out and absolutely mature decision to initiate our co-operation,' Kukliński said. 'Thank you.'

Alex Younger, the 'Chief' of MI6, placed the service's 'agents' at the heart of its operations in a speech made in December 2016, in which he explained why it was so important that intelligence operations remained secret. Put simply, the agents who worked for the intelligence services needed to know that what they did would never be betrayed. All too often they were 'traitors' to their country or a cause, assisting MI6 for a higher motive, and the good that they were doing demanded that they received protection, which could only be provided by complete confidentiality, achieved by those they were helping remaining quiet and telling no-one their stories.

'Our value depends on our ability to keep secret that which we must,' Younger said. 'Above all else, we owe that to the brave men and women who work with us to obtain the intelligence we need, often at great personal risk. These people, who we call agents ... will never enter our headquarters; they will usually not be British. Their motives for helping the UK are as diverse as the human race itself. But they have one thing in common: they take risks to make you and your families safer. More than they or you can ever know, the people of this country, and those of our allies, are deeply in their debt.'

SOURCES

Prologue

Report on the Investigation into Russian Interference in the 2016
    Presidential Election, Special Counsel Robert S. Mueller, III,
    Washington, D.C., March 2019.
Senate Judiciary Committee, Interview with Ike Thomas Kaveladze, 3
    November 2017.
Senate Judiciary Committee, Interview with Donald J Trump Jr, 7
    September 2017.
Senate Judiciary Committee, Interview with Rinat Akhmetshin, 14
    November 2017.
Senate Judiciary Committee, Interview with Anatoli Samochornov, 8
    November 2017.
Senate Judiciary Committee, Interview with Robert Goldstone, 15
    December 2017.
Testimony of Natalia Veselnitskaya before the United States Senate
    Committee on the Judiciary, 20 November 2017.

Chapter 1

Story of Samson and Delilah taken from King James Bible, Book of Judges
    16, verses 1–31.

Chapter 2

Rose Greenhow and Belle Boyd

Karen Abbott, *Liar, Temptress, Soldier, Spy*, Harper Perennial, New York, 2014.
Larissa Phillips, *Women Civil War Spies of the Confederacy*, Rosen, New York,
    2004.

Walter Christmas

The National Archives (TNA) FO1093/29 Secret Service Expenditure: Agents and Estimates.

Alan Judd, *The Quest for C*, HarperCollins, London, 2000.

Walter Christmas, *King George of Greece*, Eveleigh Nash, London, 1914.

Michael Smith, *Six: The Real James Bonds 1909–1939*, Biteback, London, 2010.

Andrei Vyshinsky

The Malign Foreigner in Russia, *The Times*, 5 July 1937.

Edward Ellis Smith

Tennent H. Bagley, *Spy Wars: Moles, Mysteries, and Deadly Games*, Yale University Press, New Haven, 2007.

Nigel West, *The A to Z of Sexpionage*, Scarecrow Press, Lanham, Maryland, 2009.

Oleg Kalugin

Oleg Kalugin, *Spymaster*, Basic Books, New York, 2009.

Midnight Climax

CIA Chief deplores CIA Brothels, *San Francisco Examiner*, 5 August 1977.

Senators Would Force Four CIA Mind-Controllers to Testify, *Washington Post*, 6 August 1977.

Mindbending Disclosures, *Time*, 15 August 1977.

Giving Love Potions to Informants, *Wilmington News Journal*, 15 October 1978.

Operation Midnight Climax: How the CIA Dosed S.F. Citizens with LSD, *SF Weekly*, 14 March 2012.

UNSCOM official

Nigel West, *The A to Z of Sexpionage*, Scarecrow Press, Lanham, Maryland, 2009.

John Vassall

Vassall Sentenced to 18 Years Imprisonment, *The Times*, 23 October 1962.

Vassall says Nonsense to Suggest there was a Plan to Meet Mr Galbraith on the Continent, *The Times*, 31 January 1963.

Vassall says no-one Sponsored him at the Admiralty, *The Times*, 31 January 1963.

'Nothing Improper' in Mr Galbraith's Relationship with Vassall – First Lord Also Cleared, *The Times*, 26 April 1963.

John Vassall, *Vassall: The Autobiography of a Spy*, Sidgwick & Jackson, London, 1975.

Roy Guindon

Nigel West, *The A to Z of Sexpionage*, Scarecrow Press, Lanham, Maryland, 2009.

Munir Redfa

Iraqi Pilot Who Defected to Israel Finds Friendly Reception, *Jewish Telegraphic Agency*, 18 August 1966.

In 1966, Israeli Intelligence Convinced an Iraqi Pilot to Defect with His MiG-21 Fighter, *The National Interest*, 28 August 2016.

Syrian pilot's defection in MiG-21 stirs Cold War memories, *The Phoenix Star*, 30 June 2012.

In 1966, Israeli Intelligence Convinced an Iraqi Pilot to Defect With His MiG-21. *War is Boring*, 28 August 2016.

Sharon Scranage

The Scranage Case, CIA, Ghana, and the [remainder of title redacted], *CIA Studies in Intelligence*, Vol. 34, Fall 1990.

CIA Employee, Ghanaian Held on Spy Charges, *LA Times*, 12 July 1985.

Officials think spying led to death of CIA informant in Ghana, *New York Times*, 13 July 1985.

Accused Spy Sharon Scranage Released to Parents' Custody, *Washington Post*, 19 July 1985.

Ex-clerk Admits She Revealed CIA Data, *SunSentinel*, 29 September 1985.

US Swaps Spy for 8 Ghanaians who Aided CIA, *LA Times*, 26 November 1985.

Former CIA employee Sharon Scranage, convicted of espionage, *UPI*, 10 April 1986.

Karl-Heinz Schneider/Gotthold Schramm/Marianne Lenzkow

Markus Wolf (with Anne McElvoy), *Memoirs of a Spymaster*, Pimlico, Bournemouth, 1997.

Nigel West, *The A to Z of Sexpionage*, Scarecrow Press, Lanham, Maryland, 2009.

Gabriele Gast

Gabriele Gast, *Kundschafterin des Friedens*, Eichborn, Frankfurt am Main, 1999.

Gabriele Gast, *Die politische Rolle der Frau in der DDR*, Bertelsmann Universitätsverlag, Dusseldorf, 1973.

Markus Wolf (with Anne McElvoy), *Memoirs of a Spymaster*, Pimlico, Bournemouth, 1997.

Pearl aus Pullach, *Der Spiegel*, 22 March 1999.

Isabelle Cheng and Donald Willis Keyser

United States of America v Donald Willis Keyser, Memorandum in Support of Motion to Find Defendant in Material Breach of Plea Agreement, US District Court for Eastern Virginia, 5 July 2006.

Arrest Shocks Former State Department Colleagues, *Washington Post*, 17 September 2004.

A Novel-Like Tale of Cloak, Dagger Unfolds in Court, *New York Sun*, 14 July 2006.

E-mails detail ex-diplomat's ties to Taiwanese spy, *Washington Times*, 23 July 2006.

Jail Sentence for Diplomat in Spy Case, *New York Sun*, 23 January 2007.

The Case of Donald Keyser and Taiwan's National Security Bureau, Stephane Lefebvre, *International Journal of Intelligence and Counter-Intelligence*, Vol. 20, Issue. 3, 2007.

Bernard Boursicot

The True Story of M. Butterfly; The Spy Who Fell in Love with a Shadow, *New York Times*, 15 August 1993.

Shi Pei Pu Dies; Convicted Spy's Affair with Man Inspired 'M. Butterfly' Play, *Washington Post*, 3 July 2009.

Shi Pei Pu, Singer, Spy and 'M. Butterfly,' Dies at 70, *New York Times*, 1 July 2009.

Shi Pei Pu, *Daily Telegraph*, 3 July 2009.

Chapter 3

Arsène Marie Verrue and Captain Bertrand Stewart

TNA WO374/65422 Army file for Captain Bertrand Stewart; FO 1093/29 Secret Service Expenditure: Agents and Estimates.

Heavy sentence on Mr Stewart, *The Times*, 5 February 1912.

Judd, The Quest for C; 'Espionage' in Germany, *The Times*, 9 August 1911.

The Alleged Espionage at Bremen, *The Times*, August 1911.

Statement by the Belgian informer, *The Times*, 14 February 1912.

Espionage trial at Leipzig, *The Times*, 1 February 1912.

The trial of Mr Stewart, *The Times*, 3 February 1912.

Poet jailed as a spy, *New York Times*, 4 February 1912.

Letter from Reginald Arkwright, *The Times*, 5 February 1912.

Hector C. Bywater and H.C. Ferraby, *Strange Intelligence: Memoirs of Naval Secret Service*, Biteback, London, 2015.

Hans Thilo Schmidt

Paul Paillole, *The Spy in Hitler's Inner Circle*, Casemate, Oxford, 2016.

Hugh Sebag-Montefiore, *Enigma: The Battle for the Code*, Weidenfeld & Nicolson, London, 2000.

W. Kozaczek, *Geheimoperation Wicher*, Karl Muller Verlag, Erlangen, 1999.

Ilyas Bazna

TNA KV6/8, Investigations into leakage of information to the German Intelligence Service from British Embassy Ankara (CICERO case).

KV 2/1171, Interrogation of Maria Clara Mathilde Molkenteller, a translator employed by German Intelligence (RSHA) in Berlin where she was given British documents to translate provided by CICERO, the spy who worked as valet for the British Ambassador in Ankara.

HW 19/240, Decrypts of German Secret Service (*Abwehr* and *Sicherheitsdienst*) Messages (ISOS, ISK and other series) Cicero Material.

GFM 33/412/738, Department Inland II: Geheim: Kaltenbrunner, Moyzisch, Papen, Arrest of members of the Foreign Service, Cicero.

FO 370/2930, Cicero Papers 1940–1964; FO 195/2661, Cicero: suspected spy; FCO 12/359, Paper concerning CICERO, background and correspondence with the Knatchbull-Hugessen family.

L.C. Moyzisch, *Operation Cicero*, Tandem, London, 1969.

Ilyias Bazna, *I was Cicero*, Chivers Press, Bath, 1985.

Goldfinger

Interview and correspondence with Tony Divall.

Coomar Narain

Western Firms Linked To India Espionage Ring, *UPI*, 20 January 1985.

Sex and hint of British link complicate the great Indian spy scandal, *The Times*, 25 January 1985.

Businessman spy ring 'kingpin', *Reuters*, 28 January 1985.

Businessman Said to Testify He Sold Secrets to France, Poland, East Germany, *AP*, 4 February 1985.

India Spy Sold Secrets for 25 Years: Says He Gave Data to France, 2nd Western Nation for $1 Million, *LA Times*, 4 February 1985.

Indian Spy Names His Clients, *The Times*, 5 February 1985.

India conveys displeasure to Polish premier over spy case, *UPI*, 11 February 1985.

19 Are Charged in Indian Espionage Scandal, *New York Times*, 16 April 1985.

14 years RI for Maneklal in Coomar Narain case, *Press Trust of India*, 18 July 2002.

Ronald Pelton

United States of America v. Ronald William Pelton, Indictment, US District Court for the District of Maryland, 20 December 1985.

United States of America v. Ronald William Pelton, US Court of Appeals
    for the Fourth Circuit, 18 December 1987.
US Suspect Held After Confession of Soviet Spying, *New York Times,*
    November 26, 1985.
FBI Says Spy Suspect Admits Selling Data, *Washington Post*, 26 November
    1985.
US holds another spy suspect, *The Times*, 26 November 85.
US Security 'damaged by spy', *The Times*, 27 November 1985.
Arrests mark the year of the spy, *The Times*, 27 November 1985.
Ex-Security Agency Employee Said to Have Admitted Spying, *New York
    Times*, 28 November 1985.
US Intelligence Reels as CIA net closes and more spy scandals loom, *The
    Times*, 28 November 1985.
Bail Refused for US Spy suspects, *The Times*, 29 November 1985.
Accused Spy Ronald Pelton Was Preoccupied with Money, *Washington Post*,
    7 December 1985.
Agent details Pelton's Sale of Spy Secrets, *Washington Times*, 29 May 1986.
Pelton Spy Case Chronology, *Washington Post*, 6 June 1986.
Matthew Aid, *The Secret Sentry*, Bloomsbury Press, New York, 2009.

Rocco Martino

Information provided to the author in confidence by representatives of two
    different Western intelligence services.
Review of Intelligence on Weapons of Mass Destruction, Report of a
    Committee of Privy Counsellors, 14 July 2004.
Report on the US Intelligence Community's Pre-War Intelligence
    Assessments, Senate Intelligence Committee, 7 July 2004.
Scarlett to Campbell, 18 September 2002, CAB 11/0071; Iraqi Weapons
    of Mass Destruction – Intelligence and Assessments, Intelligence and
    Security Committee, 9 September 2003.
French probe led to 'fake Niger uranium papers', *Financial Times*, 2 August
    2004.
Nigergate: Ex Head of CIA in Europe, Sismi Didn't Apply Any Pressure,
    ANSA, 12 May 2006.
How a Bogus Letter Became a Case for War, *Washington Post*, 2 April
    2007.
What I Didn't Find in Africa, *New York Times*, 6 July 2003.
The War They Wanted, The Lies They Needed, *Vanity Fair*, 17 October
    2006.

Chapter 4

Frederick Fairholme

Judd, *The Quest for C*; *Burke's Landed Gentry 1936*, Burke's Peerage and
  Gentry, London, 1936. I am grateful to Roger Fairholm for his assistance
  in tracking down the details of the Fairholme family.

Hector Bywater

TNA FO1093/25, Minutes of the Proceedings of a Meeting Held at the
  Foreign Office on 23 May 1911 and Minutes of the Proceedings of a
  Meeting Held at the Foreign Office on 23 November 1911.

FO1093/29, Estimates of SS Expenditure for 1 April 1911 to 31 March
  1912 and for February and March 1912.

Bywater and Ferraby, *Strange Intelligence*.

William H. Honan, *Bywater: The Man Who Invented the Pacific War*, Futura,
  London, 1991.

Judd, *The Quest for C*.

Walter Archer and Hugh Archer

TNA FO1093/29, Minutes of Meeting held at the Foreign Office on 8
  November 1912.

Navy Lists 1896–1912.

Mr Walter E. Archer CB, *The Times*, 28 September 1917.

Captain H.E.M. Archer RN, *The Times*, 6 January 1931.

Political notes, *The Times*, 3 May 1912.

Judd, *The Quest for C*; Smith, *Six: The Real James Bonds*.

Edith Cavell

TNA WO208/3242, Colonel Norman Crockatt, Historical Record of MI9.

CUST49/448, Arrangements for Bringing Body of Nurse Edith Cavell
  into England.

HO45/10794/302577, Nurse Edith Cavell: Removal of Remains from
  Belgium to UK.

KV2/822, Edith Cavell; KV2/844, Gaston Georges Quien.

MT25/32, Re-interment of Remains of the Late Miss Edith Cavell in
  England.

FO383/15, Belgium: Prisoners, Including: Miss Edith Cavell, English Nurse
  in Brussels, Arrested and Executed by the Germans for Assisting Allied
  Soldiers to Escape from Germany.

M.R.D. Foot and J.M. Langley, *MI9: The British Secret Service That Fostered
  Escape and Evasion 1939–1945*, Biteback, London, 2013.

Airey Neave, *Saturday at MI9: A History of Underground Escape Lines in North-
  West Europe in 1940–5 by a Leading Organiser at MI9*, Coronet, London,
  1971.

Phil Tomaselli, *Tracing Your Secret Service Ancestors*, Pen and Sword, Barnsley, 2009.

Revealed: New evidence that executed wartime nurse Edith Cavell's network was spying, *Daily Telegraph*, 12 September 2015.

Walthère Dewé and Herman Chauvin

Henry Landau, *Secrets of the White Lady*, Putnams, London, 1935.

Judd, *The Quest for C*; Smith, *Six: The Real James Bonds*.

Boris Bazhanov

Boris Bazhanov, *Avec Staline dans le Kremlin*, Les Editions de France, Paris, 1930.

Boris Bazhanov and David W. Doyle, *Bazhanov and the Damnation of Stalin*, Ohio University Press, Athens, 1990.

TNA FO 371/4021 General Correspondence Russia.

FO 371/4024 General Correspondence Russia; KV3/11, A Short Statement about the OGPU – SSSR, B. Bajanov, Simla, 17 May 1928.

Liddell Hart Centre for Military Archives, King's College London, GB 0099 KCLMA, unpublished memoirs of Colonel Leo Steveni.

Conrad O'Brien-ffrench, *Delicate Mission: Autobiography of a Secret Agent*, Skilton & Shaw, London, 1979.

RGVA (Russian State Military Archive) Moscow, Captured Polish Intelligence Files: Fond 453, op. 1, file 54, p.55; Fond 308, op. 2, file 39.

Charles Richards

TNA FO 371/17269 General Correspondence Russia.

KV 2/572 Michael Markovich Borodin. A prominent Soviet Communist, Borodin represented the Soviets in Peking.

Christopher Andrew, *Secret Service; The Making of the British Intelligence Community*, Heinemann, London, 1985.

'The evidence, Russian prisoner's "Confession"', *The Times*, 13 April 1933.

The Moscow charges, first day of 'trial', the Soviet case, two prisoners questioned, *The Times*, 13 April 1933.

Briton confesses at Moscow trial, five deny guilt, *New York Times*, 13 April 1933.

Marked change in 'trial', the prosecution confused, Mr Thornton's stand, *The Times*, 15 April 1933; Mystery document in Moscow trial, *Brisbane Courier*, 15 April 1933.

Moscow sabotage trial, 'Whole case a frame-up', *The Argus* (Melbourne), 17 April 1933.

Evidence for prosecution, *Sydney Morning Herald*, 17 April 1933.

The objective proofs, Mr Macdonald's confession, *The Times*, 18 April 1933.

Speeches for defence, 'discredited' witnesses, *The Times*, 19 April 1933.

The Moscow prisoners, *The Times*, 20 April 1933.

The returned engineers, a message from the King, Foreign Office visits, *The Times*, 25 April 1933.

The Moscow trial I, a new survey – Mr Monkhouse's own story, *The Times*, 22 May 1933.

The Moscow trial II – Mr Cushny and the OGPU, a personal narrative, *The Times*, 23 May 1933.

The Moscow trial III – light on the confessions OGPU pressure, *The Times*, 24 May 1933.

The Moscow trial IV – procedure of the OGPU, incidents in courts, *The Times*, 25 May 1933.

Release from Russia, prisoners on way home, trade ban raised, *The Times*, 3 July 1933.

Paul Thümmel

TNA ADM 223/838 Germany Political Reports (CX Series).

Keith Jeffery, *MI6: The History of the Secret Intelligence Service 1909–1949*, Bloomsbury, London 2010.

F.H. Hinsley, E.E. Thomas, C.F.G. Ransom, R.C. Knight, *British Intelligence in the Second World War*, Vol. 1, TSO, London, 1979.

Halina Szymańska

TNA ADM 223/838 Germany Political Reports (CX Series); Information provided to the author in confidence.

Keith Jeffery, *MI6: The History of the Secret Intelligence Service 1909–1949*, Bloomsbury, London 2010.

Ian Colvin, *Chief of Intelligence,* Gollancz, London, 1951.

Tessa Stirling, Daria Nalecz & Tadeusz Dubicki, *Intelligence Co-operation Between Poland and Great Britain During World War II*, Vallentine Mitchell, London, 2005.

Heinz Höhne, *Canaris*, Secker & Warburg, London, 1979.

C.G. McKay, *From Information to Intrigue: Studies in Secret Service Based on the Swedish Experience, 1939–1945*, Routledge, London, 1993.

Nigel West, *MI6: British Secret Service Operations 1909–1945*, Weidenfeld and Nicolson, London, 1983.

Pieter Tazelaar

Keith Jeffery, *MI6: The History of the Secret Intelligence Service 1909–1949*, Bloomsbury, London 2010.

The secret war mission that inspired Goldfinger scene, *Daily Telegraph*, 17 April 2010.

Paul Gorka

Paul Gorka, *Budapest Betrayed*, Oak-Tree Books, Wembley, 1986.

Ryszard Kukliński

CIA Electronic Reading Room, Historical Collections, Martial Law & Kukliński: CIA Deputy Director Operations to SoS, SecDef, Asst to President for National Security Affairs, Dir NSA, Polish Government Plans for the Possible Introduction of Martial Law, 11 February 1981.

CIA Deputy Director Operations to SoS, SecDef, Asst to President for National Security Affairs, Dir NSA, Soviet Polish Positions on the Declaration of Martial Law, 29 April 1981.

CIA Deputy Director Operations to SoS, SecDef, Asst to President for National Security Affairs, Dir NSA, New Draft Decree on Martial Law, Current Situation in Poland, 9 September 1981.

CIA Intelligence Information Special Report, 'Report on the Status of Preparations of the State in Case of Need to Introduce Martial Law and Basic Effects of this Measure,' 7 October 1981.

Douglas J. MacEachin, *US Intelligence and the Polish Crisis 1980–1981*, Center for the Study of Intelligence, Washington, 2000.

Adam Michnik, Hero or Traitor, *Transitions*, Prague, September 1998.

CIA had Agent on Polish General Staff, *Washington Post*, 4 June 1986.

Dongfan (Greg) Chung

United States of America vs Dongfan 'Greg' Chung, Memorandum of Decision, US District Court, Central District of California Southern Division, 16 July 2009.

David Wise, *Tiger Trap: America's Secret War with China*, Houghton Mifflin Harcourt, Boston, 2011.

A New Kind of Spy, *New Yorker*, 5 May 2014.

Katrina Leung

A Review of the FBI's Handling and Oversight of FBI Asset Katrina Leung, Department of Justice, Office of the Inspector-General, Special Report, May 2006.

David Wise, *Tiger Trap: America's Secret War with China*, Houghton Mifflin Harcourt, Boston, 2011.

Shirley A. Kan, China: Suspected Acquisition of US Nuclear Weapons Secrets, Congressional Research Service Report, 1 February 2006.

Chapter 5

Sidney Reilly

TNA AIR 76/421/184 Officer Service Record for Sidney George Reilly.

FO 371/3350, Report of Work Done in Russia.

FO 395/185, CX044633, report by ST1, 13 July 1918.

KV 2/827 MI5 Personal File of Sidney George Reilly.

WO 372/16/193799 Medal Card of Sidney George Reilly, Royal Flying Corps.

Supplement to London Gazette, 12 February 1919.

Information provided to the author in confidence.

Keith Jeffery, *MI6: The History of the Secret Intelligence Service 1909–1949*, Bloomsbury, London 2010.

Andrew Cook, *Ace of Spies: The True Story of Sidney Reilly*, History Press, Stroud, 2004.

Richard B. Spence, *Trust No One: The Secret World of Sidney Reilly*, Feral House, Los Angeles, 2002.

Gordon Brook-Shepherd, *Iron Maze: The Western Secret Services and the Bolsheviks*, Macmillan, London, 1998.

Lieut-Col Norman Thwaites, *Velvet and Vinegar*, Grayson & Grayson, London, 1932.

Judd, *The Quest for C*; Sidney Reilly, *Adventures of a British Master Spy*, Biteback, London, 2014.

Robert Bruce Lockhart, *Memoirs of a British Agent*, Putnam, London, 1932.

George Hill, *Go Spy the Land*, Biteback, London, 2014.

Juan Pujol Garcia

TNA KV 2/4190-KV 2/4214 MI5 Personal Files of Juan Pujol Garcia, alias Garbo.

Juan Pujol Garcia and Nigel West, *Codename Garbo*, Biteback, London, 2011.

Ralph Erskine & Michael Smith (eds), *The Bletchley Park Codebreakers*, Biteback, London, 2011.

Paul Fidrmuc

TNA ADM223/792, NID12 Selections from History.

KV 2/196-KV 2/201 MI5 Personal Files of Paul Georg Fidrmuc, code name Ostro.

Joseph S. Petersen

Betrayers of the Trust: Joseph Sidney Petersen, NSA Cryptologic Almanac, 24 February 1998.

Cees Wiebes, Operation 'Piet': The Joseph Sidney Petersen Jr. Spy Case, a Dutch 'Mole' Inside the National Security Agency, *Intelligence and National Security*, Vol. 23, No. 4, August 2008.

Richard W. Miller and Svetlana Ogorodnikova

Agent of the FBI Accused of Giving Secrets to Soviet, *New York Times*, 4 October 1984.

FBI Agent Charged in Espionage, *Washington Post*, 4 October 1984.

FBI Cites Cash Woes as Motive, *New York Times*, 4 October 1984.

FBI Agent in Spying Case is said to have had Problems at Work, *New York Times*, 5 October 1984.

Wild Story of sex with Andropov, *The Times*, 17 December 1984.

The FBI'S Most Unwanted Spy Case, *New York Times*, 10 February 1985.

Trial Opens for Émigré Couple Accused of Spying for Russia with an FBI Agent, *New York Times*, 20 April 1985.

'James Bond Fantasy' Told at Spying Trial, *LA Times*, 14 June 1985.

Ex-Agent of FBI tells of Spy Case 'Fantasy', *New York Times*, 14 June 1985.

Ex-Agent of FBI Faces 2D Spy Trial, *New York Times*, 13 Feb 1986.

Spy Trial Clash Turns on Motives of Émigré, *New York Times*, 12 May 1986.

Richard Miller, the only FBI agent ever charged with Espionage, *UPI*, June 19, 1986.

Agent Says He Was 'Stupid,' Not Traitorous, *New York Times*, 8 December 1989.

FBI Man Guilty of Soviet Spying, *New York Times*, 10 October 1990.

From LA With Love …, *Washington Post*, 5 May 1991; Convicted Spy Fights Deportation: Espionage: Woman who served prison sentence in Richard Miller case says she was forced to plead guilty, *LA Times*, 25 September 1995.

Convicted Spy Testifies in San Diego Murder Case, *AP*, 27 June 2002.

Russell Warren Howe, *Sleeping With the FBI: Sex, Booze, Russians and the Saga of an American Counterspy Who Couldn't*, National Press Books, Washington DC, 1993.

Aldrich Ames

Sandra Grimes and Jeanne Vertefeuille, *Circle of Treason*, Naval Institute Press, Annapolis, 2012.

Victor Cherkashin, *Spy Handler*, Perseus, New York, 2005.

An Assessment of the Aldrich H. Ames Espionage Case and Its Implications for US Intelligence, Senate Select Committee on Intelligence, 1 November 1994.

United States Tax Court, Aldrich H. Ames v. Commissioner of Internal Revenue, 28 May 1999.

The Two Million Dollar Spy, *BBC Panorama*, 1 January 2005.

Why I Spied: Aldrich Ames, *New York Times*, 31 July 1994.

Aldrich Ames Interviewed, *NPR*, 16 February 1995.

Robert Hanssen

USA v. Robert Philip Hanssen: Affidavit in Support of Criminal Complaint, Arrest Warrant and Search Warrant, United States District Court for the Eastern District of Virginia, 16 February 2001.

A Review of the FBI's Performance in Deterring, Detecting, and
  Investigating the Espionage Activities of Robert Philip Hanssen,
  Department of Justice, Office of the Inspector-General, August 2003.
David Wise, *Spy: The Inside Story of How FBI's Robert Hanssen Betrayed
  America*, Random House, New York, 2003.
Sandra Grimes and Jeanne Vertefeuille, *Circle of Treason*, Naval Institute Press,
  Annapolis, 2012.
Victor Cherkashin, *Spy Handler*, Perseus, New York, 2005.

Chapter 6

Karl Kruger

TNA ADM 137/4679, MI1c Section XVI.
ADM 223/637, various reports from agent TR/16.
ADM 337/120/119, service record of Charles Louis Power.
Judd, *The Quest for C*; Information supplied to the author in confidence.
Captain Henry Landau, *The Spy Net*, Biteback, London, 2015.
Captain Henry Landau, *All's Fair: The Story of the British Secret Service behind
  the German Lines*, G.P. Putnam's Sons, New York, 1934.
German estimate of forces, *The Times*, 6 June 1916.
Fate of the Derfflinger, *The Times*, 6 June 1916.
Britannia still rules the waves, *The Times*, 6 June 1916.
Germany and the Lützow, *The Times*, 10 June 1916.
John Campbell, *Jutland: An Analysis of the Fighting*, Conway Maritime Press,
  London, 1987.

Johann de Graaf

TNA PRO KV 3/12 CX report on Soviet Espionage Activities.
FO 369/2189, General Correspondence for China.
TNA PRO KV 3/129, Report on the activities of the Communist
  International (The Comintern).
KV 3/145, Russian Intelligence Organisation in the Far East.
FO 1093/92 The Noulens Case; National Archives and Records
  Administration (NARA) RG 263, box 7, document 96.
KGB archives, file 72240, vol. 6; India Office Library and Records
  L/P&J/12/45.
L/P&J/12/144, R.S. Rose and Gordon D. Scott, *Johnny: A Spy's Life*,
  Pennsylvania State University Press, University Park, 2010.
Michael Smith, *Foley: The Spy Who Saved 10,0000 Jews*, Biteback, London,
  2016; Peking police raid, *The Times*, 7 April 1927.
Soviet plots in China, compromising documents, *The Times*, 18 April 1927.

'Reds' in China, *The Times*, 23 April 1927; information provided to the
    author in confidence.
Lived life of intrigue, espionage, *Ottawa Citizen*, 12 January 1954.
Antony Best, *British Intelligence and the Japanese Challenge in Asia 1914–1941*,
    Palgrave, London, 2002.
William Waack, *Die Vergessene Revolution*, Aufbau, Berlin, 1994.
Charles A. Willoughby, *Sorge: Soviet Master Spy*, William Kimber, London,
    1952.
H. J. Lethbridge, *All about Shanghai: A Standard Guidebook*, Oxford
    University Press, Oxford, 1986.
Frederick S. Litten, 'The Noulens Affair', *China Quarterly 138*, June 1994.
E.H. Carr, *The Twilight of the Comintern 1930–1935*, Macmillan, London,
    1982.
Fernando Watson, *Olga*, Peter Halban, London, 1990.

Viktor Vasilyevich Bogomoletz

TNA HO 344/133 Certificate of Naturalisation.
KV2/1106 Identification of Bogomoletz as Agent 31109, previously
    HV109.
Nigel West & Oleg Tsarev, *Triplex: Secrets from the Cambridge Spies*, Yale
    University Press, London, 2009.
Keith Jeffery, *MI6: The History of the Secret Intelligence Service 1909–1949*,
    Bloomsbury, London 2010.
Alin Spanu, Colaborarea Structurilor Informative Romane cu Cele Anglo–
    Franceze in Primul Deceniu Interbelic (1919–1929), *Anuarul Arhivelor
    Mureşene*, Serie Noua Nr II (VI) – 2013.

Oleg Penkovsky

CIA Electronic Reading Room, Historical Collections: Transcripts of
    meetings with Penkovsky:
John M. Maury, Memorandum for the Record, 13 July 1961.
Penkovsky Operational Plan, Casing of Drop Site.
Letter No. 7, 10 January 1961.
The Soviet Missile Venture in Cuba, CIA/RSS/DD/I Staff Study, 17
    February 1964.
Reflections on Handling Penkovsky, *CIA Studies in Intelligence*, undated;
    Kennedy to McCone, 13 May 1963.
Helms to DCI, 8 July 1963.
Osborn to Deputy Director (Plans), 10 December 1982.
CIA Biographic Data on Colonel Oleg Vladimirovich Penkovsky.
Marshal Loses Post in Soviet over Spy, *New York Times*, 30 May 1963.
Oleg Penkovsky, *The Penkovsky Papers*, Fontana, London, 1967.
Greville Wynne, *The Man from Moscow*, Hutchinson, London, 1967.

Anthony Verrier, *Through the Looking Glass: British Foreign Policy in the Age of Illusions*, Jonathan Cape, London, 1983.

Jerrold Schecter & Peter Deriabin, *The Spy Who Saved the World*, Charles Scribner's, New York, 1992.

Gordon Brook-Shepherd, *The Storm Birds: Soviet Post-War Defectors*, Weidenfeld and Nicolson, London, 1988.

Edward Lee Howard

Turncoat former CIA agent granted asylum by Soviets, *Washington Times*, 8 August 1986.

Why Edward Lee Howard Sold Out for Money and Revenge, *Newsday*, 26 October 1986.

The Spy Who Got Away, *New York Times*, 2 November 1986.

Edward Lee Howard, 50, Spy Who Escaped to Soviet Haven, *New York Times*, 23 July 2002.

CIA Defector Edward Lee Howard Said to Have Died in Moscow, *Washington Post*, 21 July 2002.

Grimes and Vertefeuille, *Circle of Treason*.

David Wise, *The Spy Who Got Away: The Inside Story of the CIA Agent Who Betrayed His Country*, Random House, New York, 1988.

Edward Lee Howard, *Safe House: The Compelling Memoirs of the Only CIA Spy to Seek Asylum in Russia*, National, Bethesda, 1995.

Chapter 7

John Merrett

TNA FO 371/3975, Merrett to Foreign Secretary, 4 May 1920.

Bulmer to FO, 29 June 1920.

W.H. Murray-Campbell to FO, 15 July 1920.

T 161/30 letter from Paul Dukes to Under-Secretary of State at Foreign Office.

The Russian Terror, *The Times*, 24 October 1918.

Paul Dukes, *Red Dusk and the Morrow*, Biteback, London, 2012.

Edith Tudor-Hart

TNA FCO 158/27-FCO 158/28 Files of the Peach investigation [Peach was the MI5 code name for Kim Philby].

KV 2/1012-KV 2/1014 Edith Tudor Hart MI5 case files.

KV 2/1603-KV 2/1604 Alexander Ethan Tudor Hart MI5 personal files.

KV 2/4091-KV 2/4093 Edith Tudor Hart MI5 personal files.

Genrikh Borovik, *The Philby Files*, Warner, London, 1995.

Nigel West & Oleg Tsarev, *The Crown Jewels*, Harper Collins, London, 1998.

Photography in Commerce, *The Times*, 6 September 1936.

Wolf Suschitzky, Edith Tudor Hart, *Das Auge des Gewissens*, Dirk Nishen, Kreuzberg, 1986.

John Cairncross

KGB Archives, Moscow, File of Lista (Liszt) 83896, Volumes 1–5.

TNA AB 4/1014, Report by MAUD committee on the use of uranium as a source of power; CAB 104/227, Scientific Advisory Committee: investigations on the use of uranium for a bomb.

West & Tsarev, *Crown Jewels*.

John Cairncross, *The Enigma Spy*, Century, London, 1997

Letter to author from Geoffrey Robinson, 14 January 1998.

Ana Belen Montes

Review of the Actions Taken to Deter, Detect and Investigate the Espionage Activities of Ana Belen Montes, Office of The Inspector General of the Department of Defense, Deputy Inspector General for Intelligence, 16 June 2005.

Hearing before the House Committee on Foreign Affairs Sub-committee on the Western Hemisphere 'Cuba's Global Network of Terrorism, Intelligence and Warfare', Statement submitted by Michelle Van Cleave, Former National Counter-intelligence Executive, 17 May 2012.

DIA fears Cuban mole aided Russia, China, *Washington Times*, 1 February 2003.

Cuba spies sell to US foes, *Washington Times*, 26 October 2007.

Ana Montes did much harm spying for Cuba. Chances are, you haven't heard of her, *Washington Post*, 18 April 2013.

Cuba deal reveals new clues in case of Ana Montes, 'the most important spy you've never heard of', *Washington Post*, 18 December 2014.

US spy freed by Cuba was long-time asset, *Washington Post*, 18 December 2014.

The most dangerous US spy you've never heard of, *CNN*, 11 July 2016.

Islamic State

US strike believed to have killed 'Jihadi John,' Islamic State executioner, *Washington Post*, 13 November 2015.

Pentagon Says 'Jihadi John' Was Probably Killed in Airstrike, *New York Times*, 13 November 2015.

How the US and UK tracked down and killed Jihadi John, *Daily Telegraph*, 13 November 2015.

Jihadi John 'dead': MI5 on alert amid fears of Isil revenge attack, *Daily Telegraph*, 14 November 2015.

How Jihadi John was 'evaporated', *Sunday Times*, 15 November 2015.

Chapter 8

Putin orders Active Measures Campaign

James Comey, FBI Director, Testimony to the House Intelligence
Committee, 20 March 2017.

Office of the Director of National Intelligence, Intelligence Community
Assessment, Assessing Russian Activities and Intentions in Recent US
Elections, ICA 2017-01D, 6 January 2017.

Report on the Investigation into Russian Interference in the 2016
Presidential Election, Special Counsel Robert S. Mueller, III,
Washington, D.C., March 2019.

Steele Reports 2016/095, Russia/US Presidential Election: Further
Indications of Extensive Conspiracy Between Trump's Campaign Team
and the Kremlin, 20 July 2016.

Steele Reports 2016/097, Russia-US Presidential Election: Kremlin
Concern that Political Fallout from DNC E-Mail Hacking Affair
Spiralling Out of Control, 30 July 2016.

Steele Reports 016/080, US Presidential Election: Republican Candidate
Donald Trump's Activities in Russia and Compromising Relationship
with the Kremlin, 20 June 2016.

Internet Research Agency

Report on the Investigation into Russian Interference in the 2016
Presidential Election, Special Counsel Robert S. Mueller, III,
Washington, D.C., March 2019.

What We Know About Russians Sanctioned by the United States, *New York
Times*, 17 February 2018.

FSB/GRU agents in US and payments

Steele Reports 2016/095, Russia/US Presidential Election: Further
Indications of Extensive Conspiracy Between Trump's Campaign Team
and the Kremlin, 20 July 2016.

Steele Reports 2016/097, Russia-US Presidential Election: Kremlin
Concern that Political Fallout from DNC E-Mail Hacking Affair
Spiralling Out of Control, 30 July 2016.

Steele Reports 016/080, US Presidential Election: Republican Candidate
Donald Trump's Activities in Russia and Compromising Relationship
with the Kremlin, 20 June 2016.

Russia's pension money for its veterans escapes scrutiny as it flows into US,
McClatchy, 21 February 2017.

Hacking of DNC computers and email accounts

Report on the Investigation into Russian Interference in the 2016
    Presidential Election, Special Counsel Robert S. Mueller, III,
    Washington, D.C., March 2019.

Office of the Director of National Intelligence, Intelligence Community
    Assessment, Assessing Russian Activities and Intentions in Recent US
    Elections, ICA 2017-01D, 6 January 2017.

Russian government hackers penetrated DNC, stole opposition research on
    Trump, *Washington Post*, 14 June 2016.

Spy Agency Consensus Grows That Russia Hacked D.N.C., *New York Times*,
    26 July 2016.

Carter Page

Report on the Investigation into Russian Interference in the 2016
    Presidential Election, Special Counsel Robert S. Mueller, III,
    Washington, D.C., March 2019.

A transcript of Donald Trump's meeting with The Washington Post edito-
    rial board, *Washington Post*, 21 March 2016.

Steele Reports 2106/094, Russia: Secret Kremlin Meetings Attended by
    Trump Advisor, Carter Page in Moscow (July 2016), 19 July 2016.

Steele Reports 2016/134, Russia/US Presidential Election: Further Details
    of Kremlin Liaison with Trump Campaign, 18 October 2016.

Letter from Carter Page to FBI Director James Comey, 25 September 2016.

Letter from Carter Page to Voting Section, Civil Rights Division, US
    Department of Justice, 12 February 2017.

US intel officials probe ties between Trump adviser and Kremlin, *Yahoo
    News*, 23 September 2016.

Trump campaign approved adviser's trip to Moscow, *Politico*, 7 March 2017;
    Memos: CEO of Russia's state oil company offered Trump adviser, allies
    a cut of huge deal if sanctions were lifted, *Business Insider*, 27 January
    2017.

Trump adviser's public comments, ties to Moscow stir unease in both par-
    ties, *Washington Post*, 5 August 2016.

Trump campaign approved adviser's trip to Moscow, *Politico*, 7 March 2017.

Memos: CEO of Russia's state oil company offered Trump adviser, allies a
    cut of huge deal if sanctions were lifted, *Business Insider*, 27 January 2017.

Trump adviser's public comments, ties to Moscow stir unease in both par-
    ties, *Washington Post*, 5 August 2016.

Harry Reid Cites Evidence of Russian Tampering in US Vote, and Seeks
    FBI Inquiry, *New York Times*, 29 August 2016. United States of America
    v Evgeny Buryakov, aka Zhenya, Igor Sporyshev and Victor Podobnyy,
    Sealed Complaint, 23 January 2015.

Trump campaign adviser Carter Page targeted for recruitment by Russian
    spies, *ABC News*, 4 April 2017.

George Papadopoulos

Report on the Investigation into Russian Interference in the 2016 Presidential Election, Special Counsel Robert S. Mueller, III, Washington, D.C., March 2019.

United States District Court for the District of Columbia, United States of America v George Papadopoulos, Case 1:17-cr-00182-RDM, Statement of the Offense, 5 October 2017.

Code Name Crossfire Hurricane: The Secret Origins of the Trump Investigation, *New York Times*, 16 May 2018.

Paul Manafort

Report on the Investigation into Russian Interference in the 2016 Presidential Election, Special Counsel Robert S. Mueller, III, Washington, D.C., March 2019.

Secret Ledger in Ukraine Lists Cash for Donald Trump's Campaign Chief, *New York Times*, 14 August 2016.

How Paul Manafort Wielded Power in Ukraine Before Advising Donald Trump, *New York Times*, 31 July 2016.

Intercepted Russian Communications Part of Inquiry into Trump Associates, *New York Times*, 19 January 2017.

Trump Links with Russia

Fact-checking Trump's claim that he has no business ties to Russia, *Vox*, 17 February 2017.

Steele Reports 2016/095, Russia/US Presidential Election: Further Indications of Extensive Conspiracy Between Trump's Campaign Team and the Kremlin, July 2016.

US election: Trump's Russian riddle, *Financial Times*, 14 August 2016.

The Curious World of Donald Trump's Private Russian Connections, *The American Interest*, 19 December 2016.

Michael Sater

Real Estate Executive with Hand in Trump Projects Rose From Tangled Past, *New York Times*, 17 December 2007.

Former Mafia-linked figure describes association with Trump, *Washington Post*, 17 May 2016.

US Supreme Court Petition, No 14-676, Lorienton N.A. Palmer, Frederick Martin Oberlander, V. John Doe 98-Cr-01101, United States of America.

Michael Flynn

United States District Court for the District of Colombia, United States of America v Michael T Flynn, Case 1:17-cr-00232-RC, Statement of Offense, 1 December 2017.

Top Trump aide in frequent contact with Russia's ambassador, *AP*, 13 January 2017.

Flynn Was Brought Down by Illegal Leaks to News Media, Trump Says, *New York Times*, 15 February 2017.

Michael Flynn Resigns as National Security Adviser, *New York Times*, 13 February 2017.

Edward Snowden

Marc Thiessen: The danger of what Edward Snowden has NOT revealed, *Washington Post*, 1 June 2013.

Edward Snowden: the whistleblower behind the NSA surveillance revelations, *Guardian*, 11 June 2013.

Snowden sought Booz Allen job to gather evidence on NSA surveillance, *South China Morning Post*, 24 June 2013.

Edward Snowden: NSA whistleblower answers reader questions, *Guardian*, 27 June 2013.

Snowden Says He Took No Secret Files to Russia, *New York Times*, 17 October 2013.

Edward Snowden: I brought no leaked NSA documents to Russia, *New York Times*, 18 October 2013.

Snowden denies stealing passwords to access secret files, *Washington Post*, 23 January 2014.

Edward Snowden: A Timeline, *NBC*, 26 May 2014.

NSA Officials: Snowden Emailed With Question, Not Concern, *NBC*, 13 January 2015.

A Bill's Surveillance Limits, *New York Times*, 1 May 2015.

NSA Collection of Bulk Call Data Is Ruled Illegal, *New York Times*, 7 May 2015.

US Surveillance in Place Since 9/11 Is Sharply Limited, *New York Times*, 2 June 2015.

Investigatory Powers Tribunal, Bulk Data Judgement in case of Privacy International v. Secretary of State for Foreign and Commonwealth Affairs, Secretary of State for the Home Department, Government Communications Headquarters, Security Service and Secret Intelligence Service, 29 July 2016.

'Extreme surveillance' becomes UK law with barely a whimper, *Guardian*, 19 November 2016; Luke Harding, *The Snowden Files*, Guardian Books, London, 2014.

Alex Younger on Agents

Remarks by the Chief of the Secret Intelligence Service, SIS Headquarters, Vauxhall Cross, 8 December 2016.

GLOSSARY

Abwehr: German military intelligence organisation formed in 1920, initially as a counter-espionage organisation (*Abwehr* is German for defence) but expanding into foreign intelligence operations and sabotage. It was abolished in 1944 and its role taken over by the *Sicherheitsdienst*, the SS and Nazi Party security and intelligence service. (See also ***Sicherheitsdienst***)

Access Agent: A person based in an organisation such as a university or government organisation in a target country who looks for potential agents and introduces them to a Case Officer for recruitment.

Accommodation Address: A house or apartment used by the handler to communicate with an agent. (See also **Safe House**)

Actionable Intelligence: The gold standard of intelligence acquired from an agent. Intelligence that can be acted upon to further the aims of the service's government.

Active Measures: *Aktivnyye Meropriyatiya*. Multi-faceted Russian operations technique using various combinations of disinformation, deception, propaganda (including fake news merged with genuine facts), co-ordinated exploitation of various communications media, influence operations, psychological operations, false-flag operations, and so-called 'Decomposition' of target organisations and people, even extending to the death of perceived opponents, often but not always under the cover of 'natural deaths'. Russian Active Measures operations date back to the times of the Tsars and were adopted by the Bolsheviks in the wake of the Revolution to serve their own cause, in particular in the 1920s when various anti-Soviet émigré organisations were created or taken over by the OGPU in order to confuse, deceive and influence Western intelligence agencies. The complexity of Active Measures was not fully understood by the Western intelligence agencies until the 1970s and '80s with the Soviet active measures campaign to try to thwart the award of the Nobel Peace Prize to Andrei Sakharov and the highly successful campaign to oppose the introduction of US cruise missiles to Europe. They have re-emerged as a powerful weapon of the Russian state under Vladimir Putin's leadership. The expansion of the media via the internet and the widespread use of mobile telephones to access social networks has greatly increased its effectiveness, as for example during the 2016 US Presidential elections. (See also **Decomposition**)

Agent: A person who is not an official member of an intelligence service but is employed or used by that service either as a source of information or for a specific role in assisting an operation.

Agent-in-Place: An agent inside a foreign government organisation who is persuaded to remain in place rather than defecting in order to continue producing intelligence or influencing a situation.

Agent-of-Influence: A person who works within the government or media of a target country to influence national policy in a way that assists the controlling service.

Agent Provocateur: Agent employed to influence someone else into carrying out an act that will discredit them or their organisation or create a situation necessary for a specific operation.

Agent-Running: The process of recruiting, directing and managing (or 'running') an agent.

al-Amn al-'Amm: Iraqi Directorate of General Security. Iraqi internal security organisation set up in 1921 and dissolved in the wake of the 2003 US-led invasion.

ÁVH: *Államvédelmi Hatóság* (State Protection Authority). Hungarian intelligence and internal security organisation from 1945 to 1956.

Asset: An agent or other clandestine source or capability, or simply someone who assists an operation.

Babysitter: An intelligence officer or agent put in place to look after an operation or network on a temporary basis, or someone who looks after a defector or agent during a debriefing.

Bagman: Someone who makes covert payments to agents or bribes others to assist an operation.

BfV: *Bundesamt für Verfassungsschutz* (Federal Office for the Protection of the Constitution). The German internal security service.

Biuro Szyfrów: Polish inter-war Cipher Bureau that made the first break into the German army's Enigma machine cipher.

Black Bag Job: Covert entry of a building in order to obtain information. Often used in counter-espionage operations against suspected agents of a foreign intelligence service.

Blown: An intelligence officer, agent, capability or operation that has become known to the target, or more often to another intelligence service, and is therefore no longer of any operational use.

BND: *Bundesnachrichtendienst* (Federal Intelligence Service). The German foreign intelligence service set up in 1956.

Bridge Agent: An agent who acts as a courier between a case officer and an agent.

Brush Contact/Brush Meeting/Brush Pass: A brief encounter during which intelligence or other information is passed between one agent or intelligence officer and another.

Burned: When an agent is known to the other side, or their identity is deliberately disclosed to the other side, and they are therefore no longer of any operational use.

Case Officer: An intelligence officer who recruits, runs or controls agents and operations.

Chance Contact: An unplanned meeting between an intelligence officer and an agent.

Cheka: *Vserossijskaya Chrezvychajnaya Komissiya* (the All-Russian Extraordinary Commission for Combating Counter-revolution and Sabotage). Bolshevik intelligence and security service set up by Lenin in 1917 and replaced in 1922 by the GPU, which a year later became the OGPU.

CIA: Central Intelligence Agency. The US foreign intelligence service set up in 1947.

Clean: Someone who has no previous contact with an intelligence service and is therefore less likely to be detected by an opposing counter-espionage service.

Compromised: When an intelligence officer, agent, capability or operation has become known to the other side.

Contact Agent: A go-between who deals with the agent on behalf of the case officer, usually when the agent is working undercover.

Controller: The intelligence officer in overall charge of an operation or network. Often based at headquarters with no day-to-day physical contact with the agent(s).

Co-opted Agent/Co-optee: *Doverennoye Litso*. Russian intelligence term for someone who is required to act as an agent by the state because they have a specific capability needed for an operation.

Counter-espionage: Carrying out security and intelligence operations in order to protect the service's own authorities from operations mounted by a foreign intelligence service.

Counter-intelligence: US term for counter-espionage. UK term for study of foreign intelligence services.

Courier: Someone who passes secret information or money between one intelligence officer or agent and another.

Cover: An assumed persona and background used by an intelligence officer or agent to disguise his or her real activities. (See also **Legend**)

Cut-out: Someone who acts as an intermediary between intelligence officers and/or agents involved in an operation in order to avoid their detection.

CX Report: SIS intelligence report.

Dangle: A person presented surreptitiously to another intelligence agency as a potential agent in order to use that agent as a double agent or as part of a deception operation.

DCRI: *Direction Centrale du Renseignement Interièur* (Central Directorate of Interior Intelligence). French internal security service between 2008 and 2014. (See also **DST** and **DGSI**)

Dead Drop/Dead Letter Box (DLB)/Dead Letter Drop: A secret location where intelligence, money or instructions can be left for an agent or intelligence officer to retrieve. The drop is said to be 'filled' or 'loaded' by the agent and 'cleared' by the handler.

Decomposition: *Razlozheniye*. A key part of Russian '**Active Measures**' that involves inducing internal strife, dissension or tensions between members of a target organisation in order to render it ineffective, destroy its reputation and reduce its influence. Also refers to a similar process used to destroy the reputation and influence of a target individual.

Deep Cover: An intelligence officer or agent operating in a target country with the persona of an ordinary member of the public, usually including a normal job and during long-term operations even extending to marriage and a family.

Denial and Deception Operations: Actions designed to disguise the acquisition and value of 'actionable intelligence' obtained, when it was obtained and what actions were taken as a result.

Deuxième Bureau de l'État-Major Général: The Second Bureau of the General Staff, the French foreign intelligence service between 1871 and 1940. Usually known simply as the *Deuxième Bureau*.

DGSE: *Direction Genérale de la Sécurité Extérieure* (General Directorate for External Security). The French foreign intelligence service set up in 1982.

DGSI: *Direction Genérale de la Sécurité Intérieure* (General Directorate for Internal Security). French counter-espionage, counter-terrorist and counter cyber-crime organisation formed in 2014. (See also **DST** and **DCRI**)

DIA: Defense Intelligence Agency. US armed forces intelligence service.

DGI: *Dirección General de Inteligencia* (Cuban Intelligence Directorate), the country's foreign intelligence service, set up in 1961.

DIS: Defence Intelligence Staff, UK Ministry of Defence intelligence analysis organisation.

Discard: An agent used for a task that is likely to result in whoever carries it out being compromised. The discard's role is usually designed to protect another better placed agent or intelligence officer.

Disinformation Agent: *Agent-Dezinformator*. Russian term for a double agent who is being used as part of a deception operation.

Double Agent: An agent working for two separate, opposing intelligence services at the same time, usually under control of only one of those two services and feeding the second false information while at the same time gathering intelligence from the second intelligence service on behalf of the first.

Dry Cleaning: Counter-surveillance procedure designed to ensure that an intelligence officer, agent, capability or operation is not under surveillance from the opposing intelligence service.

DST: *Direction de la Surveillance du Territoire* (Directorate of Territorial Surveillance). French post-war internal security service. It was replaced in 2008 by the DCRI, *Direction Centrale du Renseignement Intérieur* (Central Directorate of Interior Intelligence). (See also **DCRI** and **DGSI**)

Exfiltration: The clandestine removal of an agent, intelligence officer or defector from hostile territory, often accompanied by their close family.

False-Flag: Technique designed to make it look as if an operation was carried out by another country, often to discredit that country. Also the recruitment of an agent under the guise of the intelligence service of a country allied to the agent's own country – as in the cases of Marianne Lenzkow and Margarethe Lubig.

FBI: Federal Bureau of Investigation. US domestic counter-espionage service and federal law enforcement agency, set up in 1908 and taking on a counter-espionage role in 1917.

Fireman: British term for an intelligence officer sent out from London to help deal with a sudden operational crisis, often when it occurs in an area where there is only limited or no SIS presence.

Freelance Agent: An agent who is prepared to work for or provide intelligence to anyone who will pay him or her.

FSB: *Federal'naya Sluzhba Bezopasnosti Rossiyskoy Federatsii* (Federal Security Service of the Russian Federation). Russian internal security organisation that replaced the FSK in 1995. Increasingly involved in operations abroad and to some extent over-shadowing the **SVR**.

FSK: *Federal'naya Sluzhba Kontrrazvedki* (Federal Counterintelligence Service). The Russian internal security service after the dissolution the Soviet Union in 1991. Replaced in 1995 by the FSB.

GC&CS: Government Code and Cypher School. The British signals intelligence organisation between 1919 and 1945, most famous for its work breaking the German Enigma ciphers at Bletchley Park during the Second World War.

GCHQ: Government Communications Headquarters. The British signals intelligence organisation. The name originated as a cover name for Bletchley Park and was adopted as a formal title when it moved first to Eastcote in North London and then to Cheltenham after the Second World War.

GRU: *Glavnoye Razvedyvatelnoye Upravleniye* (Main Intelligence Directorate). Russian military intelligence service. Operates in parallel with the **SVR** in collection of human intelligence abroad and has its own *Rezident* in every Russian embassy abroad. Specialises in collecting technical intelligence and offensive cyber operations such as the hacking of the Democrat Party's email system during the 2016 US Presidential Election.

Handler: An intelligence service case officer who runs an agent or network of agents.

Head (or Chief) of Station: The intelligence officer in charge of his service's offices in a foreign city, usually but not always in his country's embassy or mission.

Honeytrap: The use of sex to ensnare a potential agent.

Humint: Human intelligence. The use of human agents and sources in order to acquire intelligence.

HVA: *Hauptverwaltung Aufklärung* (Main Directorate for Reconnaissance). The foreign intelligence service of the former German Democratic Republic (East Germany). It was an integral part of the *Ministerium für Staatssicherheit* (Ministry for State Security), better known as the Stasi.

Illegal: Russian intelligence officer or agent living an apparently normal life under a false identity in a foreign country, often with a job and a locally acquired partner who is unaware of their covert role.

Infiltration: Gaining covert access to a country or organisation without being detected.

Influence Operation: Operation designed to influence a person, government or organisation to act in a way that is advantageous to the service's aims.

IB: Intelligence Bureau, Indian internal security service, set up in 1887.

Intelligence Officer: A full-time employee of the intelligence service as opposed to an Agent.

Joe: Slang for an Agent, implies a closeness between the Handler and the Agent.

KGB: *Komitet Gosudarstvennoy Bezopasnosti* (Committee for State Security). Soviet internal security and foreign intelligence service from 1946 to 1991.

Legend: The cover story and false identity of an agent or intelligence officer operating in a foreign country.

MfS: *Ministerium für Staatssicherheit* (Ministry for State Security). The East German intelligence and security service from 1950 to 1990. (See also **HVA** and **Stasi**)

MI1c: Cover title used by British foreign intelligence service from 1916 until 1940, deriving from the designation of the War Office department which liaised with it during that period.

MI5: Title commonly used for the British internal Security Service. It derives from a reorganisation of War Office intelligence in January 1916 which designated the counter-espionage section of the Secret Service Bureau as the fifth department of military intelligence.

MI6: Title commonly used for the British Secret Intelligence Service. It derives from the designation of the War Office department liaising with SIS between 1940 and 1964.

Mole: An agent who penetrates another intelligence service or governmental organisation.

Moscow Centre: The KGB Headquarters in Moscow. (See also **The Centre**)

Mossad: Israeli Foreign Intelligence Service, literally means the Institute, set up in 1949. Its full title is *HaMossad leModi'in ule-Tafkidim Meyu adim.*

MSS: Chinese Ministry of State Security (*Zhonghua Renmm Gongheguo Guojia Anquanbu*). The intelligence and security service of the People's Republic of China, set up in 1983.

Mukhabarat: Iraqi Intelligence Service from 1976 to 2003. Its full title was *Jihaz al-Mukhabarat al-Amma* (General Directorate of Intelligence).

Nachrichten Abteilung: The foreign intelligence service of the German Imperial Navy between 1901 and 1919.

National Security Bureau: The Taiwanese foreign intelligence service (*Zhonghua Mmguo Guojia Anquanju*), set up in 1955.

Natural Cover: A job already held by a potential agent that places him or her in a position to collect intelligence or perform a specific role for an intelligence service.

NKVD: *Narodnyi Komissariat Vnutrennikh Del* (People's Commissariat for Internal Affairs). Soviet internal security and foreign intelligence service from 1934 to 1946.

Non-official Cover: Intelligence officers working for one of their country's organisations in a target country under cover of a role that disguises their affiliation but does not have diplomatic immunity.

NSA: National Security Agency. The US signals intelligence organisation set up in 1952.

Official Cover: Intelligence officers on the staff of their country's embassies or missions in foreign countries who are given an official role that disguises their intelligence affiliation and grants them diplomatic immunity.

OGPU: *Obyedinyonnoye Gosudarstvennoye Politicheskoye Upravleniye* (All-Union State Political Administration). Soviet security and foreign intelligence organisation from the creation of the Soviet Union in 1923 until 1934.

OSS: Office of Strategic Services. The US foreign intelligence and special operations organisation during the Second World War. It was created in 1942 and dissolved in 1945.

Penetration: Placing an agent or intelligence officer inside a target organisation.

Post Box/Letter Box: An agent to whom intelligence material/reports are handed who acts as a Cut-Out between the agent and the Handler, or an address to which intelligence material/ reports can be sent.

PVDE: *Polícia de Vigilância e Defesa do Estado* (Surveillance and State Defence Police). The Portuguese internal security organisation from 1933 to 1945, commonly known as 'the International Police,' the name of its predecessor.

Raven: A male agent or intelligence officer who seduces people of either sex in order to persuade them to provide intelligence or perform some other operational role.

Research and Analysis Wing (RAW): The Indian foreign intelligence service, set up in 1968.

Rezident: **SVR** or **GRU** head of station in Russian embassies abroad.

Rezidentura: **SVR** or **GRU** station, usually, but not always, based in Russian embassies abroad.

Rolled-up: When an agent network has been broken up and the agents arrested by the opposing counter-espionage service.

Safe House: A location controlled by an intelligence service which provides a secure haven for the interrogation or debriefing of an agent or defector.

SB: *Służba Bezpieczeństwa* (Security Service). Polish internal security service from 1956 to 1989.

SD: *Sicherheitsdienst*, the security and intelligence service of the SS and the Nazi Party. Its full title was *Sicherheitsdienst des Reichsführer-SS* (Security Service of the Head of the SS). It was set up in 1932 and dissolved in 1945 when it was officially designated a criminal organisation by the Allies.

Secret Service Bureau: British intelligence and counter-espionage service set up in 1909 in response to exaggerated reports of German espionage in Britain. The origins of both the British Security Service (MI5) and the Secret Intelligence Service (SIS), also known as MI6.

Security Service: British internal security service commonly known as MI5, set up in 1909. (See also **Secret Service Bureau** and **MI5**)

SSI: (*Serviciul Special de Informaţii*). Romanian foreign intelligence service from 1908 to 1948.

Shin Bet: *Sherut ha'Bitachon ha'Klali* (General Security Service). The Israeli internal security service set up in 1949.

Sigint: Signals Intelligence. The collection of various wireless transmissions for intelligence purposes. Originally focused largely on radio communications or other military transmissions such as radar but now extended to include the collection of phone calls, emails and internet communications.

Signal Site: A pre-arranged location where a mark or sign can be left in order to inform the agent or the handler of a certain issue. It might be a signal that a drop has been made elsewhere or a call for a meet, or indeed any other issue related to the operation.

SIS: Secret Intelligence Service. British foreign intelligence service set up in 1909, although its official title did not become SIS until 1919. It is now better known as MI6.

SISMI: *Servizio per le Informazioni e la Sicurezza Militare* (Military Intelligence and Security Service). It was the Italian foreign intelligence service from 1977 to 2007.

Sleeper: Agent living under **Deep Cover** in a target country. He or she behaves as if they are a normal citizen of the target country until activated for a particular operation.

Special Agent: *Spetsialnyy Agent.* An agent of the Soviet intelligence services who – between 1924 and 1954 – carried out operations and tasks that would now be performed by an intelligence officer.

Stasi: Nickname for the *Ministerium für Staatssicherheit* (Ministry for State Security). The East German intelligence and security service from 1950 to 1990. (See also **HVA** and **MfS**)

Stringer: An intelligence agent based in a foreign country or city, usually in a location where the intelligence service he or she works for has no other presence.

Sub-agent/Sub-source: An agent or source run by another agent and often unaware of his or her role.

Support Agent: An agent who performs a background role within an operation.

StB: *Státna Bezpečnost.* Czechoslovak State Security Service between 1945 and 1990.

SVR: *Sluzhba Vneshney Razvedki*. The Russian Foreign Intelligence Service set up after the dissolution of the Soviet Union in December 1991.

Swallow: A female agent or intelligence officer who seduces people of either sex in order to persuade them to provide intelligence or perform some other operational role.

Take: The intelligence product from an agent, network, operation or capability.

Talent-spotting agent: *Agent-Navodchik*. Russian term for an agent who spots potential recruits in target countries or organisations. (See also **Access Agent**)

The Centre: Moscow Headquarters of the Russian foreign intelligence service.

Throwaway: An agent who is considered expendable. (See also **Discard**)

Unconscious Agent: An individual who is exploited by an intelligence service to provide intelligence or carry out actions useful for an operation or favourable to the service's own government but remains completely unaware of their own role.

Unwitting Agent: US term for an **Unconscious Agent**.

Walk-in: An agent who volunteers his or her services as an intelligence source or an agent-in-place, often quite literally walking into the embassy of the country he or she wants to work for.

Watchers: MI5 name for covert surveillance officers.

Work Name: An alias used by an intelligence officer or agent during an operation.

ACKNOWLEDGEMENTS

Inevitably when writing a book such as this there will be readers who find that their favourite spy stories have been omitted. The purpose of this book has not been to produce the most famous, the most popular, or even the most important spy stories in history, if such a choice is even possible to make. The stories that have been included in this book have been designed to demonstrate why spies spy. As a result, many will be new to some readers, others like that of Aldrich Ames, for example, are better known but recounted from the perspective of why they chose to spy rather than a simple retelling of what they did. The purpose of this book is not to recycle old spy stories; it is to analyse what makes someone betray their country or their friends. I would like to thank the following people for their assistance: Kees Jan Dellebeke, Bruce Jones, Alan Judge, Mark Lowe, Dan Mulvenna and a number of other former intelligence officers from various countries who have chosen not to be named. Despite their invaluable help, any opinions expressed and errors made in this book are mine and mine alone. I would also like to thank Jennifer Barr, whose idea this book was, the editorial staff at The History Press, and my agent, Tom Cull. On a personal basis, it would be remiss not to thank my wife, Hayley, my children and my grandchildren, who as ever were patient and supportive throughout the long process of writing this book.
Michael Smith, June 2019

THE AUTHOR

Michael Smith is the best-selling author of a wide variety of books on spies and special forces. He served in British military intelligence before becoming an award-winning journalist, working for the BBC, the *Daily Telegraph* and the *Sunday Times*. His many books include, *Killer Elite: The Inside Story of America's Most Secret Special Operations Team; Foley: The Spy Who Saved 10,000 Jews; The Secrets of Station X: How Bletchley Park Codebreakers Helped Win the War; The Debs of Bletchley Park* and *The Secret Agent's Bedside Reader.* He is a member of the Historical Advisory Group of the Bletchley Park Trust and a Visiting Fellow at Kellogg College, Oxford.

INDEX

The History Press

The destination for history
www.thehistorypress.co.uk